The Essential CFO

Founded in 1807, John Wiley & Sons is the oldest independent publishing company in the United States. With offices in North America, Europe, Asia, and Australia, Wiley is globally committed to developing and marketing print and electronic products and services for our customers' professional and personal knowledge and understanding.

The Wiley Corporate F&A series provides information, tools, and insights to corporate professionals responsible for issues affecting the profitability of their company, from accounting and finance to internal controls and performance management.

The Essential CFO

A Corporate Finance Playbook

BRUCE NOLOP

WILEY

John Wiley & Sons, Inc.

Published by John Wiley & Sons, Inc., Hoboken, New Jersey.

Published simultaneously in Canada.

For general information on our other products and services or for technical support, please contact our Customer Care Department within the United States at (800) 762-2974, outside the United States at (317) 572-3993 or fax (317) 572-4002.

Wiley also publishes its books in a variety of electronic formats. Some content that appears in print may not be available in electronic books. For more information about Wiley products, visit our web site at www.wiley.com.

Library of Congress Cataloging-in-Publication Data:

Nolop, Bruce, 1950–
   The essential CFO: a corporate finance playbook/Bruce Nolop.
      pages cm.—(Wiley corporate F&A)
   Includes index.
      ISBN 978-1-118-17304-6 (pbk.); ISBN 978-1-118-22689-6 (ebk);
   ISBN 978-1-118-24003-8 (ebk); ISBN 978-1-118-26463-8 (ebk)
   1. Chief financial officers.   2. Corporations—Finance—Management.   I. Title.
   HG4027.35.N65 2012
   658.15—dc23   2011048566

Printed in the United States of America

V10003275_081018

To my mother, Barbara Sandager Nolop

Contents

PART VI: ACCOUNTING AND CONTROLS

PART VII: LEADERSHIP

Introduction

THE ROLE OF THE CHIEF FINANCIAL OFFICER (CFO) has evolved at a breathtaking pace in the twenty-first century. As the last century came to a close, financial engineering was in vogue and the recent winners of *CFO* magazine's prestigious "Excellence in Finance" awards—along with glowingly positive stories—included Scott Sullivan of WorldCom, Andrew Fastow of Enron, and Mark Swartz of Tyco International. This proved embarrassing when all three of these award winners were later indicted for their malfeasance.

EVOLVING JOB DESCRIPTION

Not surprisingly, it wasn't too long before the era of the "Financial Engineer" CFO gave way to the "Trusted" CFO. Since then, we have seen a further evolution in CFO fashions from "Trusted" to "Super Accountant" to "Risk Manager" and, most recently, to "Strategic Partner" in the attributes that are most in demand by recruiters. As expressed by one recruiter, "With the accounting and controls side of the house now in order, a new CFO profile has emerged: a strategic, operationally oriented finance executive who can serve as the business partner to the CEO."[1]

To a large extent, the evolution of the CFO position has been fueled by external events such as the Enron and other corporate scandals; the passage of the Sarbanes-Oxley legislation; the introduction of the Fair Disclosure rule; the advent of enterprise risk management; the proliferation of new accounting standards; and, most notably, the widespread fallout from the financial meltdown and credit crisis that exploded on the scene in 2008. Furthermore, companies have experienced new demands arising from enlivened regulatory authorities and from activist shareholders, including the escalating influence of hedge funds and private equity investors.

STRATEGIC CFO

Without question, the CFO position has expanded dramatically in its breadth, complexity, and criticality. In a word, CFOs have indeed become more *strategic*, reflecting enhanced opportunities to impact a company's program for delivering shareholder value.

In 2005, CFO Research Services prepared a report in collaboration with Booz Allen Hamilton entitled "The Activist CFO—Alignment with Strategy, Not Just with the Business." In a prescient conclusion, the report noted the following:

> And as CEOs are challenged by the external market and their boards of directors, they increasingly need a trusted adviser to help develop and execute corporate strategy. Thus CFOs are poised to take on an expanded and increasingly activist role within their companies. As part of this activist role, CFOs are increasingly aligning their function not just with the business but with the company's overall strategy. And by doing so, they are not just supporting the business with information and analyses, but also ensuring that the entire enterprise delivers on its commitments.[2]

This report also classified activist CFOs within four groups:

1. **"Growth navigators:** CFOs who work closely with CEOs to map out an aggressive course to profitable growth through acquisition or organic channels."
2. **"Execution maestros:** CFOs who focus on operational excellence and instill in their companies a value discipline that enables them to do more with less."
3. **"Turnaround surgeons:** CFOs who step in under close scrutiny to make difficult decisions that others often will not make—with the goal of restoring ailing companies to financial health."
4. **"Business model transformers:** CFOs who identify opportunities for strategic innovation and take advantage of them by recasting their companies' business models and organizations."[3]

More recently, CFO Research Services published another report in collaboration with KPMG entitled "A New Role for New Times" that largely reaffirmed the trends that it outlined in its earlier study. The 2011 report concluded that "The finance function has come to contribute more substantively to developing and executing business strategy at a great many companies in recent years."[4]

And the focus on strategy was further highlighted in 2011 when *The Wall Street Journal* convened the inaugural annual meeting of its "CFO Network." The large company CFOs who attended this conference ranked *"Become a Strategic CFO"* as their top priority.[5]

Undoubtedly, these shorthand descriptions of the CFO position can be misleading in their overemphasis of certain aspects of the job. However, they do highlight the seemingly inexorable trend toward a CFO who is more integral to shaping and executing a company's strategic and business priorities.

EXPANDED ROLES

It's also indisputable that the CFO's roles are expanding: as new responsibilities are added, the previous responsibilities don't go away. And the CFO usually is expected to take on these additional duties while continuously reducing the finance organization's headcount and cost structure.

Deloitte addressed the challenges for CFOs in managing their expanding scope of responsibilities in a posting on its CFO Learning Center website. It described the "four faces" of a CFO's time allocation—Strategist, Catalyst, Steward, and Operator—and compared the desired allocation—as indicated by a survey among CFOs—with the amount of time that actually is allocated to each of these four roles. Deloitte concluded that "while CFOs desire to spend 60 percent of their time as a Strategist or Catalyst, in reality they average only 42 percent of their time in these roles."[6]

As indicated by Deloitte's analysis, while being a Strategist or Catalyst may be their preferred vehicles for adding value, CFOs nevertheless must be continuously focused on all of the other responsibilities that come with the job. It's analogous to a figure skater who executes a triple axel to compete for a gold medal, but who must also spend countless hours in perfecting the less glamorous compulsories that constitute much of the judges' scoring.

CFOs must focus on several things at once and respond appropriately to the priorities of the moment. In the real world, it's hard to perform as a Strategic CFO in the face of an accounting restatement, a controls breakdown, or a liquidity crisis. In addition, their emphasis will reflect the talents of their team, since no CFO can do everything alone and the team inevitably will comprise complementary strengths and weaknesses.

Finally, it's worth emphasizing that the CFO's roles are still evolving. For example, CFOs have been taking a more prominent role with the financial media, helping to satisfy the insatiable appetite of broadcasters and websites for 24/7 content.

Although it's unlikely that the job will evolve into the "Telegenic" CFO, it does seem inevitable that media relations will become a growing priority for the future.

ABOUT THIS BOOK

This book is organized around the seven *essential* roles of the modern CFO—the core responsibilities that, to a greater or lesser degree, are likely to be part of every CFO's job description. These roles encompass responsibilities for strategy, capital allocations, mergers and acquisitions, funding, performance, accounting and controls, and leadership.

Although not intended to be a "day in the life" of the CFO position, this book highlights the breadth of responsibilities and discusses some of the strategies, techniques, and best practices that CFOs employ in addressing their expanding roles. It provides a framework—a corporate finance *playbook*—for organizing and executing their game plan.

This playbook explicitly recognizes that there are no cookie-cutter answers and that the optimal game plan inevitably will reflect the specific facts and circumstances of the particular CFO and company involved. Nevertheless, systematically reviewing their contemporary roles and responsibilities should be a beneficial exercise for both new and experienced CFOs. More important, this playbook can be an invaluable tool for all finance professionals and business students who aspire to financial leadership—highlighting the spectrum of skills that will be required for their long-term advancement.

At the same time, it should prove useful to accountants, attorneys, bankers, brokers, consultants, technology vendors, and anyone else who offers products and services to CFOs and their financial organizations. In fact, it's hoped that it can benefit anyone who is interested in learning more about business and finance from the CFO's vantage point.

This book is divided into seven parts and twenty-four chapters. Summary overviews are provided below.

Strategy

Part One describes the CFO's role in defining and communicating the company's strategic plan—achieving alignment around business and financial objectives that are designed to produce total shareholder return. It also discusses how the CFO focuses on enterprise risks, which goes hand in glove with the development of the strategic plan.

Articulating a Strategic Plan

Chapter 1 discusses the process of developing a strategic plan. It argues that this plan should guide all of the company's business and financial strategies and form the basis for the company's communications with investors and other stakeholders. The plan should incorporate business objectives, strategic themes, financial objectives, and acquisition strategies—all with target shareholders in mind.

This chapter also describes the creation of a long-term financial model—translating the strategic plan into a financial framework and confirming that the strategies will, in fact, create shareholder value. This value creation is encapsulated in the company's goal for delivering total shareholder return, which reflects a combination of share price appreciation and dividend yield.

Communicating and Achieving Alignment

Chapter 2 provides an overview of the CFO's role in communicating the strategic plan, stressing the need for consistency and transparency in achieving seamless alignment among both internal and external stakeholders. It argues that CFOs should provide input to the design of incentive compensation programs, which can reinforce the strategic plan's objectives.

This chapter also describes the CFO's mission in communicating the company's story to investors and the media, arguing that this has become a higher priority due to investor appetite for more information and the burgeoning of media outlets. It stresses that the CFO should help to frame the message points and coordinate consistent messaging throughout the various communication channels.

Assessing Enterprise Risks

Chapter 3 addresses the CFO's role in assessing enterprise risks. It describes the implementation of an enterprise risk management program and highlights the unique perspectives that CFOs can bring to the program.

This chapter also highlights some of the risk areas that have become more salient in the current environment. It argues that CFOs should seek to maximize the benefits from "rewarded" risks, while protecting the company from "unrewarded" risks.

Capital Allocations

Part Two reviews the CFO's role in allocating capital, which is critical to the implementation of the strategic plan. This requires dexterous navigation among competing priorities, including investment projects, acquisitions, dividends, and share repurchases.

Estimating the Cost of Capital

Chapter 4 describes the process of estimating a company's cost of capital, including the determination of "betas" and the other variables used in the capital asset pricing model. It also discusses the potential use of a "hurdle rate," including the possibility of adding a fudge factor or varying risk premiums.

This chapter advocates that CFOs should use a consistent cost of capital to evaluate all of the company's investment projects and acquisitions—without adding a fudge factor or risk premiums—and should emphasize subjective judgments in comparing the alternatives.

Prioritizing Capital Investments

Chapter 5 focuses on the prioritization of capital investments, describing the iterative process for establishing a capital investment budget and allocating this budget among potential projects. It reviews the evaluation criteria and emphasizes that the investment priorities should reflect a number of factors besides net present values, including both financial and non-financial considerations.

This chapter also highlights the CFO's role in monitoring projects after they are approved, including the value to be harvested from "real options" and the information to be gleaned about the credibility of project sponsors and the company's track record by type of project.

Considering Dividends and Repurchases

Chapter 6 focuses on returning cash to shareholders through either dividends or share repurchases. It discusses the pros and cons of alternative dividend policies and reviews the tradeoffs between paying dividends versus repurchasing shares, as well as the methods for implementing a share repurchase program.

This chapter also discusses the possibility of retaining "strategic" cash. It cites the potential benefits from greater financial flexibility—while highlighting the potentially negative reactions from shareholders—and stresses adherence to approved investment policies.

Mergers and Acquisitions

Part Three outlines the creation of value through mergers and acquisitions, which can be quicker, cheaper, and less risky alternatives to purely organic growth. It also describes the CFO's role in executing divestitures and spinoffs and potentially responding to a takeover offer or other strategic proposal.

Identifying Acquisition Candidates

Chapter 7 discusses the identification of acquisition candidates, highlighting the ways that CFOs can increase the odds of a successful transaction—including sticking to adjacent spaces, taking a portfolio approach, exercising patience and flexibility, and requiring a business sponsor who is personally accountable for the transaction. It also describes the importance of clearly identifying the strategic purpose for an acquisition, drawing distinctions among consolidation, bolt-on, platform, and transformative transactions.

This chapter argues that CFOs should facilitate—but not drive—the transactions and that the acquisitions should be motivated primarily by strategic rather than financial considerations.

Evaluating Acquisition Candidates

Chapter 8 describes the criteria for evaluating an acquisition candidate, including valuation methodologies—such as discounted cash flows, comparable companies, precedent transactions, leveraged buyout, and premiums paid analyses—as well as pro forma financial analyses. Other criteria include the impact on the company's stock price and whether the proposed transaction will exacerbate or mitigate enterprise risks.

This chapter advocates determining both the target's standalone value and the net value of synergies and then calculating how much of the value created is retained by the acquirer.

Executing a Merger or Acquisition

Chapter 9 reviews the CFO's role in executing a merger or acquisition, including conducting due diligence; preparing a business plan; determining pricing parameters; arranging acquisition financing; and negotiating contract terms. It also describes the integration of an acquisition, including monitoring of results against the business plan.

This chapter describes the CFO's role in determining the deal terms and stresses that, to avoid overpaying, the acquirer should not be too anxious to do a deal or too fixated on a particular target.

Executing Divestitures and Spinoffs

Chapter 10 outlines the reasons for pursuing a divestiture and then reviews the process for executing the transaction, including the decisions whether to hire an investment banker, conduct an auction or a negotiated transaction, and structure it as a stock or asset deal. It also discusses the possibility of a tax-free spinoff (including a "Morris Trust" variation) as well as "split-up" and "equity carve-out" alternatives.

This chapter argues that CFOs can add considerable value by regularly pruning a company's business portfolio and through their quality of execution in a divestiture or spinoff scenario.

Responding to Takeover Offers

Chapter 11 discusses the CFO's role in a company's response to a takeover offer, including the preparation of financial projections and coordination of external advisors. It also describes the expanded responsibilities if the board of directors decides to pursue a sale transaction.

This chapter emphasizes that CFOs should be fully prepared in advance of a potential proposal, including understanding the company's governance provisions, maintaining an up-to-date long-term financial model, and continuously reviewing possible strategic or financial actions to add shareholder value.

Funding

Part Four reviews the CFO's role as the primary architect and manager of the capital structure, including establishing capital structure objectives; developing financing strategies; analyzing financing alternatives; and obtaining short-term and long-term financing.

Establishing Capital Structure Objectives

Chapter 12 describes the criteria for setting capital structure targets, including the ratio of debt to market capitalization and other leverage ratios used by analysts in the company's industry or contained in its debt covenants.

This chapter also describes the implications of obtaining alternative debt ratings from the major rating agencies, especially the distinction between investment grade and speculative debt. It discusses the criteria used by the rating agencies and stresses that CFOs should maintain an active dialogue with the agencies.

Developing Financing Strategies

Chapter 13 discusses the CFO's role in determining the financing mix in the company's capital structure. It advocates core financing principles—keep it simple, preserve flexibility, continue to evolve, and react opportunistically—and describes debt and equity financing alternatives, as well as off balance sheet financing.

This chapter also describes debt maturity objectives, fixed versus floating rate debt tradeoffs, financing in a foreign currency, maintenance and incurrence debt covenants, debt refinancings, debt for equity exchanges, and bankruptcy.

Ensuring Short-Term Liquidity

Chapter 14 highlights the CFO's responsibility for ensuring adequate liquidity. This involves cultivating banking relationships, establishing revolving credit lines and other sources of short-term financing, instituting rigorous cash planning processes, and developing contingency plans for unanticipated liquidity needs.

This chapter also describes the CFO's role in working capital management, including regularly monitoring liquidity ratios and actively managing accounts receivable, accounts payable, inventory, and cash to enhance cash flow from operations.

Obtaining Long-Term Financing

Chapter 15 reviews the potential sources of long-term financing, including venture capital, private equity, initial public offerings, subsequent equity issuances (secondary, follow-on, and ATM offerings), bank term loans, syndicated bank loans, investment grade securities, high yield securities, and strategic alliances.

This chapter discusses the pros and cons of each of the alternatives and argues that CFOs should strive to strike the right balance between cost and flexibility.

Performance

Part Five describes the transition of CFOs from serving as scorekeepers to becoming players who help to deliver business and financial results. This includes generating organic revenue growth; reducing the cost structure; using budgets, forecasts, and metrics to drive performance; and managing financial risks and taxes.

Driving Business Performance

Chapter 16 reviews the CFO's role in producing organic revenue growth and managing the cost structure. It argues that CFOs should partner with the business leaders and share ownership for achieving the company's performance targets. This includes adopting a mindset for encouraging growth and taking an active interest in customer relationships.

This chapter also describes the numerous tools that CFOs can use to reduce costs, ranging from short-term contingent actions to long-term reengineering of functions and processes. It advocates attacking company-wide cost categories and adopting fixed versus variable cost strategies that complement the strategic plan objectives.

Providing Planning and Analysis

Chapter 17 highlights the ability of CFOs to drive results through their leadership of the budgeting and forecasting processes and the establishment of performance metrics, including non-financial measures that are enablers of the strategic plan. It also describes the processes for preparing budgets and forecasts and the systems for measuring business unit performance.

This chapter advocates a focus on cash as well as accounting results—including regular cash flow forecasts—and argues for fewer and simpler performance metrics, with a bias toward actionable items rather than voluminous details.

Managing Financial Risks and Taxes

Chapter 18 focuses on the risk management activities that are directly managed by the CFO, including the development and administration of cost-effective insurance programs. It also discusses strategies for managing interest rate, currency, commodity, inflation, and pension fund risks.

This chapter discusses the CFO's oversight of the tax planning functions, emphasizing the establishment of clear management objectives—such as avoiding excessive risk, reducing complexity, performing holistic analyses, and ensuring compliance—as well as a focus on potential areas of opportunity—such as net operating losses, transfer pricing, and special credits.

Accounting and Controls

Part Six discusses the establishment of accounting and control processes and the ways that CFOs are responding to the challenges arising from additional regulations and new accounting pronouncements. It also describes the CFO's leadership role in preparing for an earnings announcement.

Establishing Accounting Processes

Chapter 19 reviews the CFO's need for robust financial reporting processes—producing financial statements that are timely and accurate and that effectively communicate the company's results. It discusses the factors that can affect the accounting environment, including automation, technology tools, documentation, various checks and balances, and the overriding importance of having good people.

This chapter also describes recent trends in Securities and Exchange Commission (SEC) filings and argues for active coordination with the external auditors and the audit committee.

Communicating Financial Results

Chapter 20 discusses the preparations for quarterly and annual earnings announcements. It emphasizes a rigorous focus on identifying business and financial issues; crystallizing the company's response to these issues; and ensuring alignment in communications with investors, the media, and all stakeholders, especially employees. It also argues for transparent communications.

This chapter also addresses two topics that are top-of-mind among CFOs: the use of non-generally accepted accounting principles (GAAP) measures and whether to provide earnings guidance.

Implementing Sarbanes-Oxley

Chapter 21 discusses the procedures adopted by CFOs in their implementation of Sarbanes-Oxley. It enumerates the main provisions of the act and focuses specifically on three provisions: requiring auditor independence; certifying financial statements; and testing the adequacy of financial controls, including the identification of deficiencies, significant deficiencies, and material weaknesses.

This chapter also describes the CFO's challenge in reaping benefits from the Sarbanes-Oxley requirements, while at the same time minimizing bureaucracy and incremental costs.

Reinforcing Compliance and Controls

Chapter 22 describes the CFO's role in reinforcing compliance and controls. It describes proven management practices—such as establishing a strong tone at the top, promulgating a code of conduct, and adopting a zero tolerance standard—and argues that the company's internal and external auditors as well as its audit committee can be powerful allies in this effort.

This chapter also describes the new Dodd-Frank whistleblower awards and the need for companies to focus on their internal whistleblower processes. It argues that given the explosion of regulations, CFOs should seek to reduce the company's cost of compliance by consolidating activities and streamlining processes.

Leadership

Part Seven discusses the CFO's role as leader of the financial organization. This includes fostering effective communications throughout an organization that is becoming more complex and increasingly global; driving effectiveness and efficiencies as a continuing priority; and developing a talent base to meet the challenges of the current environment, as well as the anticipated requirements for the next phases of the company's evolution and growth.

Achieving Finance Transformation

Chapter 23 describes the CFO's overarching objective of achieving "finance transformation." This usually is a shorthand term used by CFOs to encompass their goals of revising the organizational structure, implementing new technology systems, reengineering processes, utilizing outsourcing arrangements, and emphasizing analysis over data.

This chapter argues that the transformation should be implemented incrementally and that its success requires strong support from the top and superior project management skills. The benefits—which can include enhanced effectiveness, greater efficiencies, and strengthened controls—can more than justify the disruptions and risks that inevitably come with major changes in the organizational structure and transactional capabilities.

Developing Financial Talent

Chapter 24 discusses the CFO's role in developing finance professionals, starting with strategies for recruiting talent through either entry level or lateral positions. It then discusses development objectives—emphasizing expertise, experience, and leadership skills—and reviews the panoply of programs and tools that CFOs are using to achieve these development objectives.

This chapter argues that CFOs should demonstrate visible leadership in crafting creative programs for winning the fierce and escalating competition for financial talent. It concludes with some observations concerning the qualities and skills that will be required among the financial leaders of the future.

NOTES

1. Heid, Michele, "What's expected now of CFOs?" (March 1, 2010, www.heidrick.com/blogs).
2. CFO Research Services in collaboration with Booz Allen Hamilton, "The Activist CFO-Alignment with Strategy, Not Just with the Business" (April 2005, CFO Publishing Corp.), p. 3.
3. Ibid., pp. 5–6.
4. CFO Research Services in collaboration with KPMG, "A New Role for New Times—Opportunities and Obstacles for the Expanding Finance Function" (March 2011, CFO Publishing Corp.), p. 5.
5. *The Wall Street Journal* (June 27, 2011): C6. The top five priorities were (1) Become a strategic CFO; (2) Drive value through capital allocation; (3) Develop a financial leadership pipeline; (4) View cash as a strategic tool; and (5) Provide short-term and long-term balance.
6. Deloitte, "CFO insights: Crossing the chasm: From operator to strategist" www.deloitte.com/us/cfo center (2011, Deloitte Development Center).

The Essential CFO

PART ONE

Strategy

1

Articulating a Strategic Plan

EVERY COMPANY HAS A STRATEGIC PLAN. It may not be documented or well-defined, but it can be seen in the accumulated actions of employees, management, and the board of directors.

At the other extreme, a company may have extraordinarily detailed strategic plans that are scattered throughout the various business units and geographic locations, but no clear understanding that unites everyone around core objectives.

And then there's the "Goldilocks" company that gets it just right—a plan that achieves alignment around an overarching strategic framework, with detailed strategies that are developed and implemented throughout the company. This should be the CFO's goal.

Whatever the status of a company's planning efforts, CFOs can play an important role in helping to articulate a strategic plan and analyze its effectiveness. In particular, the CFO can help answer such big picture questions as:

- Will the plan deliver the company's *shareholder return* objectives?
- Can it be executed successfully by the company's *management* team?
- Is it consistent with the company's core *values* and tolerance for *risk?*
- Does the company have the *financial wherewithal* to execute the plan?

- Can it be effectively *communicated* to shareholders, customers, employees, and other key stakeholders?

Most important, CFOs can help to articulate the plan's business objectives; strategic themes; financial objectives; acquisition strategies; and target investors.

 ## BUSINESS OBJECTIVES

The CFO's first task is to define and confirm the business objectives that form the building blocks for creating shareholder value. This typically encompasses a systematic review of the company's historical performance, its positioning against the competition, and the strategies being emphasized by each of the company's business units and product lines.

The goal is to sift through the information—which usually is voluminous —and condense it into a top-down overview, describing the company as it is today and predicting what it will look like at the end of the planning horizon.

The business objectives should summarize the company's strategic positioning, financial characteristics, and business and geographical mix— answering basic questions that broadly describe the current and future company. Some examples of questions are provided below, but CFOs will want to determine the questions that are most relevant for their company.

Typically, these questions will have been discussed in various strategic and operational reviews and the answers will be generally well understood by the management team and board of directors. Nevertheless, the discipline of defining and confirming the consensus in a summary format can be a useful exercise, helping to ensure clarity and consistency in the objectives being pursued.

- **Strategic Positioning.** What is the mission or vision statement? What is the competitive positioning? What are the areas of competitive advantage? What are the critical factors for success? What are the key criteria for entering or exiting a business or product line?
- **Financial Characteristics**. What is the cyclicality or volatility of results? What is the capital intensity? What is the underlying growth rate? Is the profit margin likely to increase, decrease, or stay the same in the next five years?
- **Business and Geographical Mix.** What is the current business mix? What are the sources of growth? Which businesses will grow faster than average

and which will grow more slowly? What is the projected business mix at the end of the planning period? What is the current percentage breakdown by geographical region for revenue and operating profit? Which countries will be emphasized for growth? What is the projected geographical mix?

STRATEGIC THEMES

In addition, CFOs should distill the business objectives into their thematic essence, establishing a shorthand communication for the way that the company is going to create value. A company may have one overriding strategic theme, but more likely it will focus on three or four.

Some examples are provided below, but by no means do they exhaust the possibilities—which should be tailored for each company. The key point is that it's usually helpful if the CFO can boil down the company's business strategies into a few bullet points that can be communicated succinctly and remembered easily. It's a good way to ensure that everyone's on the same page.

- **Develop Superior Products:** Offer products or services that are considered superior to those of competitors.
  Example: *Toyota*
- **Establish Brand Leadership:** Maintain a marketing and pricing advantage through a superior brand image that translates into new markets.
  Example: *Coca-Cola*
- **Achieve Operational Excellence:** Offer quality products or services through management focus on flawless execution.
  Example: *FedEx*
- **Maintain Market Leadership:** Achieve and sustain a significant market share in a large and growing business.
  Example: *Google*
- **Invent New Products:** Invest in research and development to produce new products that establish market leadership or develop new markets.
  Example: *Apple*
- **Develop Line Extensions:** Use market research to develop line extensions in an existing product category.
  Example: *Colgate-Palmolive*
- **Expand in Emerging Markets:** Market a company's products in developing countries that have superior growth potential.
  Example: *Caterpillar*

- **Lower Cost Structure:** Achieve a competitive edge and higher operating margins through cost reductions and efficiencies.
  Example: *Walmart*
- **Sell More Products to Customers:** Expand the breadth of products or services that are offered to the existing customer base.
  Example: *IBM*
- **Exploit Economies of Scale:** Invest in major projects that require significant capital expenditures and diversification of risk.
  Example: *ExxonMobil*
- **Introduce a Better Distribution Model:** Use Internet or other distribution technologies to change the industry dynamics.
  Example: *Amazon*
- **Leverage a Disruptive Technology:** Expand the customer and revenue base through a new technology that is transforming a business.
  Example: *Netflix*
- **Create More Consumer Demand:** Invest in marketing and advertising to generate more customers for products or services.
  Example: *Capital One*
- **Anticipate a Cyclical Upside:** Position a business to reap the benefits when economic conditions improve in the future.
  Example: *Alcoa*
- **Effect a Turn Around:** Take decisive actions to improve a company's financial results, often with a new CEO and management team.
  Example: *Ford*
- **Make Accretive Acquisitions:** Establish a track record for executing acquisitions that enhance growth and earn superior returns.
  Example: *Danaher*
- **Consolidate an Industry:** Rationalize a fragmented industry to achieve economies of scale and greater pricing power.
  Example: *International Paper*
- **Maximize Free Cash Flow:** Manage a mature company to maximize free cash flow for paying dividends and repurchasing stock.
  Example: *Altria*
- **Transform the Company:** Transition to a new business with better growth prospects and greater long-term profitability.
  Example: *Kodak*
- **Break up the Company:** Gain greater focus and higher stock market valuations by spinning off business units.
  Example: *Kraft*

LONG-TERM FINANCIAL MODEL

The CFO's next challenge is to translate the business objectives into long-term financial projections, converting the strategic framework into a tangible financial plan. These projections can confirm whether the business strategies will produce shareholder value and can help to formulate the company's financial objectives—including a target for delivering total shareholder return and a tentative plan for allocating capital.

Modeling Methodologies

In contrast to an annual budget, a company's long-term financial projections usually involve more top-down assumptions and a longer time period (typically three to five years). The modeling also is more oriented toward "finance" rather than "accounting" perspectives, which means that it relies more on mathematical formulas—such as historical and expected revenue growth rates and projected changes in operating margins—and focuses more on cash flow assumptions and metrics.

For example, the model usually calculates the amount of capital expenditures and working capital requirements as a percentage of revenue growth for each of the company's product lines rather than through a full bottoms-up analysis of specific investment plans.

Modeling Formats

In developing their models, CFOs can either adapt sophisticated software packages that are available from technology vendors or else develop their own in-house version from scratch. Whether purchased or home-grown, the model should encompass the following attributes:

- *Sufficiently detailed* to capture the key drivers of the company's performance in each of its businesses and product lines.
- *Easily updated* through automated calculations that are based on correlations and interdependencies that are both logical and verifiable.
- *Analytically oriented* to show a wide range of accounting, cash flow, and rate of return measures, including estimated stock prices and total shareholder return.

CFOs also may want the financial model to be relatively consistent with the formats used by the sell side and buy side financial analysts in the company's industry. This conformity can be especially valuable to investor communications, helping to foster congruity with investor expectations concerning the drivers of future performance and the types of returns that can be generated.

Valuation Measures

The model's output should include agreed-upon valuation measures to determine the amount and the sources of shareholder value creation over the planning horizon. The stock prices usually are estimated by performing discounted cash flow analyses or by employing valuation multiples used by industry analysts.

For example, the market values may be estimated using a multiple of earnings per share, free cash flow per share, or book value per share. Another common technique is to assume a multiple of EBITDA (earnings before interest, taxes, depreciation, and amortization) to determine the company's *enterprise value* and then to subtract debt less cash (net debt) in deriving the market value for its equity.

In addition, the model should show other valuation benchmarks that are used in the industry or that are incorporated in the company's incentive compensation plans. Some examples include:

- **Market Value Added:** Market value of the company's equity securities in excess of their book value.
- **Organic Revenue Growth:** Year-over-year change in revenue excluding the effects of currency and any acquisitions or divestitures during the latest 12 months.
- **Net Income Growth:** Year-over-year change in after-tax earnings (or earnings per share) from continuing operations (either generally accepted accounting principles [GAAP] or "adjusted" earnings).
- **Free Cash Flow Yield:** Cash flow from operations less capital expenditures as a percent of market value.
- **Return on Capital:** Net income plus after-tax interest as a percent of book capitalization (shareholders' equity plus net debt).
- **Economic Profit:** Net income plus after-tax interest less a capital charge on average book capitalization.
- **Return on Equity:** Net income (GAAP or "adjusted") as a percent of book equity.
- **Operating Margin:** Earnings before interest and taxes (EBIT) as a percent of revenue.
- **Net Income Margin:** Net income as a percent of revenue.

Strategic Metrics

In addition to the valuation benchmarks, CFOs should include some performance drivers that relate to the company's business strategies. Examples might include:

- **Cost Reduction:** General and administrative expense as a percent of revenue.
- **Emerging Markets:** Revenue from Asia-Pacific, Latin America, and Africa as a percent of total revenue.
- **Innovation:** Revenue from new products as a percent of total revenue.
- **Technology:** Research and development spending as a percent of revenue.
- **Market Leadership:** Marketing and advertising spending as a percent of revenue.
- **Cross-Selling:** Revenue or products per customer.
- **Superior Products:** Gross margin on revenue.
- **Operational Excellence:** Number of customers.
- **Cyclical Upside:** Pricing on key products.

Sensitivity Analysis

The model should also permit a fulsome understanding of the sensitivities to the primary external and company-specific performance drivers. Therefore, CFOs will want the model to have the capability to vary these assumptions.

For example, the model might contain the ability to change assumptions for economic conditions, interest rates, foreign exchange rates, product pricing, and raw material pricing, and it might be useful to build in variables related to the inflation rate and assumed wage increases.

While the strategic plan should focus primarily on factors within management's control, CFOs will want to develop an appreciation for the exogenous variables that may overwhelm their efforts. Moreover, the sensitivity analyses can inform their preparation of contingency plans and their assessments of enterprise risks.

Potential Acquisitions

Although unidentified acquisitions typically are not included in a company's base case projections, CFOs should analyze the sensitivities to alternative acquisition scenarios. For example, they may want to examine the potential impact on the company's revenue and earnings growth rates, its return on capital, and the availability of cash to pay dividends or repurchase shares.

These sensitivity analyses can help CFOs to understand whether the company's financial objectives are attainable given different acquisition assumptions and the extent that they may need to raise additional long-term funding—either debt or equity financing.

 TOTAL SHAREHOLDER RETURN

In parallel with their financial modeling, CFOs also should be defining and confirming the company's target for total shareholder return (TSR), which is the ultimate measure of the shareholder value created per share of common stock. It's equal to the annual percentage growth rate in the stock price plus the value of dividends received (including any shares distributed through a spinoff).

For example, a company might deliver an annual TSR of 12 percent, of which 9 percent is derived from stock price growth and 3 percent from dividends.

Analysis of Projections

The long-term financial projections will largely determine the TSR target, providing CFOs with answers to key questions such as:

- **Earnings Definition:** How will the company's earnings growth rate be defined (for example, by GAAP net income, "adjusted" net income, or free cash flow)?
- **Earnings Growth Rate:** What growth rate in earnings (however defined) can be achieved over the planning period?
- **Sources of Earnings Growth:** What is the expected contribution to the earnings growth rate from organic revenue growth and the expected contribution from margin improvements (growing costs at a slower rate than organic revenue)?
- **Earnings Multiple:** What is the expected valuation multiple on earnings (market value divided by earnings) and is it likely to increase, decrease, or stay the same?
- **Shares Outstanding:** What is the projected annual increase or decrease in shares outstanding (the net of share issuances and share repurchases)?
- **Acquisitions:** What is the possible impact from potential acquisitions (accretion or dilution to earnings per share)?
- **Dividend Payments:** What is the expected return that will be derived from dividend payments (current yield, plus dividend rate increases)?

Alternatives for Delivering Total Shareholder Return

The total return to shareholders can come from various combinations of earnings growth, dividend payments, and share repurchases, as well as by changes in a company's earnings multiple. For example, consider three companies with the following characteristics:

- Company A is a relatively high-growth company that does not pay a dividend. It expects to grow its earnings at an average 16 percent rate over the next five years and to maintain a constant price/ earnings multiple of 20X over the planning period. It anticipates that shares outstanding will increase at a rate of 2 percent per year due to issuances through its incentive compensation programs.

- Company B is a moderate-growth company that expects to grow its net income by 10 percent per year and to maintain a price/earnings multiple of 14X over the planning period. It plans to maintain a dividend yield of 3 percent and to reduce its shares outstanding by 1 percent each year through share repurchases.

- Company C is a cyclical company that expects to maintain a dividend yield of 2 percent and maintain a constant amount of shares outstanding. Its net income is presently depressed due to a cyclical downturn, but the company expects it to double over the five-year period as the economy recovers. However, it also expects to see a decline in its presently inflated price/earnings (P/E) ratio of 15X (due to its low earnings) to a more normalized 12X.

A simplified comparison of the components of their total shareholder returns shows the following:

	Company A	Company B	Company C
Stock Price Today	$100	$100	$100
Stock-Price Impact From:			
-Earnings Growth	+80%	+50%	+100%
-Change in Shares	–10%	+5%	—
-Change in P/E Ratio	—	—	–40%
Stock Price in 5 Years	$170	$155	$160
Average Annual Increase	14%	11%	12%
Plus Dividend Yield	—	3%	2%
Total Shareholder Return	14%	14%	14%

TSR Considerations

CFOs should seek to define a TSR target that is aspirational but attainable. Usually, they will establish an internal target that is at the high end of, or even above, a range that is communicated externally. For example, they might set a goal of 12 to 14 percent internally, but state a public goal of 10 to 12 percent. This conservatism reflects a strong desire not to overpromise and underdeliver—which is anathema to stock market analysts.

The lower bound of the range should be equal to or greater than the company's cost of equity (which is estimated through the capital asset pricing model). For example, if the company's cost of equity is 10 percent, the bottom end of the target range should not extend below this number.

The target range should reflect realistic estimates of the earnings and cash flows that will be produced by the company's business and financial strategies, taking into account expectations for key macroeconomic or company-specific economic variables (including assumptions related to gross domestic product (GDP) growth rates and the key supply/demand assumptions that affect product pricing).

The long-term financial model is an invaluable tool for analyzing the possible range of outcomes under alternative scenarios. The sensitivity analyses can affect the level of target that is established or the way that it is communicated—perhaps adding a caveat such as "assuming normalized economic conditions."

CFOs should also analyze their company's historical track record for delivering TSR—on an absolute basis and in comparison with both a market index (such as the S&P 500) and an industry peer group. This historical perspective can provide insights concerning the market's expectations and the credibility of the company's projections.

In analyzing TSRs, CFOs should be aware of the alternative methodologies for computing the impact of dividends. In a conventional discounted cash flow model, dividends are implicitly assumed to earn the company's cost of capital. In contrast, calculations of stock market TSRs usually assume that dividends are reinvested in the company's stock; this methodology implicitly ascribes more value to dividends when the company enjoys strong stock price appreciation and less value when its stock price declines.

Finally, CFOs should strive to establish a TSR target that will remain valid over an extended period. Maintaining a consistent target reinforces the strategic plan's focus on long-term objectives and not on reactions to transitory conditions.

Example of TSR Target

After analyzing the historical and projected financials, CFOs should be in a good position to recommend a target for TSR, including its assumed components. For example, the annualized target might look something like the following:

Organic revenue growth	5.0–6.0%
Margin improvement	3.0–4.0%
Earnings growth	8.0–10.0%
Reduction in shares	1.0%
Earnings per share growth	9.0–11.0%
Change in P/E multiple	—
Dividend payments	3.0%
Total Shareholder Return	12.0–14.0%

The range could be communicated publicly as 10 to 12 percent, giving the company some cushion for unforeseen events. Or, alternatively, the company could communicate a less precise target—such as a "double digit" return—or choose not to make a public pronouncement.

In this example, the price/earnings multiple is assumed to remain constant, which is the assumption that CFOs normally use in their long-term financial modeling. However, if the company is in a cyclical business, the CFO may want to assume a more normalized valuation.

In addition, CFOs may consider a higher valuation multiple to be a potential upside from achieving greater consistency and growth in earnings. For example, increasing the price/earnings ratio from 12X to 15X would be equivalent to around 5 percentage points of annualized total shareholder return over a five-year period. However, the potential leverage from a change in the valuation multiple also highlights the downside if the company fails to perform up to expectations.

The example also does not include any incremental earnings accretion or dilution due to acquisitions, which implicitly assumes that any impact is subsumed in the earnings growth target. This is the typical assumption, except in cases where acquisitions are integral to the company's business strategies, such as private equity firms or certain industrial conglomerates.

Private Company TSRs

Although the calculation of TSR is based on stock price movements, the basic conceptual framework is applicable to private as well as public companies. The only difference is that the value of a private company's stock must be estimated.

Many private companies compute estimates of their share prices in connection with equity compensation programs or their share values may be indicated by a secondary market. If these estimates do not exist, private company CFOs can calculate their estimated market values based on discounted cash flows or extrapolations from comparable public companies. Alternatively, they can engage a third-party advisor to analyze their historical and projected TSRs.

 ## CAPITAL ALLOCATION STRATEGIES

The long-term financial model also will highlight the amount of cash flow from operations that the company expects to generate over the planning period. CFOs can help to define tentative priorities for allocating this capital among capital expenditures, dividend payments, share repurchases, and acquisitions.

For example, CFOs may want to depict the targeted allocation in a simple pie chart such as the one shown in Figure 1.1.

They then can analyze the tentative allocation strategies through the long-term financial model, showing the pro forma effects on the financial results and valuation measures. Furthermore, this analysis can help them to determine the reasonableness of the company's TSR target.

CFOs can also employ a similar format in analyzing the company's actual allocations of capital over an historical time period (say, the past three or five years). This analysis can indicate whether the target allocations are consistent with, or a departure from, the company's capital allocation strategies in the recent past.

The strategic plan should incorporate an assumed dividend policy—whether the company intends to pay no dividend, pay a token dividend, achieve steady increases in the dividend rate, establish a target payout ratio, or focus on a target dividend yield. In most cases, the CFO will assume a continuation of the current policy.

In addition, the plan should highlight whether the company intends to make regular share repurchases—perhaps to offset any dilution due to incentive compensation programs—or pursue share repurchases opportunistically, depending on the availability of surplus cash and the relative valuation of the company's stock.

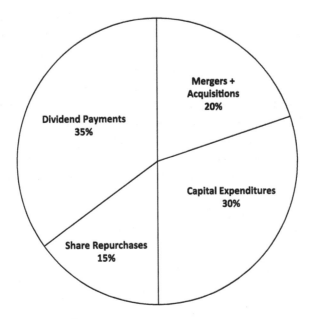

FIGURE 1.1 Capital Allocations

 ## ACQUISITION STRATEGIES

The strategic plan should include an overview of the expected role of acquisitions in fulfilling the company's business and financial objectives. Obviously, the specific transactions will not be known, but CFOs can help to clarify the types of acquisitions that will be considered—especially if they are an essential rather than a discretionary component of the strategic plan.

In addition, a company's acquisition strategies may have a profound effect on its growth potential, cash allocation priorities, and risk profile—which can influence the types of investors to target for the company's shareholder base or even whether the company should be publicly or privately held.

Acquisition Parameters

Some of the questions to be addressed should include: How big are the acquisitions likely to be? What is the estimated range of outlays for acquisitions over the planning period? What are the strategic purposes likely to be? For example, will they be vehicles to add new customer bases, enter new markets, obtain new technologies, realize cost savings, or enhance market leadership?

It also helps if the CFO can articulate the types of acquisitions that the company will be targeting—including the extent to which the company intends to emphasize:

- *Consolidations* that involve mergers or acquisitions in a mature or fragmented industry, usually to strengthen market leadership, reduce costs, or expand products and services to existing customers.
- *Bolt-ons* that involve the swift and complete integration of a target into an existing business, usually to obtain cost synergies or to save time and expense in adding customers, technologies, products, brand names, or geographical presence.
- *Platforms* that involve a target that facilitates entering a business or product line with good growth prospects, usually to obtain the target's management knowhow, market presence, brand name, or customer base.
- *Transformations* that involve major transactions that shift the company's focus toward a new business with greater growth prospects, usually to transition from a business that is stagnant or in decline.

Most important, CFOs should relate the acquisition strategies to the company's business objectives: Acquisitions should not be pursued as financial transactions, but rather as ways to accomplish business objectives more quickly, more cheaply, or with less risk.

As a rule, CFOs should not be too specific in communicating their acquisition strategies to the investment community. However, investors will appreciate reassurances that acquisitions will be pursued only if they fulfill business objectives, make economic sense, and compare favorably with alternative uses of capital—especially versus dividend payments or share repurchases.

Acquisition Financing

In addition, investors will be interested in the potential impact to the company's capital structure. Therefore, CFOs should have some tentative thoughts concerning acquisition financing—in particular, whether the company plans to issue equity in connection with the acquisition program (and if so, will it repurchase the shares?). Another important question is whether the acquisitions can be funded without impairing the company's debt ratings.

Obviously, the actual financing transactions will be largely dependent on the size and nature of the acquisitions that are ultimately undertaken, as well as the availability of other possible sources of cash, such as the proceeds from a divestiture. Nevertheless, the strategic plan should reflect the CFO's best preliminary thinking about the potential impact on the company's capital structure objectives.

 ## TARGET SHAREHOLDERS

In articulating a strategic plan, it usually helps if the company has a target shareholder profile in mind. The business and financial strategies should be viewed through the lens of current and potential shareholders in the company—answering the question: Will they perceive the stock to be an attractive investment? CFOs should view investors as their customers, who will need to buy into the company's strategies for delivering shareholder value.

For private companies, focusing on target shareholders involves learning the investment objectives of the specific individuals or institutions who directly own the company. CFOs of private companies usually can engage in a direct dialogue with their shareholders—gaining an understanding of their rate of return objectives, liquidity needs, tax situations, and risk tolerances.

For CFOs of public companies, the process of targeting shareholders is usually more nebulous. Although they can communicate with investors directly in many cases (e.g., in one-on-one meetings), they also will be marketing their investment story to a large number of existing and potential investors with whom they may not have had much, if any, direct contact in the past. Therefore, CFOs typically will classify target shareholders in much the same manner that a company focuses on customer segments in its marketing strategies.

Institutional Investors

Most institutional investors—such as mutual funds, money managers, and pension funds—will adopt investment styles that strongly influence and constrain the types of stocks in which they invest. By analyzing the investment styles of institutions in their existing shareholder base, CFOs can gain a pretty rich understanding of the criteria that these shareholders will consider in deciding whether to retain or add to their holdings.

In addition, CFOs can determine the types of institutional investors that are likely to be interested in their stock. They then can identify segments and institutions that are currently underrepresented in their stock ownership, comprising a fertile field to cultivate new shareholders.

As another technique, CFOs can compare their shareholder composition with those of peer group companies—thus identifying institutions that may be predisposed to embrace their investment thesis. It is a useful exercise to examine the shareholder bases not only of competitors, but also companies in other industries that have comparable investment characteristics, such as similar growth rates, P/E ratios, and dividend yields.

Investment Styles

The investment styles can vary significantly among institutional investors—and even among portfolio managers within an institution—making it difficult to categorize them with much precision. However, in an admittedly simplified model, the alternative investment styles can be defined by the following stock preferences:

- **Growth:** Stocks that offer above-average growth in earnings relative to the market; these stocks typically have relatively high price/earnings multiples and usually pay no or relatively low dividends.
- **Income:** Stocks that pay steady dividends and offer a relatively high dividend yield in comparison with other stocks in the market.
- **Value:** Stocks that tend to trade at low valuation multiples in comparison with the market and that are viewed as potentially undervalued due to company-specific issues or as a result of industry or macroeconomic conditions.
- **Growth at a Reasonable Price (GARP):** Stocks that offer a combination of consistent earnings growth at above market averages and valuation multiples that are considered reasonable in comparison with other stocks in the market.
- **Growth and Income:** Stocks that offer balanced returns from stock price appreciation and dividend yield; these stocks are relatively stable and often serve as core holdings in a portfolio.

Furthermore, the investment styles can vary by degree (such as "high" growth or "deep" value) and there are subcategories within each (such as "tax advantaged").

Hedge Funds

The growth in the size and influence of hedge funds is one of the most important developments in the investment world over the past decade. While few companies have purposely set out to cultivate hedge funds as their preferred investor base, CFOs should recognize that they are a powerful and growing force in the market—especially influencing stock valuations over the short term—and account for a disproportionate percentage of the liquidity in most listed stocks.

Unlike traditional institutional investors, hedge funds usually are unabashedly focused on short-term gains—with a year being a relatively long time for them to hold a position—and they are as prone to be short as long a stock. They typically seek to understand not only the fundamentals of a company's business, but also the potential near-term "catalysts" that can cause a meaningful upside or downside to the stock price. If a company is considering a significant change in its business or financial strategies, the CFO should be acutely aware of the potential reaction of this investor group.

Given the extraordinary expansion in electronic trading and derivative transactions in recent years, hedge funds are playing a larger role in providing liquidity to the market—and thus can serve as a buffer that may temper wild swings in a company's stock price. Consequently, CFOs are increasingly including hedge funds among the investor segments that they are targeting through their investor relations strategies. They simply are too important to ignore.

Index Funds

Index funds are becoming a larger percentage of most public companies' shareholder base—largely due to the increase in investors who have adopted the philosophy that it is better to pay lower fees for average returns than to pay higher fees for returns that may or may not exceed the average (and usually don't!). Furthermore, the amount of shares held by passive investors is increasing due to the explosive growth in exchange traded funds (ETFs), which offer investors a basket of stocks that reflect market or industry indexes.

Index funds and most ETFs are passive managers of their portfolios—simply reflecting the price movements in their baskets of stocks. Therefore, CFOs should not focus on them as a priority investor segment. However, CFOs should explicitly consider them if contemplating a change in a business or financial strategy that will cause their company not to qualify for the index or ETF in the future.

For example, a company may no longer fit a fund's criteria due to a significant change in its business mix, dividend yield, trading volume, or debt ratings. And if the company is removed from an index or ETF, the CFO should be prepared for some short-term downside pressure on the stock as the fund sells its shares into the market.

This market dislocation likely will dissipate over time. Nevertheless, CFOs don't want to be caught unawares by this potential volatility and will want to inform the CEO and board of directors in advance of the proposed action.

Individual Investors

CFOs historically have not emphasized individual investors in their marketing efforts. However, they can be a source of relatively stable holders. In addition, more retail investors are investing directly in stocks and ETFs through online brokerages, which continue to gain market share versus the traditional brokerage community.

Because the worldwide web has greatly facilitated the ability of companies to communicate their story directly to individual investors—rather than relying on brokerage firm analysts—targeting retail investors has become a more viable strategy, especially for companies with a well-known consumer franchise.

Investor Relations Programs

Of course, the actual mix of shareholders in a company's stock will be a composite of several different investment styles and is largely outside the company's control. Nevertheless, by focusing on target shareholders, CFOs can enhance the effectiveness of their investor relations programs.

For example, establishing a target mix can help determine which investor conferences to attend and which institutions to emphasize in road show visits. Moreover, having target shareholders in mind can guide the preparation of investor communications, indicating message points that should be highlighted and reinforced.

 ELEVATOR PITCH

After determining their target shareholders, CFOs should tailor a succinct investment story—an "elevator pitch"—that piques investor interest in their stock. In particular, they should craft answers to the three questions that investors seem invariably to ask in one-one-meetings. To paraphrase these questions, they are:

- How will I make money in this investment?
- What will be the catalyst for a higher stock price?
- What are the risks to my realizing the expected return?

As described by Malcolm Gladwell in his book *Blink* (Little, Brown, 2005), people often make snap judgments based on limited information—but are amazingly accurate in their assessments. Investors epitomize this phenomenon, quickly forming first impressions that determine whether they will take the time and make the effort to learn more about a company. CFOs should acknowledge this short attention span and be ready to make a compelling argument that will induce investors to perform a full investigation of a potential ownership stake.

PLAN REVISIONS

Although the strategic plan is intended to be enduring, it also should be a "living" document that adapts to changing conditions and shifting priorities.

As a best practice, boards of directors usually revisit the strategic plan at least annually, often via an offsite retreat. This provides the board members an opportunity to assess management's progress in implementing the plan—highlighting what is going well and what is proving to be a challenge. It also gives the board members an opportunity to make suggestions and voice concerns, which may cause some revisions in thinking.

In addition, the plan will evolve in response to specific strategic decisions. In a process that is analogous to the way that courts will interpret and shape the law in response to specific cases, the consideration of potential strategic actions—such as an acquisition opportunity—can bring clarity to a company's priorities. For example, a bank that has a business objective to increase cross-selling might consider whether acquiring an insurance company would make sense. It likely fits the broad strategic criteria, but it may be too expensive for the value created or too difficult to implement successfully.

Finally, the plan will be reviewed thoroughly in response to landmark corporate events such as the appointment of a new CEO, significant changes in the competitive environment, the introduction of a disruptive technology in the market, the loss of a major customer, a precipitous decline in the stock price, a takeover offer, or a shareholder activist proposal.

2

Communicating and Achieving Alignment

O NE OF THE PRINCIPAL BENEFITS OF A well-articulated strategic plan is that it can foster alignment among the company's investors, board of directors, chief executive officer (CEO), management team, and employees: It's a great way to get everyone singing from the same hymnal.

The strategic plan also provides milestones through which the CFO and the financial organization can monitor, measure, and evaluate the company's financial performance and forms the basis for the company's incentive compensation programs. CFOs can add considerable value in the design and implementation of the compensation programs, which are powerful tools in driving performance.

In addition, CFOs today typically play an indispensable role in interfacing with the investment community and a growing role with the financial media. Given the powerful developments in communications technology and the explosion of both traditional and online sources of information, it's more important than ever that companies project consistent messaging to the external world, especially with respect to their business and financial strategies. The CFO's playbook should emphasize this priority.

CONSISTENCY AND TRANSPARENCY

CFOs can play an integral role in achieving alignment, emphasizing consistency and transparency in the company's messaging—all the time reinforcing a focus on the strategic plan's business and financial objectives.

Consistent Communications

The strategic plan should be described consistently in all strategic communications, although the degree of specificity will vary depending on the audience and the type of communication (e.g., a regulatory filing, a press release, a media interview, an investor conference, or a town hall meeting). The general counsel typically will also review presentation materials to ensure that the company doesn't inadvertently violate a securities regulation.

In addition to consistency, CFOs should emphasize *repetition* in their communications. By repeating key message points, they can reinforce the company's commitment to its business and financial objectives and achieve greater alignment throughout the company and with external constituencies.

Transparent Communications

The investment community is looking for greater transparency concerning a company's strategic objectives, as well the metrics and sensitivities that will drive the company's performance. Therefore, CFOs are trending toward providing more information with respect to the key variables that will create or destroy shareholder value.

CFOs should evaluate what metrics to disclose regularly to investors, either in connection with their quarterly results or through a separate communication, including posting the results on the company's website. It is one of the best ways to achieve greater appreciation for the relationship between the company's near-term performance and its long-term strategic objectives.

It can also be argued that greater transparency will enhance shareholder value; investors abhor uncertainty and may ascribe a higher valuation to a stock if they believe management is being open and candid with them. Therefore, although some information may be sensitive in light of competitor or customer concerns, CFOs generally should be biased toward transparency—withholding information only if they have good reason to believe that the potential downsides of disclosure will outweigh the potential benefits.

Stakeholder Communications

CFOs generally have broadened and escalated their communications efforts in recent years, not only with investors, but also with other external and internal constituencies. For example, they often meet with customers, vendors, and government officials to describe their companies' strategic objectives and to provide perspectives concerning their historical financial results and expectations for the future. Furthermore, they meet regularly with bankers and the rating agencies; make frequent presentations to the board of directors and board committees; and speak regularly to management and employee groups.

The challenge for CFOs is not only to maintain consistency in their communications across the various constituencies, but also to cater their presentations for the specific audience that is being addressed—striking the right balance to inform and motivate. Recruiters at search firms confirm that these communication skills are becoming increasingly important in evaluating CFO candidates.

 INCENTIVE COMPENSATION PROGRAMS

Incentive compensation programs are especially important tools in achieving alignment around the strategic plan objectives. As a result, many CFOs are involved with establishing the criteria for these programs; it is integral to their playbook for delivering shareholder value.

While the chief human resource officer usually provides the primary staff support for the compensation committee of the board of directors, CFOs can play a role in recommending the metrics used for determining bonuses and other incentive compensation, establishing the definitions for these metrics, calculating the performance against these metrics, and providing input concerning the type of compensation that is paid. They can also help assess whether the compensation programs will incentivize behaviors and actions to achieve the company's strategic objectives.

Incentive Compensation Metrics

CFOs should provide input into the frameworks for the compensation programs. These frameworks usually reflect a mix of criteria that are either quantitative or qualitative and that are judged either according to a formula or left to the committee's discretion.

The discretionary portion of the framework can reflect the "degree of difficulty" in achieving the targets. For example, economic conditions may have improved or grown worse since setting the financial targets. They can also accommodate judgments concerning qualitative objectives that don't lend themselves to formulaic determinations.

An example of a hypothetical framework might be expressed in the following three-by-two matrix:

	Formulaic	Discretionary
Financial Metrics:	50%	20%
Non-Financial Metrics:	20%	—
Qualitative Objectives:	—	10%

CFOs can express views concerning the metrics to be included, as well as the percentage breakdown among quantifiable financial metrics (e.g., earnings per share); quantifiable non-financial metrics (e.g., customer satisfaction surveys); and qualitative objectives (e.g., implementation of a management development program). They can also recommend relative weightings for the criteria—especially the percentage breakdown between financial and non-financial metrics—as well as the amount of discretion that can be applied.

The criteria and their weightings should reinforce the strategic plan, including the business and financial objectives.

Absolute versus Relative Performance

Another key decision is whether the financial metrics should be evaluated on an absolute or relative basis. For example, if total shareholder return is to be a key performance measure, how should it be evaluated?

- As an *absolute target* (say, 12 percent)?
- In comparison with a *market index*?
- In comparison with an industry *peer group*?
- Or as a *combination* of an absolute target, with a market index or industry peer group modifier?

Range of Possible Outcomes

CFOs also can offer their perspectives concerning the ranges for the performance metrics—such as the minimum threshold to receive a bonus and the upper target to earn the maximum bonus. Also, should the range be symmetric or asymmetric from the target? For example, it may make sense to have a wider range for the upside potential and a narrower range for the downside risk.

By analyzing the company's historical data and performing sensitivity analyses, CFOs can help the compensation committee arrive at a sound judgment concerning the best way to structure the incentive payments for a range of possible outcomes.

Metric Definitions

CFOs should ensure that the definitions of the performance metrics are consistently applied and that they reinforce the strategic plan. For example, they should consider questions such as:

- **Capital Charge:** Should a capital charge be applied to the financial results?
- **Currencies:** Should non-U.S. operations be evaluated using local currency, budgeted exchange rates, or actual exchange rates?
- **Restructurings:** Should the costs and benefits of restructuring programs be included in the financial results?
- **Pension Funds:** Should the financial targets include the incremental costs of defined benefit plans due to changes in stock market values and interest rate levels?
- **Non-recurring Items:** Should the results include one-time benefits or costs such as a large investment gain or a litigation settlement?
- **Strategic Transactions:** Should the results include the costs and benefits of incremental acquisitions and divestitures?

Compensation Mix

CFOs may also want to express a point of view concerning the proportion of incentive compensation relative to salaries. For example, they may recommend a higher percentage of variable compensation as a way to gain more consistency in the company's financial results or to lessen its vulnerability to economic cycles.

As another example, CFOs may advocate restricted stock versus stock options if the company is paying a rich dividend and emphasizing the stability and predictability of its results. In contrast, stock options (or stock appreciation rights) may be more appropriate if the company is pursuing a high growth strategy in a relatively risky or volatile industry.

INVESTOR ALIGNMENT

Given their dual responsibilities in strategy and investor relations, CFOs are uniquely positioned to help achieve investor alignment around the strategic plan objectives. As much as possible, they should emphasize transparency in their communications of the company's strategic and financial objectives and the metrics that are used in the company's incentive compensation programs.

At the same time, they should *manage expectations*. It is critically important that CFOs establish credibility with investors and cultivate a reputation for delivering on their promises. The commonly expressed goal is to *underpromise* and *overdeliver*.

As a result, CFOs will always face a delicate balance between their desire to communicate openly about the company's objectives and their need to set realistic expectations about what can be accomplished within a given time frame.

Compensation Metrics

In particular, investors are increasingly focused on the metrics that drive incentive compensation programs—often considering them to be crucial in their decisions whether to own a stock. This focus has been heightened by the enhanced disclosures in proxy statements, particularly the relatively new requirement to provide a compensation discussion and analysis (CD&A).

The disclosures concerning incentive compensation can be a source of tension with shareholders; companies often prefer not to provide the specifics of their compensation metrics due to competitive concerns, while investors want to know the agreed-upon formulas that are incentivizing management. Furthermore, boards of directors often do not want to be constrained by a strictly formulaic approach to their compensation decisions—preferring to preserve some flexibility to account for the business environment and competitive conditions—while investors often desire certainty, especially in cases where the company has underperformed in the past.

Given the differing approaches to compensation, CFOs should be prepared to describe to investors not only the facts concerning their company's incentive compensation program, but also the compensation committee's rationale in designing and disclosing the management incentive metrics.

Form of Consideration

In addition, investors often have strong views concerning the form of consideration provided to management. For example, they may prefer that management receive equity securities rather than cash—thus giving management more "skin in the game." Or they may prefer that a company issue restricted stock rather than options so as to expose management to the same downside risks as investors and to eliminate a potential disincentive for increasing dividends on the stock (due to the negative impact on the Black-Scholes valuation of options).

Therefore, CFOs should evaluate whether the mix of consideration in the incentive compensation programs is consistent with the company's strategies and its target shareholders. If not, they may want to express this point of view to the compensation committee.

ANALYST RELATIONS

Analyst relations are at the heart of investor communications and central to the CFO's goal of achieving alignment. Between earnings announcements, public companies generally try to maintain an active dialogue with both sell side and buy side financial analysts, although subject to the "Fair Disclosure" restrictions (which prohibit selective disclosure of material information).[1] This dialogue typically begins in the immediate aftermath of the earnings call, when the company's investor relations professionals will answer detailed questions from the analysts to clarify the points made on the call.

Typically, most of the analysts' questions relate to their earnings models, which are updated to reflect the new information that has been communicated by the company. The sell side analysts usually will publish research notes that summarize the messages conveyed by the company on the earnings call, give some commentary about their reaction to the earnings announcement, and provide any updates with respect to their investment ratings on the company or their stock price expectations going forward.

Because of the significant decline in the number of sell side analysts during the past decade, as well as the sizable increase in the number of companies that each analyst covers, CFOs have become less reliant on sell side analysts to communicate their company's story to investors. The analysts simply do not have the bandwidth to fulfill this mission in today's financial environment. Therefore, maintaining sell side relations is a necessary, but not sufficient, strategy for keeping investors informed.

In response, CFOs and their investor relations teams are placing greater emphasis on communicating directly with current and prospective investors—focusing on both buy side analysts and institutional portfolio managers. This is a trend that has been underway for several years and shows no signs of abating.

For CFOs, it means being readily accessible to investors and recognizing that every interaction is important given the relatively close-knit investment community; major investors often will share their impressions with each other and the media.

Sell Side versus Buy Side Analysts

Sell side analysts are employed by brokerage firms to communicate with investors concerning an industry and companies within that industry. They typically will provide some fundamental research on the industry, maintain earnings models, and publish projections for earnings per share and other key financial data. They also will rate the company's stock (along the lines of a buy, sell, or hold recommendation) and usually provide a stock price target (the expected price within twelve months).

They formerly were closely identified with investment banking and played active roles in soliciting and executing equity financings. However, as a result of the reforms instigated by then New York Attorney General Elliot Spitzer in 2002, they now are separated from underwriting activities and are expected to generate revenue from trading commissions and fees paid by investors to the brokerage firm.

Buy side analysts, in contrast, are employed by institutional investors (such as investment managers, mutual funds, pension funds, and hedge funds) to analyze industries and companies and to recommend investments (either purchases or short sales) to the portfolio managers or other decision-makers. They do not publish their research and their investment ideas are considered proprietary.

Industry Analysts

In addition to their relations with financial analysts, CFOs also may help to cultivate the relations with industry analysts who form opinions concerning a company's business strategies and product lines. They include industry experts and consultants who provide proprietary commentary on industry developments. These thought leaders are especially prominent in high technology industries, where a number of well-known firms can exert significant influence among customers and investors.

At a minimum, CFOs should be aware of the analysts' opinions and should be alerted to any significant commentaries—both favorable and unfavorable—that may be forthcoming. This early warning allows CFOs to consider the potential impact on the company's financial results and the likely reaction among investors.

Furthermore, CFOs should make sure that any information provided to industry analysts is consistent with that provided to the investment community. And they may want to be actively involved in presentations to the analysts. For example, they can help to communicate the company's acquisition strategies or provide updates concerning the company's financial condition and its performance metrics.

 ## INVESTOR PRESENTATIONS

CFOs usually play a primary role in coordinating the priorities and content of investor presentations, which can include investor conferences, group meetings, investor days, and road shows. In addition, they often make the presentations.

Investor Conferences

The most common way to foster direct communications with investors is to make presentations at conferences that are sponsored by brokerage firms, often hosted by a sell side analyst who covers the company. The number of conferences that companies attend can vary a great deal, but around three or four a year is probably the norm. Usually the presentations are made by the CEO or CFO, although chief operating officers or business leaders can also be featured at these conferences.

Participating in investor conferences can offer several advantages:

- **Broad Dissemination:** The formal presentation is webcast, thus enabling the communication of new information without running afoul of the Fair Disclosure restrictions. This represents an effective way to highlight recent developments and gives more prominence to the communications than the alternative of issuing a press release.
- **Small Group Meetings:** The firm sponsoring the conference usually will arrange several small group or one-on-one meetings with investors. This is a highly efficient way to have intimate conversations with investors without the need to travel among dispersed locations.
- **Competitor Presentations:** The conferences typically feature presentations by competitors or by companies with similar investor profiles, thus providing a window into their current status and positioning with the investment community.

- **Investor Feedback:** They afford a chance to learn what is on investors' minds. Listening to their points of view can be of tremendous help in calibrating the company's messaging or even refining its financial strategies.

CFOs often use their presentations at investor conferences as an opportunity to educate analysts concerning their *earnings model*. This education can go a long way toward establishing effective communications with the financial community, especially when there are significant and rapid changes in business or economic conditions. If analysts and investors have a thorough comprehension of the earnings model, it is much easier for them to understand how changes in the macroeconomic environment likely will affect the company's results—thus reducing the possibility of negative surprises.

Most CFOs believe that participating in selected conferences is a worthwhile investment of their time and a superb opportunity to stay current with both equity and debt investors. However, they also recognize that the presentations can require considerable advance preparation and that they are generally most effective when the company has some new information to convey.

Group Meetings

Another common practice is to meet informally with a group of investors who have been convened by a sell side analyst, typically over a breakfast, lunch, or dinner. The usual format is for the CEO or CFO to make brief remarks and then to entertain questions and answers. The investors usually like to hear what's on the minds of other investors, which makes the Q&A format especially popular.

Unlike the investor conferences hosted by brokerage firms, these informal meetings are not webcast and thus are subject to the Fair Disclosure constraints. Nevertheless, they can provide an excellent opportunity for a constructive dialogue with investors, helping to clarify and reinforce the messages that have been previously delivered and giving the company's management a chance to hear directly from investors about their expectations and concerns.

Investor Day

Many CFOs have found it valuable to host an investor day, which is an opportunity to showcase the management team and to provide updates concerning the company's strategic objectives. Typically, these are half-day events that are simultaneously broadcast over the web.

In contrast to investor conferences, an investor day is sponsored by the company itself rather than by a brokerage firm; the company is the sole attraction—which has the advantage of gaining investors' undivided attention for the presentations and question-and-answer sessions. In addition, it can be an effective vehicle for exposing investors to the company's product offerings, including new product launches.

Some companies schedule an annual investor day that is held around the same time each year, often based on their planning cycle. This has the advantage of predictability and avoids raising expectations that an important announcement will be made.

The other approach is to host an investor day from time to time, usually when there is something new to report to investors. This helps the company deliver rich content, but may lead to disappointment if investors have high expectations for a dramatic announcement of some sort. Also, the scheduling of this kind of event can lead to anticipatory market activity in the company's stock and options, which can affect the way that the company's messaging is received, especially if the company is not making a major announcement.

As a general rule, investor days are generally well-received by shareholders and can facilitate a more in-depth understanding of the company's strategic objectives—including the financial performance that it expects to achieve over the long run and the sensitivities of its performance to exogenous factors and company-specific growth drivers. If done well, they also can relieve some of the pressure to meet quarterly expectations, with investors able to take a longer-term view with respect to the company's financial performance.

Road Shows

From time to time, companies will visit one or more cities for a series of one-on-one meetings and usually one or two group meetings. Although more time consuming than an investor conference, the visits to the investors' places of business can facilitate the attendance by portfolio managers, as well as buy side analysts, and can give the CFO a good feel for the various objectives and concerns among the decision-makers at significant institutions. The cities typically visited can range from U.S. locations such as New York, Boston, Chicago, San Francisco, Los Angeles, Denver, Minneapolis, Houston, Dallas, Atlanta, Philadelphia, or Baltimore or non-U.S. locations such as London, Edinburgh, Frankfurt, Paris, Milan, Tokyo, Hong Kong, or Shanghai.

The format typically comprises some brief remarks by the CEO or CFO, followed by questions and answers, although if it's a first-time meeting with the institution, presentation materials may be used to provide an overview of the company. These meetings are subject to the Fair Disclosure constraints.

Often a road show is arranged in connection with a securities offering, which adds another layer of legal constraints concerning the information that can be conveyed by the company.

Companies often ask sell side analysts to sponsor these visits. It is a way for CFOs to recognize the contributions of the brokerage firm analysts in communicating the company's messages to investors. Furthermore, the brokerage firms have the knowhow for arranging these visits, including taking care of the logistics (which can be especially valuable in an unfamiliar city). Most important, their salespeople will follow up with the investors subsequent to the meetings.

Some institutions will permit the sell side analysts to attend the meetings, but increasingly they are excluding the analysts from their one-on-one sessions with management. However, the analysts usually will attend the group meetings and will accompany the company's management in traveling to and from the various institutions. The analysts frequently will write a report subsequent to their trip, which means that the company's management should consider their conversations with the analyst to be "on the record" and subject to the Fair Disclosure rule.

The institutions to be visited usually will be a combination of existing and prospective shareholders. The sell side analysts typically will determine the itinerary, which sometimes can create a conflict with the company's investor relations objectives. For example, the analysts often will want to include hedge fund investors—who are responsible for much of the brokerage firms' trading volumes—while companies may prefer that the visits be focused on longer-term investors. Therefore, it is important that CFOs work closely with the analysts in arranging the visits so as not to have miscommunications and disappointments in their itinerary.

In the case of a securities offering, the lead underwriters will arrange the road show, including the recommendations of cities and institutions to visit. They also will coordinate the follow-ups to "indications of interest" by the institutions that are visited.

Virtual Road Shows

Despite the giant strides in communication technologies, most road shows are still done in person and investment banks generally will advocate that physical travel is necessary, especially in connection with initial public offerings or other issuances of securities. They argue that investors want to get a good feeling for the company's management, which is difficult to accomplish over the phone or through a screen.

Nevertheless, there has been some movement toward conducting virtual road shows from remote locations and, given the rapid advances in communication technologies, it would seem inevitable that we will be seeing more virtual road shows in the future.

For example, one technique is to have a conference call where the company communicates prepared remarks around a series of slides that are posted on the web. Then, similar to an earnings call, the management team answers questions from the group. Subsequent to this general presentation, the company then holds a series of one-on-one conference calls or video meetings with selected institutions.

Major Announcements

Companies usually will arrange a special communications program for major announcements, such as a merger or a significant acquisition or divestiture. Often working with a public relations firm that specializes in strategic communications, companies will typically engineer a multifaceted program consisting of a press release, a webcast presentation, several investor meetings or calls, and media interviews—all well-coordinated around targeted message points.

These communication programs can be extremely important to investors' perceptions of major events, often determining whether an announcement is well-received and the initial impact on the company's stock price. Consequently, it is vitally important that in preparing for the announcement, CFOs have anticipated the potential questions from investors and the media, and to the extent possible, have crafted answers that can be communicated clearly and concisely to a relatively broad audience.

 COMPANY WEBSITE

All of the company's financial communications come together on the website, which has become the bedrock of effective investor communications. It provides one-stop convenience for investors, allowing them to obtain Securities and Exchange Commission (SEC) filings, earnings press releases, earnings and other conference calls, investor presentations, webcasts, and other essential information about a company. Websites are especially important vehicles for communicating with individual investors, who appreciate the breadth of information.

CFOs typically use third-party services to help develop and maintain their investor relations websites, with considerable focus on the design of the home page. However, the technology and best practices are evolving quite rapidly, which means that CFOs should ensure that their practices are staying up-to-date. Also, to the extent that they can add features such as answers to frequently asked questions, the website can free up investor relations people to focus on higher value added activities.

SOCIAL MEDIA

To date, CFOs generally have not actively embraced social media in their investor communications strategies and investor relations professionals have been wary concerning their potential use. Encouraging visits to the company's website continues to be the primary focus of their electronic communications with investors.

This reluctance to utilize social media at least partly reflects the potential legal ramifications. The SEC has made it clear that all communications made by, or on behalf of, the company are subject to securities laws. Furthermore, the SEC has admonished companies to establish controls and procedures and to monitor all of the company's activities on the web. Thus, even if companies are not proactively using social media in their investor relations strategies, their general counsels will need to stay abreast of actions by the marketing departments or other areas that may be accessing these outlets.

In addition, CFOs will want to stay current concerning the use of social media by investors to communicate with each other. For example, a posting by an individual in a blog or on a chat board—irrespective of whether the information is true or false—can trigger a rumor and cause volatility in the company's stock price.

Furthermore, shareholders may use social media to organize their efforts to propose a strategic action by the company or to effect a change in its governance—which could have serious consequences to the company if it allows them to gain proxy access or otherwise advance their agenda. This is a trend worth watching, especially when combined with other changes in the corporate governance landscape.

The bottom line is that the use of social media—as well as the Internet in general—is likely to have far-reaching implications for investor communication strategies in the future. CFOs—as well as CEOs, general counsels, and board members—will need to stay abreast of these developments to maximize their positive impact, but also to safeguard against their potential to do harm.

MEDIA RELATIONS

Most companies believe that it is advantageous to have their CFOs play an active role in media relations, which is a prime example of how the CFO's playbook is expanding. And it seems reasonable to assume that this responsibility will continue to grow in importance, indicating additional skill sets that will be desirable—or, more likely, essential—for the CFOs of the future.

Integral to Investor Relations

With the growth of financial media beyond the traditional print sources—including specialist broadcast networks like CNBC, Fox Business, and Bloomberg, as well as financially oriented websites like Yahoo Finance, Google Finance, Motley Fool, Seeking Alpha, and The Street—more investors are obtaining information from third-party sources than previously. The lines between media and investor communications are continuing to blur, with investors obtaining information from the various media outlets and with the media following market developments with more intensity.

Therefore, CFOs should ensure that the media relations strategies are synchronized with the investor relations strategies—helping to accomplish their common objectives—and should consider their involvement in media relations as integral to their investor relations efforts.

Substitute for CEO

In most cases, the media would prefer to interact with the CEO. However, it is virtually impossible for the CEO to satisfy all of the requests due to conflicting demands on his or her time. The CFO typically is considered a credible substitute for the CEO, capable of discussing the company's strategies and financial objectives and of representing the company with a broad audience. In addition, CFOs can be a desirable subject for an interview due to their particular expertise with respect to strategic or financial topics.

In light of the increased skepticism about corporate financial statements and the public's heightened interest concerning corporate investment plans—especially why they are not reinvesting in more job-creating projects—CFOs can be desirable public relations representatives. Next to the CEO, the CFO is usually the best alternative to serve as the public face for the company—capable of addressing questions concerning the company's policies and plans.

Need for Immediate Responses

Given the fast pace of the 24/7 news cycle, the corporate communications group often needs to provide an immediate response to a media inquiry, possibly relating to activity in the company's stock price or to rumors concerning its financial results. CFOs are often in the best position to provide this response, which can make a big difference in ensuring that the company's point of view is represented from the outset.

POTENTIAL MEDIA PITFALLS

Nevertheless, although CFOs are increasingly expected to add value through their active participation in media relations, they should be wary of the downside risks in playing this role.

SEC Restrictions

For public company CFOs, anything that they say to the media is subject to the anti-fraud provisions under the securities laws. Therefore, it is important that CFOs stick to messages that are consistent with the company's communications strategies—as would be the case for an investor presentation. Moreover, depending upon the publication or news outlet, the CFO must be careful not to violate the Fair Disclosure rule. This could occur if a statement is not deemed to be broadly disseminated through the media—such as a specialist blog or website—and is considered material information provided to a select group of potential investors.

Marketing Coordination

Comments to the media are likely to be heard or read by customers; therefore, anything that the CFO says about products or services should be consistent with the company's marketing communications. In particular, CFOs should be careful in discussing product launch dates or sales expectations—which could upstage the marketing plans.

Stakeholder Concerns

Even with the proper caveats, a CFO's comments may upset a stakeholder group who may translate the comment more strongly than intended or take it out of context. For example, if a CFO says that a plant shutdown or additional outsourcing could be a potential cost reduction strategy, this might prematurely or unnecessarily alarm employees or communities about the possible impact to them.

Predictions of the Future

Because there usually is a delay between an interview and the publication of an article or the airing of a feature, the CFO's comments about the future may seem out of touch in light of intervening events—an especially acute risk due to the volatile and unpredictable financial environment in recent years. As Yogi Berra said, "It's hard to make predictions, especially about the future."

 ## COORDINATING COMMUNICATIONS

To maximize the benefits and to ameliorate the potential downsides, CFOs should work closely with their company's public relations and corporate communications people and any media advisors. They can help to screen and prioritize interviews, establish appropriate ground rules, and accompany the CFO to any interviews or appearances.

In some cases, it may be helpful to establish a direct or dotted line reporting relationship between corporate communications and the CFO. However, regardless of the reporting structure, it is important for the CFO to forge a close working relationship between the finance organization and the people who communicate regularly with the media.

 ## INTERVIEW FORMATS

Some interview formats have more risks for CFOs than other formats. For example, a live broadcast interview is more controllable than one that is edited. And if ground rules are established for the interview—such as a prior review of facts and quotes before they are published—that can be a good check against wrong information or erroneous transcriptions, although it usually won't allow the CFO to retract a quote unless the journalist agrees. Also, a "deep background" interview that doesn't mention the CFO by name is certainly less risky than going on the record in a documented conversation.

Furthermore, the type of publication or broadcast outlet can make a real difference. For example, specialist publications such as finance magazines tend

Ernst & Young's "Media Relations: 10 Tips for the CFO"

1. Prepare for the unexpected.
2. Have clear goals for an interview.
3. Keep it simple.
4. Don't be afraid to dig in.
5. Ask for feedback.
6. Get to know journalists and their agendas.
7. Prepare for everyday situations—not just a crisis.
8. Make the time for media training.
9. Work in tandem with the corporate communications team.
10. Recalibrate your measure of successful media relations.

Source: Excerpted from "Back seat or center stage? CFOs and the Media," which was published in 2010 as part of Ernst & Young's "The Master CFO Series" at www.ey.com.

to be more favorable to the CFO than national publications, which may have a less balanced agenda. The simple fact is that a journalist can make CFOs look bad, no matter how much they stay on message.

In addition, it certainly helps to know the track record of the journalist or, even better, to have dealt with him or her in the past. The best defense against an unbalanced interview is to deal with a journalist with a reputation for integrity and fairness.

Finally, CFOs will want to be sure that they are comfortable with the subject matter, especially if it's on a technical subject—like an accounting standard or a technology strategy—where the interview is likely to get into details.

The main point is that CFOs should be circumspect about granting an interview, making sure that it is likely to result in a story that advances the company's overall communications and media relations strategies, as well as enhancing its brand image with investors, customers, employees, and other stakeholders. When in doubt, don't do it.

 MEDIA TRAINING

As CFOs become more involved in their company's media relations, they are well advised to undergo some media training. Either in-house or external experts can help CFOs to achieve impactful interviews and avoid some common pitfalls. For example, media training can provide helpful tips such as the suggestions described below.

Stick to Message Points

Although politicians are often ridiculed for their slavish devotion to prepackaged messages, there is wisdom in their goal of answering the questions that they want to answer rather than necessarily the ones that they are asked. Message points also can help to prevent rambling or to avoid drifting into unfamiliar or dangerous territory.

Do Not Repeat a Leading Question

Media training can sensitize the CFO to journalist techniques such as the "have you stopped beating your wife" type of question. For example, if a journalist asks "Are you cooking the books?" and you reply, "We are not cooking the books," you are apt to see a headline like the following: "CFO Says that Company XYZ is Not Cooking the Books."

Avoid Extraneous Subjects

A journalist may ask you about a current event that essentially amounts to a political question. Unless the CFO can resist the temptation to offer a personal opinion, he or she may inadvertently embroil the company in a controversial topic and risk alienating a segment of the company's customer or employee base. It is usually better to avoid extraneous subjects at all times, but especially when they have not been considered in advance.

Keep It Simple

The audience for a media interview is usually less sophisticated about financial matters than an investor group. Therefore, CFOs should avoid using acronyms or jargon and try to communicate in a manner that is clear, concise, and easily understood. The goal is not to sound smart—it is to communicate the company's message points in a way that connects with the audience.

Be Self-Confident

If nothing else, media training will bolster CFOs' self-confidence and sense of being in control. This will increase the probability that their involvement in media relations will be a positive experience for both them and their company.

NOTE

1. The Securities and Exchange Commission adopted the Fair Disclosure regulation (Regulation FD) on August 15, 2000 to "address the selective disclosure of information by publicly traded companies and other issuers." The rule provides that "when an issuer discloses material nonpublic information to certain individuals or entities—generally, securities market professionals, such as stock analysts, or holders of the issuer's securities who may well trade on the basis of the information—the issuer must make public disclosure of that information." http://www.sec.gov/answers/regfd.htm.

CHAPTER THREE

Assessing Enterprise Risks

R ISK MANAGEMENT HAS BEEN RECEIVING much more focus in recent years. Companies have been stepping up their risk procedures, the rating agencies are considering risk management in their credit evaluations, and boards of directors are devoting more of their agendas to risk oversight. Risk is now considered fundamental to a company's strategy; the best practice is to consider risk assessments as integral to strategic plan reviews.

 ## ENTERPRISE RISK MANAGEMENT

This heightened focus on risk has been encapsulated in enterprise risk management (ERM) programs that take a systematic approach to identifying, monitoring, and mitigating risk exposures. Much of the impetus for ERM programs has come from regulatory pressures—notably from the Sarbanes-Oxley Act and the New York Stock Exchange's corporate governance rules—but undoubtedly they also have been motivated by recent events in the business, financial, and political environments—where so-called black swan events have challenged previously held beliefs concerning the predictability of the future. Furthermore, the financial crisis has caused considerable introspection concerning the degree to which incentive compensation may be causing behavior that is inimical to a company's long-term financial health—let alone to the overall economy.

Against this backdrop, CFOs are plunging head first into risk—reviewing its implications for strategy and analyzing its potential to create both downside and upside to shareholder value. And they are becoming actively involved with ERM programs, which are now essential to the CFO's playbook.

COSO Enterprise Risk Management-Integrated Framework

The Committee of Sponsoring Organizations of the Treadway Commission (COSO) published an ERM framework in 2004 that established eight components and four categories.

- **Components:** Internal Environment, Objective Setting, Event Identification, Risk Assessment, Risk Response, Control Activities, Information and Communication, Monitoring
- **Categories:** Strategy, Operations, Financial Reporting, and Compliance

In January 2011 COSO published a white paper entitled "Embracing Enterprise Risk Management" by Mark L. Frigo and Richard J. Anderson. This paper noted the following seven "underlying themes that have proved valuable in successful ERM initiatives":

- **Themes:** Support from the Top is a Necessity, Build ERM Using Incremental Steps, Focus Initially on a Small Number of Top Risks, Build on Existing Risk Management Activities, Embed ERM into the Business Fabric of the Organization, and Provide Ongoing ERM Updates and Continuing Education for Directors and Senior Management

---

 ## IMPLEMENTATION OF ERM

In implementing their ERM programs, companies generally proceed along the following path, although their actual processes can vary considerably by industry and by company.

- **Identify Risk Incidents.** Canvass people throughout the company to identify the major strategic, operational, financial, and compliance risks.

- **Quantify the Exposures.** Prioritize the greatest exposures by a combination of the probability of their occurrence and the likely impact if an incident occurs.
- **Assess the Current Status.** Determine to what extent action plans have been put in place to reduce the probability or the potential impact of an occurrence.
- **Assign Oversight Responsibilities.** Make someone accountable for assessing, monitoring, and developing action plans for each of the risks.
- **Establish a Governance Framework.** Institute a review process involving an overall ERM leader, an ERM steering committee, and oversight by the board of directors.
- **Prioritize Risk Exposures.** Focus the board's review on the risk exposures that represent the greatest threats to the company.
- **Analyze Mitigation Strategies.** Continuously consider potential action steps to mitigate existing or new risk exposures, including appropriate cost/benefit analyses.
- **Consider Potential Upsides.** Review ways that the company can use risk as a source of competitive advantage and financial rewards.

RISK IDENTIFICATION

Typically, the identification of risk incidents begins with a large assortment of potential exposures, which then need to be reduced to a manageable number.

For banks and financial services companies, the processes for identifying and managing risks have been well-established, with a predominant focus on asset portfolio risks and liquidity risks. For them, the establishment of an ERM program has meant a broadening of the risks that are managed and more formalization of the reporting arrangements, especially to the board of directors.

For non-financial companies, internal audit reviews traditionally have covered such topics as disaster recovery, supply chain exposures, regulatory compliance, fraud, stewardship of assets, and availability of liquidity. For these companies, implementing ERM has meant not only a broadening of the risks being monitored, but also a shift in emphasis toward business risks that heretofore have not been a priority for internal audit reviews.

As they identify risks, companies are challenged to focus on the new exposures that may arise in the future rather than on events that have occurred in the past. In other words, they need to look toward the horizon and not through the rear-view mirror.

RISK QUANTIFICATION

After accumulating potential exposures, the next step is to categorize and quantify them. For example, many companies evaluate the risks through a heat map that ranks the risks according to a 1 to 5 scale on two dimensions: the probability of an occurrence and the magnitude of the potential impact. See Figure 3.1 for an example.

In quantifying the *probability of an occurrence*, it is usually helpful to establish a time frame for when the event could occur—such as within the next five or 10 years. Otherwise, if the time frame is indefinite or infinite, the probability of a precipitating event (such as an earthquake or an economic meltdown) can reach close to 100 percent, which makes it a meaningless exercise.

In quantifying the *magnitude of the impact*, some risks can be estimated in terms of lost revenue or incremental costs. For these risks, their potential impact can be analyzed as a percentage of the company's overall revenue or profit and the risk numbers can be assigned according to the relative dollar amounts of the exposure.

However, in the case of other risks (such as a cyber attack), it may be very difficult to make credible financial estimates, and there could be a wide discrepancy between their immediate impact and their long-term implications. Therefore,

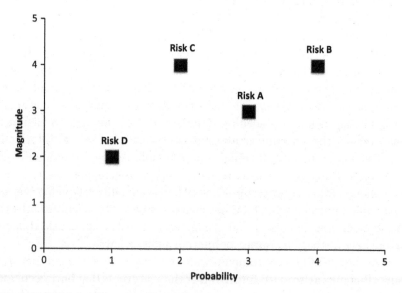

FIGURE 3.1   Quantifying Enterprise Risks

an alternative way to quantify the risks is to assign a numerical ranking based on the *amount of disclosure* that would be required in the event of an occurrence.

For example, an impact might be rated a "1" if it needs to be reported to the ERM steering committee; a "2" if it is reported to the CEO; a "3" if it is reported to the board of directors; a "4" if it should be included in the company's next 10-Q or 10-K filing; and a "5" if it requires an immediate press release and 8-K filing.

ERM programs are generally evolving toward more subjectivity in their risk assessments, including risks that have a seemingly remote probability of occurring or that are difficult to quantify.

MAJOR EXPOSURES

When ERM was first introduced within a broad group of companies, much of their focus was on traditional balance sheet and financial risk exposures. However, after implementing ERM, they have gained more appreciation for the truly material threats to their well-being. As a result, managements and boards have escalated their focus on big picture risks, such as disruptive technologies, data security, reputation and brand image, government regulations, natural disasters, and long tail events.

Disruptive Technologies

Companies have become more conscious of their exposures to potential technology breakthroughs that could seriously threaten the viability of their business models. It has become increasingly clear that the best way to reduce risk is to innovate continuously and perhaps to lead the cannibalization of their existing ways of doing business.

ERM can help companies to overcome their natural reluctance to take a short-term hit to profitability for a long-term gain in their competitive positioning.

Data Security

Companies have also become more sensitized to the potential threats to their data networks due to deliberate or accidental actions, especially when they can compromise personally identifiable information. The deliberately destructive hacking of company data systems by organized groups has been especially disconcerting to information technology experts, whose apprehension has been exacerbated by the proliferation of cloud computing and other external applications.

Furthermore, their concern over cyber security has been reinforced by SEC guidelines published in October 2011 that require disclosures of actual cyber incidents (including their costs), potential cyber risks (including those related to outsourcing), and their degree of insurance coverage for cyber risks.

In addition to the specific risks related to cyber security, companies are also generally concerned about inadvertent misuses of customer or employee data. This has led to more focus on passwords and other security protections and greater requirements for encrypted data in laptops and other portable devices.

Reputation and Brand Image

Companies have become keenly aware that a business setback (such as a product recall) can cost much more than the direct costs if it damages the company's reputation and brand image. Furthermore, it's not only actual, but also rumored events that can jeopardize a company's reputation in the marketplace. The rapid dissemination of information through electronic media makes this threat all the more real and alarming.

Given the high-profile issues that have arisen for some of the world's largest and most prestigious corporations, boards of directors and management teams have recognized that risk issues have the potential for creating much greater damage than their immediate financial impact. Indeed, fortifying their reputation and brand image can be considered the umbrella objective that drives their risk management programs.

In addition, companies are paying closer attention to sustainability and other measures of their corporate social responsibility. In many cases, CFOs are taking the lead in developing metrics and targets for their company's efforts in areas of social concern.

Government Regulations

With the recent proliferation of burdensome legislation and regulations, companies have concluded that some of their greatest risks can emanate from governments and their agencies. This is crystal clear in the financial services industry—with the impending Dodd-Frank rules and the additional capital requirements being imposed on their activities by various regulatory authorities—but the threat of constraining and costly regulations is a common theme throughout all industries and all countries.

Not coincidentally, companies are stepping up their government relations activities and adding board members with political and regulatory experience. This can alleviate exposures to their bottom lines and help to ensure that their strategic and business objectives will not be thwarted by external constraints.

Natural Disasters

As evidenced by the Japanese earthquake and tsunami—as well as the floods in the United States and Thailand—the world seems to be going through a phase where natural disasters are increasing in their frequency and severity. Climate change has raised the stakes, creating much more uncertainty concerning risk exposures that can devastate a company's future prospects.

Natural disasters are definitely risks that companies need to understand fully, including their potential exposures to supply chain and other operational risks, and they need to take proactive steps to reduce the potential magnitudes of loss.

Long Tail Events

As evidenced by the financial crisis and recent natural disasters, the quantification of risks needs to account for the "long tail" possibilities—risks that have a remote probability based on normal standard deviations, but that can have catastrophic effects. Consequently, companies are focusing more attention on these potential calamities (which are also called "black swan" or "fat tail" events) and that heretofore have not been captured adequately by value at risk or other quantitative models.

Companies are also examining the interdependencies of their risks across the globe. While a specific risk occurrence may not be material to a single location, it may cross the materiality threshold if it occurs simultaneously in several locations or if it is combined with other risk occurrences that arise from the same event.

Although investors generally can diversify their exposures to economic and market conditions through the composition of their portfolios, they cannot protect themselves from the dislocations and incremental costs resulting from a company's financial duress or potential bankruptcy. Consequently, CFOs should be especially focused on the interdependencies of exogenous events—such as the potential contagion resulting from sovereign debt defaults or the possibility of a worldwide recession—that could compromise the company's viability as a going concern.

Deloitte's "10 Fatal Faws of Conventional Risk Management"

1. Counting on false assumptions.
2. Failing to exercise vigilance.
3. Ignoring velocity and momentum.
4. Failing to make the key connections and manage complexity.
5. Failing to imagine failure.
6. Relying on unverified sources of information.
7. Maintaining inadequate margins of safety.
8. Focusing exclusively on the short term.
9. Failing to take enough of the right risks.
10. Lack of operational discipline.

Source: Funston, Frederick, Wagner, Stephen, and Ristuccia, Henry, "Risk Intelligent decision-making: Ten essential skills for surviving and thriving in uncertainty" Summer 2010 www.deloittereview.com (2010 Deloitte Development LLC), p. 4.

 MITIGATION STRATEGIES

After identifying their risk exposures, companies then determine which risks should be retained and which should be mitigated either through purchasing third-party insurance or by taking action steps to prevent an occurrence or to reduce the potential magnitude of loss.

Preventing an Occurrence

The first priority in mitigating enterprise risks is to prevent an occurrence in the first place. CFOs should encourage action steps such as:

- **Business Decisions.** For example, not locating a nuclear plant in an earthquake-prone location.
- **Technology Investments.** For example, purchasing software that detects and prevents cyber attacks.
- **Management Practices.** For example, implementing procedures to enhance the quality of products or services.

- **Training and Education.** For example, sponsoring training programs in safety and preventative maintenance.
- **Management Oversight.** For example, establishing credit committees to monitor investment policies.

Mitigating an Occurrence

The second priority is to mitigate the potential impact in the event of an occurrence. CFOs should consider action steps such as:

- **Insurance Policies:** For example, purchasing property and casualty policies that include business interruption.
- **Disaster Recovery Plans:** For example, reviewing the status of disaster recovery plans as part of internal audit reviews.
- **Contractual Limitations:** For example, establishing limits in liability exposures for outsourcing or consulting services.
- **Backup Arrangements:** For example, identifying an alternative supplier in the event of a supply chain interruption.
- **Rapid Responses:** For example, developing contingency plans to respond quickly to potential threats to the company's reputation.

REWARDED VERSUS UNREWARDED RISKS

The purpose of ERM can be misconstrued as intending to eliminate all material risks, whatever the costs. Instead, the primary purposes of ERM are to understand a company's risk exposures and to adopt risk strategies that reflect the company's considered judgments concerning the appropriate risk and reward tradeoffs—often embracing the retention of risk as an appropriate business strategy.

Within the risk management community, this distinction is often described as "rewarded" versus "unrewarded" risks. Unrewarded risks do not provide any upside to the company and typically should be managed to minimize their potential impact. In contrast, rewarded risks can be managed to realize their potential upside. It is akin to the distinction between "good" and "bad" cholesterol.

For example, pursuing a new technology may cannibalize a company's existing products, but give it greater long-term potential (such as Netflix's introduction of direct streaming of videos); expanding aggressively in a cyclical downturn can pay off handsomely if the market recovers (such as ExxonMobil's investments in natural gas); or assuming contractual liabilities may allow a company to expand its market share (such as offering product warranties for medical devices or providing performance guarantees in an outsourcing contract).

The basic point is that it may be difficult to earn superior returns without incurring some incremental risks. The question is not so much whether a strategy involves risk, but whether this risk is likely to be rewarded through greater growth or higher returns.

Diversifiable Risks

In analyzing the potential for retaining rewarded risks, CFOs should make a distinction between risks that shareholders can mitigate through diversification versus those risks that investors would expect to be protected against.

For example, investors who invest in a utility may seek exposure to nuclear energy, even though they know that it involves inherent financial and operational risks. Within the context of their diversified portfolio, the tradeoff makes sense. However, investors do not want risk exposures from locating a plant in a dangerous place or from implementing inadequate maintenance procedures.

In other words, investors can accept strategic decisions that are carefully analyzed and fully communicated, but they will be unforgiving where management has failed to take reasonable precautions or has been negligent in execution.

Opportunity Costs

CFOs also should be mindful of potential opportunity costs from pursuing risk mitigation strategies. For example, a company that is concerned about cyber security may constrain the use of electronic equipment, such as forbidding employees from using mobile devices when traveling to certain countries. While this helps to mitigate the risk, it also makes it harder for employees to function, with possible consequences to revenue and profit.

Mitigation strategies should be cost-effective and reasonable, with a balanced consideration of the pros and cons. The goal is not to minimize or eliminate risks, but to manage them intelligently.

 ## GOVERNANCE OF ERM

Companies have adopted a variety of governance models for their ERM programs. The programs usually are led by a chief risk officer, the CFO, or by the head of compliance, and include a committee consisting of representatives from the business units as well as staff areas. The goal is to have a broad enough group to encompass the key risk areas, but to be small enough to require individual accountabilities.

Recent surveys have indicated that more companies are identifying the chief risk officer as the person who assumes primary responsibility for their ERM programs. Risk professionals are especially likely to play a leadership role in regulated industries (e.g., financial services) or in companies where risk management is core to their business models (e.g., energy companies).

Board Oversight

In overseeing the ERM program, boards of directors typically employ one of the following two primary alternatives:

1. Managing all of the risks by either a dedicated risk committee or the audit committee.
2. Assigning oversight of the program to the audit committee, but delegating management of the various risks to either the entire board or to one of the board committees.

Involving the full board and all its committees has a number of advantages. First, it frees up time for the audit committee, which has seen its scope of responsibilities expand considerably in recent years. Second, some of the risks are better placed in alternative committees, such as financial risks in the finance committee and reputational risks in the corporate responsibility committee. Third, it avoids the need to establish a risk committee in a non-financial company. And fourth, given the importance of risk management as a strategic imperative, it makes sense that the whole board should be accountable.

Strategic Plan Coordination

As a best practice, the board should explicitly address risk implications when conducting strategy reviews with management. Also, the compensation committee should assess whether the incentive compensation programs are appropriately balanced from a risk perspective. Especially for financial services companies, it is critically important that the compensation programs avoid asymmetric incentives that encourage excessive risk-taking through their upside rewards without commensurate exposures in downside scenarios.

Furthermore, a relatively new SEC rule mandates that public companies analyze and disclose compensation practices that are reasonably likely to have a material adverse effect.

 ## CFO'S ROLE IN ERM

Irrespective of the management reporting structure, CFOs should play a leadership role in ERM, bringing their unique abilities to influence the program's success.

Linkage to Strategy

Probably the most compelling reason is the linkage to strategy. Given their role in articulating the strategic plan, it makes sense for CFOs to play an active role in assessing the risk implications.

CFOs should determine whether the strategies will exacerbate any enterprise risks and, if so, whether and how the company should mitigate these exposures. In addition, they should evaluate potential upsides from assuming greater risks in implementing the strategies. For example, the company could assume greater risks by accelerating the launch dates for new products. The question is whether the expected upsides to shareholder value outweigh the increased exposures to risk.

Financial Organization

The financial organization usually is aware of potential issues throughout the company and has formal communication channels through Sarbanes-Oxley, including a disclosure committee that meets at least quarterly. CFOs can tap into this financial network and encourage the free flow of relevant information through both formal and informal communication channels—serving as an early warning system concerning potential risk exposures.

External Contacts

In identifying risks, ERM strives to identify not only existing risks, but also those that may be emerging. Because of their external contacts, CFOs have a good vantage point for identifying potential threats and opportunities.

For example, CFOs can obtain valuable intelligence from both equity and fixed income analysts, who often have a window into emerging technologies, possible competitor actions, or impending regulatory changes. It's a good bet that if an issue is surfaced by a buy side analyst, it is probably something that's worth investigating.

Likewise, the CFO's relationships with investment bankers, regulators, rating agencies, and other CFOs can be fertile sources concerning issues that may be coming down the pike.

Market Intelligence

In a similar manner, financial markets may be indicating a heightened risk exposure. For example, a rumor may cause a material change in the company's stock price or options pricing. The CFO can follow up to determine whether there is any truth to the rumor and determine if it requires a response.

As another example, the company's bond prices or its pricing in the credit default market may be indicating a credit issue that is arising from external actions, such as a competitor's introduction of a new technology or a significant merger in the industry.

Mitigation Expenses

CFOs have the tools and processes for analyzing potential mitigation strategies, including the purchase of insurance or investments in risk avoidance technologies. In particular, they can evaluate the potential investments against other priorities in the investment budget.

This includes comparing projects that produce a fairly predictable rate of return with mitigation strategies that produce an extremely uncertain rate of return (such as investments that protect the company against catastrophic consequences from a highly improbable event).

Another example is investing in government affairs and lobbying to protect against regulatory risks throughout the world. It's hard to quantify a rate of return, but this very well could be a good use of capital, especially for companies in regulated industries. CFOs can help to evaluate the potential investment from the shareholder's perspective.

Investor Interest

Investors want to understand a company's risk management strategies. In virtually every one-on-one or small group meeting, they will ask management about the company's exposures to material risks, often couching the question as "What keeps you up at night"?

By being actively involved in ERM, CFOs can provide a powerful response to this boiler-plate question by describing the robustness of their company's ERM program and their efforts to mitigate the most significant risks. This can be very reassuring to investors, reinforcing their decision to own the company's stock or debt.

Rating Agency Criteria

The rating agencies have taken a keen interest in the status of companies' risk management processes and now are explicitly considering ERM as part of their ratings criteria. They view ERM as one of the hallmarks of superior management and emblematic of good governance practices. They also are specifically asking about the processes for defining the company's risk appetite.

By including ERM as part of their regular presentations to the rating agencies, CFOs can engage in a rich discussion concerning risk strategies and perhaps gain insights concerning the best practices being implemented by other companies.

PART TWO

Capital Allocations

CHAPTER FOUR

Estimating the Cost of Capital

T HE COMPANY'S ESTIMATED COST OF CAPITAL is the fundamental building block for capital allocations—providing analytical consistency across the potential investment alternatives and facilitating comparisons among alternatives that have differing time horizons and risk profiles.

It also provides a basis for comparing reinvestments in the business through capital expenditures or acquisitions versus the return of cash to shareholders through dividends or share repurchases. Unless an investment or acquisition earns the company's cost of capital, shareholders would be better off to receive the cash.

WACC FORMULA

Today most companies estimate their cost of capital through the *capital asset pricing model.* This model uses a relatively straightforward and well-accepted formula to arrive at an estimate of the company's *weighted-average cost of capital (WACC).* The variables in this formula can be expressed as follows:

L: The targeted percentage of debt leverage in the company's market capitalization

R: The risk-free rate of interest, typically measured by the 10-year Treasury rate

C: The pre-tax cost of debt, reflecting the company's estimated marginal interest rate for debt financing

M: The market's expectation for equity market returns, typically assumed to be 6 to 7 percentage points over the risk-free rate of interest

B: The company's beta, which is a measure of the correlation of its stock price with the market

T: The company's marginal tax rate

Using the above variables, the algebraic formula for the company's WACC can be shown as follows:

$$\text{Cost of Debt} = C \times (1 - T)$$

$$\text{Cost of Equity} = B \times (M - R) + R$$

$$\text{Cost of Capital} = L \times (\text{Cost of Debt}) + (1 - L) \times (\text{Cost of Equity})$$

Example of Cost of Capital Calculation

Let's assume that the risk-free rate is 3 percent; the company's pre-tax cost of debt is 6 percent; the market's expectation for equity returns is 10 percent; the company's beta is 1.25; and the company's marginal tax rate is 35 percent. In this case, if the company is targeting 30 percent of its capital structure as debt and 70 percent as equity, its cost of capital can be estimated as follows:

$$\text{Cost of Debt} = 6.00\% \times (1.00 - .35) = 3.90\%$$

$$\text{Cost of Equity} = 1.25 \times (10.00\% - 3.00\%) + 3.00\% = 11.75\%$$

$$\text{Cost of Capital} = .3 \times 3.90\% + .7 \times 11.75\% = 1.17\% + 8.23\% = 9.40\%$$

Updates and Validation

CFOs will update their cost of capital calculations periodically, not only for changes in the market environment, but also to reflect any revisions in the company's capital structure strategies—such as the target percentage of debt in its market capitalization—and to incorporate a more recent calculation of the company's beta.

In addition, they may seek third-party validation of their WACC estimates from time to time, asking investment bankers or consultants to make an independent calculation.

Betas

Betas vary among industries and companies, reflecting differences in their sensitivity to the economic or financial environment. A beta over 1.00 means that a stock moves more than the market, indicating greater market risk, while a beta less than 1.00 means that a stock moves less than the market, indicating lower market risk.

Betas are also affected by company-specific factors, including the company's debt leverage, with greater leverage correlating with a higher beta. And they can fluctuate over time, reflecting both industry and company-specific developments and trends.

Comparison of Industry Betas

Shown below is a comparison of betas for industry sectors in the S&P 500 as of the end of 2010:

Materials	1.30
Industrials	1.25
Financials	1.23
Energy	1.19
Consumer Discretionary	1.13
Information Technology	1.11
Utilities	0.86
Healthcare	0.79
Consumer Staples	0.72
Telecom Services	0.69

Source: Bloomberg

Sources of Betas

For public companies, CFOs can obtain betas from third-party providers of market data who compute the correlations of a company's share price movements with the stock market, as measured by a broad market index such as the S&P 500. The sources for betas include Bloomberg, FactSet, and Thomson Reuters.

For private companies or divisions of public companies, CFOs can extrapolate their beta from comparisons with the betas for public companies in similar industries and businesses. However, they need to adjust for differences in debt leverage.

Unlevered Betas

In adjusting for differences in debt leverage, CFOs should compute an unlevered beta and then relever the beta to reflect the target capital structure for the private company or division. The steps can be summarized as follows:

$$\text{Unlevered Beta} = \text{Beta} / [1 + (\text{Debt} / \text{Equity}) \times (1 - \text{Tax Rate})]$$

$$\text{Relevered Beta} = \text{Unlevered Beta} \times [1 + (\text{Debt} / \text{Equity}) \times (1 - \text{Tax Rate})]$$

Example of Unlevered Beta

Let's assume that the company has a beta of 1.25, a target debt leverage ratio of 30 percent, and a marginal tax rate of 35 percent. The unlevered and relevered betas can be calculated as follows:

$$\text{Unlevered Beta} = 1.25/[1 + (30/70) \times .65] = 0.98$$

$$\text{Relevered Beta} = 0.98 \times [1 + (30/70) \times .65] = 1.25$$

Prospective versus Historical Betas

CFOs normally rely on betas that are calculated using historical market data. In contrast, some analysts and bankers prefer to use a *prospective beta*. This concept was pioneered by Barra (now MSCI Barra), which uses market data and regression analyses to predict the future market correlations. This approach can yield some interesting insights—especially in managing investment portfolios—but lacks the objectivity and precision that CFOs normally prefer in their financial analyses.

Nevertheless, CFOs may want to adjust their historical beta to reflect a significant change in their target debt ratio or business mix—perhaps due to a major acquisition or divestiture. In this case, the CFO could calculate the unlevered betas, then combine them into a blended unlevered beta, and then relever the blended unlevered beta to reflect the new target debt ratio.

For example, let's assume that the company's beta is 1.25 (unlevered = .98); it is acquiring a business with a beta of 1.40 (unlevered = 1.10) that will comprise 20 percent of the combined company; and that, to finance the acquisition, it is increasing its target debt leverage from 30 to 40 percent. In this case, the calculations would be as follows:

$$\text{Blended Unlevered Beta} = (.8 \times 0.98) + (.2 \times 1.10) = 1.00$$

$$\text{Blended Relevered Beta} = 1.00 \times [1 + (40/60) \times .65] = 1.43$$

 ## HURDLE RATES

In applying their cost of capital to investment decisions, CFOs often choose to round up to the nearest whole percentage point and then add a few percentage points to establish a "hurdle rate" for assessing potential projects. They normally justify adding this "fudge factor" to offset the tendency for project sponsors to be optimistic in their projections; they believe that this will help the company to prioritize its investment alternatives—weeding out lower return projects.

However, while setting a higher hurdle rate may seem like a conservative approach and a way to facilitate the rationing of a company's scarce capital, it can produce very misleading results. Because of the complex manner in which the discount rate can affect present value calculations, using a higher hurdle rate may be either overcompensating or undercompensating for the perceived optimism in the forecast.

Furthermore, adding too much of an increment to the cost of capital may incentivize excessive risk taking in the types of projects that are pursued or cause project sponsors to be unrealistically aggressive in their business and financial assumptions.

 ## RISK PREMIUMS

Another common approach is to vary the cost of capital to reflect the perceived risk of a proposed investment. CFOs will either assume higher betas for riskier projects or simply add incremental risk premiums to their cost of capital. For example, they might require a higher hurdle rate for investments in new technologies or for projects that are located in developing countries.

Applying differing risk premiums certainly can be justified as a valid theoretical approach; it's often described in academic textbooks as the preferred methodology for prioritizing among competing investment proposals, with their relative ranking determined by their risk-adjusted net present values.

However, while applying differentiated risk premiums may make theoretical sense, most CFOs tend not to apply explicit risk adjustments. Instead, they usually employ a consistent cost of capital for evaluating their investment alternatives.

Less Arbitrary

First, it is very difficult to estimate the likely impact that an incremental investment will have on the company's cost of capital; the assignment of additional risk premiums can be relatively arbitrary, especially when the competing uses of capital are going to be considered within the context of a company's diversified portfolio of investments.

Better Projections

Second, if risk premiums are added, they may cause a bias toward more aggressive assumptions. As every CFO has observed, discounted cash flow projections are often manipulated to achieve the hurdle rate; after all, no project sponsor wants to put forth a discretionary proposal that does not show it earning the company's cost of capital. Moreover, CFOs can still apply subjective judgments in comparing projects—in other words, it's better to apply subjective judgments to objective projections than objective judgments to subjective projections.

Less Complicated

Third, the evaluation techniques that are based on the cost of capital—notably net present value calculations—can be extremely sensitive to myriad assumptions that drive the underlying cash flows. Adding risk premiums to the analysis makes it harder for decision makers to distinguish the extent to which the comparisons among projects are being driven by their cash flows versus the impact due to varying their risk premiums. It is usually better to show alternative discount rates as a sensitivity analysis than to bake different rates into the base case comparisons.

Investor Diversification

Fourth, the company's appraisal of project risks may be inconsistent with the views of its shareholders, who can diversify the risks through their investment portfolio. For example, the company may perceive greater risk in its investments in developing countries, while shareholders may welcome the greater exposure to alternative markets and economies.

Staffing Constraints

Finally, CFOs typically lack the staff resources to analyze and determine discretionary risk premiums. Given the significant and increasing demands on the financial organization and the pressures to reduce headcount, CFOs may conclude that the potential benefits from applying risk-adjusted discount rates are usually outweighed by the incremental costs.

 ACQUISITION COST OF CAPITAL

A related question surrounds the cost of capital to be used in analyzing acquisitions. According to financial theory, an acquisition should be evaluated using the cost of capital for the target's industry or line of business. In the case of a public company, the acquisition can be evaluated using the target's actual beta, while for a private company or division, the target's beta can be extrapolated from those of comparable public companies.

In theory, a company's beta will reflect the composite of its businesses and if it adds a new business, its beta will adjust for its new business profile; in other words, adding the target's beta will cause the acquirer's beta to increase or decrease proportionately. However, from a practical standpoint, except in the case of very material transactions, a change in beta is usually extremely hard to discern.

Furthermore, evaluating acquisitions using differing costs of capital is fraught with the same issues that can complicate the evaluation of investment projects. The potential benefits from applying more analytical precision to the calculations may be more than offset by the more arbitrary and less transparent nature of the methodology and by the extra time and effort involved—especially if the company is acquiring several targets in similar or related businesses.

Therefore, unless they are considering a major—perhaps transformational—transaction in a business that is demonstrably distinct from the acquirer's current profile, CFOs should use the company's existing cost of capital for evaluating acquisitions.

However, they should consider the relative riskiness of an acquisition as one of the criteria in deciding whether to proceed—including their focus on execution risks and other considerations that aren't captured in the target's beta. They should also be attuned to the sensitivities of the projected returns to alternative scenarios and alternative discount rates.

Major Transactions

In the case of a major transaction, CFOs can use the target's cost of capital to analyze its discounted cash flows. An alternative approach is to compute a new blended cost of capital for the company. To compute the blended cost of capital, the CFO would revise the company's beta, use the new capital structure target, and reflect any change in the company's cost of debt.

For example, let's assume that the company makes a major acquisition that causes its cost of equity to increase from 11.75 percent to 13.00 percent; its debt leverage target to increase from 30 percent to 40 percent; and its pre-tax cost of debt to increase from 6.00 percent to 6.50 percent. Its new cost of capital can be computed as follows:

	Prior	Revised
Cost of Debt	3.90%	4.22%
Cost of Equity	11.75%	13.00%
Debt Leverage	30%	40%
Cost of Capital	9.40%	9.50%

CHAPTER FIVE

Prioritizing Capital Investments

T HE CFO TYPICALLY MANAGES a company's process for determining how much funding should be allocated to capital expenditures over a planning period and then prioritizing the potential investments within the company's funding constraints. It is a rare company, indeed, that does not have more proposals than can be funded.

This is another example where the real world deviates from theory. In theory, a company should invest in all the projects whose returns exceed its risk-adjusted cost of capital. However, capital budgeting is usually subject to practical constraints that limit how much can and should be reinvested in the business.

Prioritizing capital investments is one of the most challenging missions in the CFO's playbook, but also one of the best opportunities to preserve and grow shareholder value.

 ## CASH FLOW PROJECTIONS

The process for allocating capital begins with the cash flow projections. Using the company's long-term financial model, the CFO estimates the *cash flow from operations* over the planning period, with a particular focus on the budget year.

Cash flow from operations consists of net income, plus non-cash expenses—such as depreciation of fixed assets, amortization of intangibles, and deferral of taxes—less net working capital requirements for inventories, receivables, prepaid expenses, and payables.

The next step is to measure *free cash flow,* which is equal to cash flow from operations, less capital expenditures. The CFO will calculate the amount of capital expenditures that already have been approved—spending that is carried over from prior years—and show the preliminary estimate of the free cash flow that remains to be allocated. For example, the preliminary projections might look something like the following:

	Year 1	Year 2	Year 3	Year 4	Year 5
Cash Flow from Operations	$1000	$1100	$1200	$1300	$1400
Approved Capital Expenditures	200	100	50	25	0
Available Free Cash Flow	800	1000	1150	1275	1400

The "available free cash flow" indicates the amount of cash that is available for discretionary uses, which, in addition to capital expenditures, can include dividends, share repurchases, and acquisitions.

INVESTMENT BUDGET

Using the preliminary free cash flow projections as a starting point, the CFO then will develop a tentative investment budget for the current year and the rest of the planning horizon.

The tentative investment budget will reflect an estimate of the total cash funding for discretionary projects. In most cases, the projected spending will be shown as increases in capital expenditures. However, to the extent that the spending is expensed (such as research and development or marketing and advertising investments) the after-tax amount will be shown as a reduction in cash flow from operations. In either case, the net effect is to reduce the amount of free cash flow—thus decreasing the funds available for dividends, share repurchases, and acquisitions.

Tentative Projections

After determining the tentative investment budget, the CFO updates the projections to show the new calculations of free cash flow. As a simplified illustration, the projections might show the following:

	Year 1	Year 2	Year 3	Year 4	Year 5
Cash Flow from Operations	$1000	$1100	$1200	$1300	$1400
Approved Capital Expenditures	200	100	50	25	0
Tentative Investment Budget	*350*	*500*	*600*	*650*	*700*
Free Cash Flow	450	500	550	625	700

The CFO then can analyze the availability of free cash flow in relationship to the company's projected uses of cash for dividends, share repurchases, and acquisitions, as well as the company's availability of surplus cash or unused debt capacity.

CFOs also should be mindful of investor expectations for the absolute levels and growth rates in free cash flow. Investors often base their valuations of a stock at least partially, if not largely, on this measure; it provides the input for their discounted cash flow analyses and they often relate the free cash flow per share to the company's stock price.

For example, if the company's free cash flow per share is $1.00 and its stock price is $10.00, the stock is *yielding* 10 percent in cash that theoretically could be paid to shareholders.

Iteration of Alternatives

Determining the actual investment budget almost invariably becomes an iterative process—starting with the tentative investment budget, but then considering alternative levels of investment spending. By arraying the numbers in a scorecard that is easily reviewed and updated, the CFO can facilitate a dialogue about the tradeoffs among alternative budget assumptions and provide a context for reviewing the investment projects.

In parallel with this dialogue on the investment budget, the CEO and the management team will be reviewing the proposed projects—considering such factors as their criticality to the company's strategic objectives, their expected returns on investment, and their impact on the company's near-term and long-term financial performance. The CFO normally facilitates this review and provides analytical materials.

As they review the projects, the CEO and management team may decide that because the company has so many essential and attractive projects, they should seek to expand the investment budget—asking the CFO to increase the size of the pie to be allocated.

Increasing the Investment Budget

CFOs have several potential levers for increasing the amount of capital that can be allocated to discretionary investments in the business. These levers generally fall into four categories:

1. Increase cash flow from operations: The company can accelerate revenue growth (e.g., by bringing a product to market more quickly), implement cost reduction measures (e.g., by deferring some discretionary programs), or reduce working capital requirements (e.g., by focusing on accounts receivable collections).
2. Reduce other capital allocations: The company can choose to reduce the capital that it intends to allocate to dividend increases, share repurchases, or acquisitions—although the allocations should remain consistent with the framework for capital deployments that have been communicated to investors.
3. Use surplus cash: If the company has a balance of excess cash, it may be more inclined to make discretionary investments due to their relatively low opportunity cost. However, any projects should still be subject to the constraint that they achieve the company's cost of capital.
4. Obtain incremental financing: The company may be able to take advantage of attractive financing markets, giving it more short-term flexibility to expand its investment program—but careful not to deviate too much or for too long from its capital structure objectives.

Driving the Process

Managing the iterative process for determining the investment budget clearly is more art than science, with a goal of striking the right balance between near-term and long-term priorities. The CFO should drive this process; if not closely managed, it can turn into an infinite loop, making it impossible to implement the detailed investment programs on a timely basis. It is important to establish deadlines, force decisions, and not become buried in minutiae.

Reinvestment Rates

As another tool in evaluating the size of their investment budget, CFOs may find it useful to calculate their company's historical and projected "reinvestment rate," which is defined to be the total of capital expenditures, acquisitions, research and development, and other investments as a percentage of earnings before interest, taxes, depreciation, and amortization (EBITDA) plus research and development and other investments, less taxes. They then can compare trends in their reinvestment rate from year to year and perhaps benchmark this ratio against peer group companies.

According to a study performed by the consulting firm Fortuna Advisors, the reinvestment rate has been positively correlated with total shareholder return. Fortuna reached this conclusion from an analysis of 748 non-financial U.S. companies over the 2000 to 2009 time period, finding the correlations shown in Figure A.

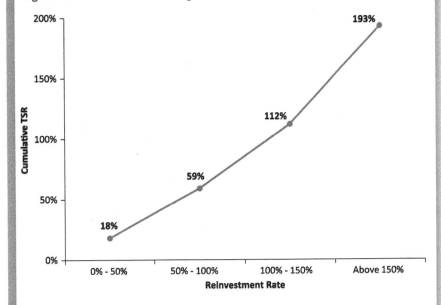

FIGURE A   Reinvestment Rates and Total Shareholder Returns: 2000–2009

Source: Chapelle, Tony, "To Boost TSR, Boost the Reinvestment Rate" (July 5, 2011, www.AgendaWeek.com), pp. 1 and 10. The study by Fortuna Associates was originally described in Milano, Gregory V., "Are You Reinvesting Enough?" CFO.com (March 4, 2011, CFO Publishing LLC).

EVALUATING PROJECTS

In parallel with the review of the investment budget, the CFO will organize a process for allocating this budget among the proposed projects. The CFO typically accumulates summary information for each of the various proposals, including the amount of investment, the time frame, the non-financial resources required, and the projected financial impact. The CEO and management team then can objectively assess and prioritize the projects, keeping in mind the tentative investment budget and the alternative uses for this cash, including acquisitions.

This review process provides the opportunity to sharpen the company's business strategies—deciding what concrete action plans will be pursued versus those that will be modified or deferred. Thus, the CFO should view potential projects through the lens of the company's strategic plan and ensure that the project evaluations focus on strategic as well as financial considerations.

Return on Investment Criteria

Of course, return on investment measures will usually constitute the most important criteria in the evaluation of investment proposals. In most cases, it makes sense to show the return from the perspective of three core methodologies: net present value, internal rate of return, and payback. Each of these methodologies has complementary strengths and weaknesses, making their collective use much more informative than relying on any one of them alone.

Net present value (NPV) is arguably the most valuable of the three methodologies: It is the purest measure of the amount of shareholder value that is being created. It is also easy to compare among projects, and it can flexibly incorporate decision tree inputs, including "real options," as well as sensitivity analyses for each of the key variables.

However, NPV has limitations when used in the context of a limited investment budget. A project may produce a large NPV, but use up most of the budget; this may result in a suboptimal allocation of capital and, more important, may cause other strategic priorities to be neglected or deferred.

Furthermore, net present value calculations are highly dependent upon their terminal value. While a project may produce an attractive net present value, it may take a long time to show positive net income and cash flow benefits.

Internal rate of return (IRR) can be a good complement to net present value by showing the magnitude of the expected return and can help optimize the returns on a limited investment budget. Moreover, IRR is not driven by a discount rate, which can facilitate a comparison of projects with differing risk characteristics. For example, if one project has a 20 percent return and another a 15 percent return, the decision maker can assess whether a 5 percentage point difference is worth the incremental risk.

However, IRR has its shortcomings as well. In particular, a high return project may be too small to have much impact on the company's results, but require as much management focus as a lower return, but much larger, project. Also, similar to the NPV methodology, it may favor a project that has negative net income and cash flow for the foreseeable future.

Payback shows the amount of time (expressed in years) it takes to get the company's cash investment back. This allows more focus on the near-term consequences of an investment. It is an especially instructive methodology for cost reduction projects, which normally should be expected to produce a relatively quick return. Many CFOs impose a minimum payback period for cost reduction projects (say, two or three years) as a means of prioritizing investment spending and ensuring that the company focuses on growth.

The major disadvantages of payback are that it does not consider the results after the payback threshold has been achieved and it does not account for the time value of money. The latter disadvantage can be addressed by a *discounted payback*, which computes the breakeven point where a project has earned an economic return on the cash investment.

Other Financial Criteria

In evaluating their investment priorities, companies may be more constrained by the forecasted impact on their net income than by the availability of cash or financing. For example, while investments in marketing and advertising or research and development can be expected to generate future revenue and profit, their accounting treatment as a current expense can make them problematic in meeting earnings expectations.

Therefore, the CFO's evaluations should address not only the economic desirability of a potential investment (does it exceed the company's cost of capital?) but also the impact on the company's *reported accounting results*, answering questions such as: What is the pro forma impact on operating margins, return on book capital, and earnings per share? Will this cause the company to compare unfavorably against analyst expectations or versus its competitors?

The CFO should also consider the likely impact of the investment program on the company's *market valuation*. Are the investment projects consistent with the strategic objectives that have been articulated to investors? Will investors have confidence in the company's ability to execute the program? Will the projected investment returns seem credible?

Non-Financial Criteria

While CFOs apply standardized financial criteria as the cornerstones of their reviews, they also recognize that non-financial criteria—such as the availability of *human or technology resources*—should supplement or, in some cases, even supersede the financial criteria. This acknowledges that while additional resources can be added over the long term, they usually represent a practical constraint over a shorter time horizon.

Moreover, a proposed investment may have a low or unquantifiable rate of return, but produce significant benefits to the company's *competitive positioning* or its *risk exposure*. For example, investments in technologies to safeguard customers' personal information can result in enormous benefits if, in fact, they prevent a compromising breach of the company's data network. However, it is usually difficult to forecast high returns for this kind of preventative investment because of the relatively low probability of an occurrence. Its IRR may be low, but its criticality may be irrefutable.

Finally, CFOs should consider the *interdependencies* among projects—whether an investment will increase the probability of success in other projects; or conversely, whether the deferral of an investment will be beneficial due to the greater focus and concentration of resources on higher priority projects.

Information Technology Projects

It is especially important for CFOs to take a holistic, long-term approach to the evaluation of information technology projects. If IT projects are evaluated as discrete investments, the company may end up with a series of disjointed investment decisions that may make sense on a stand-alone basis, but that can result in a suboptimal—or even dysfunctional—IT configuration over the long run.

Instead, the better approach is to develop a long-term IT strategy that encompasses a series of investments over time—accommodating future as well as current requirements. This IT strategic plan should include a long-range capital budget, as well as a staffing road map, including a breakdown between employees and contracted or outsourced resources. Specific projects should still be evaluated—to ensure that they make economic sense—but within the context of an overarching IT vision.

 ## CATEGORIZING PROJECTS

After accumulating and summarizing the various investment proposals, CFOs usually will group the projects into various categories. For example, they may categorize the potential projects among those that are mandatory in response to regulatory requirements, those that are considered essential to achieving the company's strategic objectives, and those that are considered attractive, but truly discretionary, investments.

They also will categorize the projects by business segments, business units, geographies, and product lines. These categories can help CFOs identify where resources are being directed and what areas are being deemphasized. This analysis can be especially instructive if the CFO also shows the free cash flow that is generated or used by each of the categories.

Another popular approach is to categorize the projects by the purpose to be achieved. For example, the CFO may identify the amount of spending that is directed toward generating organic revenue growth, improving the infra-structure, and reducing the cost structure.

These categorizations can help CFOs to clarify the tradeoffs and focus attention on the big picture implications of the company's investment strategies—much in the manner that they would review a stock portfolio. In this way, they can analyze whether the composite picture represented by the allocations is consistent with the company's strategic plan as articulated to investors. This analysis also can reveal any excessive concentrations of risk and whether the projects, taken as a whole, strike the right balance between short-term and long-term priorities.

 ## MONITORING PROJECTS

CFOs should establish processes to monitor the implementation of the approved projects—especially whether they come in within budget and whether their anticipated benefits are in fact realized. The CFO usually dis-tributes regular status reports on the projects to the CEO and management team, as well as summary reports that are provided periodically to the board of directors.

These reports can provide advance warning concerning projects that may be getting off track, prompting remedial actions, or even abandonment. This can help avoid the propensity of struggling projects to become sink holes for continued funding.

Also, business leaders may not apply the same rigor in managing capi-talized expenses that they apply to expenses that have an immediate impact on their income statement. This can be especially true for spending on inter-nally developed software, which is required by the accounting rules to be capitalized—creating the risk of future write-offs.

Value of Real Options

A tangible benefit from the monitoring of projects is that it can facilitate intensive scrutiny at critical decision junctures. This review at designated intervals is consistent with the concept of "real options," and can result in significant financial benefits.

Real options are based on the nodes in a decision tree that provide opportunities to analyze a project, deciding whether to continue the project as originally planned or whether it should be abandoned, modified, deferred, or expanded. This analysis considers the incremental cash flows from that point onward: Any spending that has been incurred to date represents "sunk costs" that are not relevant to the economic analysis going forward.

The benefits from real options arise from the opportunity to take a different path along the decision tree than the original plan, resulting in increased discounted cash flow returns. Some examples include:

- **Abandonment:** Dispassionate project reviews can mitigate the all-too-human tendency to invest good money after bad. Although abandonment is not the preferred alternative—and certainly not what was expected when the project was initiated—it can preserve shareholder value if the incremental investments will not earn the cost of capital.
- **Modification:** A company may decide to continue a project, but to modify its original design. Because of the information gleaned since the project's inception—such as market or customer data—the project sponsor can make changes that enhance the incremental returns.
- **Deferral:** The project review may indicate that continued investments should be deferred until specified criteria are met. For example, the market for a new product may not be developing as quickly as anticipated. In this case, a deferral can create shareholder value due to the time value of money.
- **Expansion:** Real options can also indicate potential sources of value beyond the project in question. For example, a project may involve investments in a technology platform that is applicable to other products. In this case, the sunk costs from the initial project may allow these additional projects to become viable—because their incremental benefits now exceed their incremental costs.

CFOs should make sure that real options are analyzed with the same discipline as the initial decisions to proceed with the project. Furthermore, for major projects, they may want to incorporate the value of real options in their original calculations of net present values and internal rates of return, perhaps performing a full decision tree analysis.

Although few CFOs explicitly calculate the value of real options in all of their discounted cash flow projections—especially for smaller projects—they should at least consider them subjectively in their rankings of potential investments. The fundamental point is that a project that has discrete decision points has more economic value than a project that requires all of its spending to occur without the opportunity to revisit its initial assumptions.

Value of Accumulated Information

Another advantage of regularly monitoring projects is that it captures valuable information that can inform evaluations of future investment proposals. For example, the data can indicate the project sponsor's credibility and project management skills. Furthermore, it can highlight the types of projects that are more likely to achieve their expected benefits. For example, a company may have much more predictable success from line extensions than from investments in new product categories.

In other words, by establishing processes for monitoring the status and results of investment projects, CFOs can play a constructive role in orchestrating fact-based decision making—providing useful insights concerning the company's probability of success with respect to a given sponsor and type of project.

 PENSION FUND CONTRIBUTIONS

When reviewing potential reinvestments in the business, CFOs should consider voluntary contributions to defined benefit plans as alternative uses of capital. First, the economic return on investment can be attractive. The company receives a tax deduction on the investment and the future earnings can compound tax free.

Second, the investment can produce favorable accounting results, generally equal to the expected investment return that the company assumes for its pension fund accounting. For example, companies typically assume an investment return of about 8 percent, which implies an after-tax return of about 12 percent.

Third, the company reduces an unfunded liability on its balance sheet, which the rating agencies generally will treat as a reduction in net debt. In addition, it gives the company more flexibility in its strategies for managing the pension fund, including shifting more of its assets to long-term fixed income securities. This can reduce the volatility in the company's pension fund expense and future funding requirements.

However, voluntary contributions also have disadvantages. The investments generally cannot be withdrawn and the plan may become overfunded in the future. For example, the plan could become overfunded if interest rates rise appreciably from their current levels, causing a decrease in the plan's liabilities.

CHAPTER SIX

Considering Dividends and Repurchases

I N REVIEWING THE COMPANY'S INVESTMENT PROGRAM, CFOs will be mindful of the alternative uses of capital to pay dividends to shareholders or to repurchase the company's shares. They will implicitly compare reinvesting cash in the business versus returning cash to shareholders and will seek the best combination to deliver shareholder value.

The alternatives for returning cash to shareholders include:

- Initiating a regular dividend payment
- Increasing an existing dividend rate
- Paying a one-time special dividend
- Repurchasing shares via a tender offer
- Repurchasing shares in the open market

The CFO will evaluate these alternatives in light of the company's dividend policy; the inherent trade-offs between dividends and share repurchases; and the company's strategies for delivering total shareholder return.

DIVIDEND POLICY ALTERNATIVES

Establishing and communicating a dividend policy is fundamental to a company's investor value proposition. The basic alternatives are not paying a dividend, paying a token dividend, maintaining a constant dividend, achieving consistent growth, targeting a payout ratio, targeting a yield, or varying with cash requirements.

Not Paying a Dividend

By not paying a dividend, a company is essentially communicating that it has higher return uses for its capital. This policy is often associated with technology and other high-growth companies, but it is also employed by highly leveraged and economically sensitive companies or by smaller companies that have limited access to the capital markets.

It maximizes the company's financial flexibility, but introduces greater uncertainty concerning the company's total shareholder return—which usually translates into more volatility in the stock price and a higher cost of equity.

Paying a Token Dividend

A company that has historically not paid dividends may declare a relatively small dividend that produces a very modest dividend yield. This signals to investors that it is primarily a growth company, but that it is also focused on shareholder value.

This policy indicates a company in transition—and likely to raise its dividend fairly rapidly as the business matures.

Maintaining a Constant Dividend

A company that wants to preserve cash may choose to maintain its existing dividend, but not plan any increases for the foreseeable future. This is often the path followed by companies in stagnant or declining businesses or companies that have recently made a large cash investment—such as a major acquisition.

This policy avoids disappointing investors with a dividend cut, but the company is essentially treading water over the near term.

Achieving Consistent Growth

Achieving consistent dividend growth is a common strategy among well-established companies that have relatively predictable cash flows and a solid balance sheet. They typically will tout the number of consecutive years that they have increased their annual dividend.

This policy reinforces an image of stability, attracting investors who are seeking income protection as well as growth and who expect the dividend to keep up with inflation.

Targeting a Payout Ratio

Companies often will relate their dividend to a targeted percentage of net income (or free cash flow). It communicates an intention to increase the dividend, but proportionate to its growth rate in earnings per share.

This policy signals the company's intention to achieve long-term dividend growth, while preserving its flexibility concerning the timing and size of the increases.

Offering an Attractive Yield

Companies that are owned primarily by yield-oriented investors may base their dividends on comparative yields in the market—not only in comparison with other stocks, but also in comparison with fixed-income alternatives, such as Treasuries or municipal bonds. It is often employed by companies in mature businesses that have ample financial flexibility.

This policy treats the dividend as fundamental to the company's strategy for delivering total return to its shareholders and generally is associated with a less volatile stock.

Estimating Cash Requirements

Another approach is to make the dividend conditional on the company's cash sources and uses, essentially paying any "residual" cash as a dividend. This has some appeal in theory, but is impossible from a practical point of view for most public companies. One-time dividends are generally not favored by investors and share repurchases represent a much more efficient alternative for returning surplus cash.

However, in determining the dividend policy, the company's long-term earnings and cash flow projections are certainly criteria that should be considered. For example, if the projections show the company with negative free cash flow, it probably would be unwise to initiate a dividend, while substantial free cash flow would indicate greater flexibility.

In addition, establishing a dividend policy based on residual cash can make a great deal of sense for private companies, helping their shareholders to manage their equity commitments and providing them with a source of liquidity.

DIVIDEND POLICY CONSIDERATIONS

CFOs should be mindful of a number of considerations that can influence the choice among dividend policy alternatives and the decision between dividends and share repurchases.

Long-Term Commitment

Most public companies want to maintain their existing dividend rate, at minimum. Reducing their dividend is generally considered a serious breach with investor expectations and unless signaled well in advance for legitimate business reasons—such as a clearly superior use for the funds—it can result in a dramatically negative impact on the stock price. In the case of private companies, their shareholders also have expectations concerning dividend payments and they likewise may be upset if these expectations are not fulfilled.

Therefore, CFOs should analyze the company's ability to pay the dividend—even during downturns in the economy—and regard the dividend as equivalent to a fixed obligation. Indeed, this is the primary advantage of returning cash to shareholders through share repurchases rather than dividend payments; it creates much less of an obligation and thus preserves the company's flexibility.

In addition, the rating agencies will consider the payment of dividends to be an obligation that can affect the company's debt ratings, especially in comparison with an open market share repurchase program. However, this is usually a relatively minor factor in their assessments of credit quality—provided that the company's free cash flow can clearly accommodate the payments and the company does not reduce or suspend its dividend, which the agencies will view as symptomatic of underlying credit or liquidity issues.

Management Signal

Maintaining or increasing the dividend rate not only provides a tangible return to investors, but also signals management's confidence in the company's future outlook. Because investors know that companies are extremely reluctant to reduce future dividend payments, they perceive that the company expects relatively stable or growing earnings over the long run.

This signal can result in a positive reaction from investors. However, it can also create the possibility of disappointing them if the dividend is subsequently suspended or reduced. This is an especially important consideration for companies that are in decline and whose dividends may be perceived as unsustainable.

In addition, if a high-growth company initiates a dividend, it can signal that it no longer has attractive reinvestment opportunities, which can temper investor enthusiasm for the stock.

Market Norms

As a benchmark, CFOs should be aware of the typical payout ratios and dividend yields in the stock market. For example, the average annual dividend yield for the S&P 500 tends to cluster around 2 percent, but exceeded 3 percent during the market meltdown in 2008. The average annual payout ratio tends to be around 40 to 50 percent, although this ratio can deviate wildly from year to year.

In addition, CFOs should be mindful of the typical payouts and yields in their industry. If a company's dividend policy deviates too much from competitors' policies, it may distort comparisons by equity analysts.

For example, many analysts use a shorthand calculation of a company's price/earnings ratio in comparison with its earnings growth rate (the *"PEG" ratio*). This can penalize a company that pays a high dividend yield in comparison with a competitor that does not pay a dividend.

Payout Ratios and Dividend Yields for the S&P 500

	Payout Ratio	Dividend Yield
2010	50%	1.87%
2009	53%	2.11%
2008	101%	3.16%
2007	89%	2.01%
2006	38%	1.77%
2005	48%	1.80%
2004	70%	1.92%
2003	98%	1.56%
2002	66%	1.81%
2001	47%	1.35%

Source: Bloomberg

Shareholder Base

The choice of dividend policy should be consistent with the company's shareholder base. For example, if the CFO is targeting "value" or "yield" investors as potential shareholders, instituting or increasing a dividend is likely to be attractive to them.

In addition, certain mutual funds and other institutional investors have investment criteria that prefer, or even require, regular annual increases in the company's dividend. Therefore, CFOs may want to consider annual increases—even if relatively small—as part of their dividend policy. This can be especially helpful in attracting "growth and income" investors.

Dividend Discount Model

Many investors use the dividend discount model in their evaluation of stocks. This model essentially says that the value of the stock is a function of its annual dividend, the growth rate for the dividend, and the company's cost of equity capital. For example, if a company pays a dividend of $1.00, grows its dividend in perpetuity at 5 percent, and has a 10 percent cost of equity capital, its stock is worth $20.00 ($1.00 / [10% −5%]).

Therefore, if a company can convince investors that it will grow its dividend consistently at a given rate, this will be reflected in its stock market valuation. However, investors tend to be skeptical that a growth rate can be sustained into perpetuity. They usually will project the dividend growth rate for a foreseeable period (say, five to ten years) and then assume a lower rate of growth into perpetuity (say, 2 to 4 percent per annum).

Earnings Growth Rate

Investors will also factor the dividend payout ratio into their expectations for a company's growth rate in earnings. They will analyze a company's return on equity and compute the percentage of its earnings that will be reinvested in the business.

For example, if a company earns a 15 percent return on its equity capital and is targeting a payout ratio of 40 percent, the implied earnings growth rate is 9 percent (15% × .6).

Stock Options

A significant increase or decrease in the dividend will affect the value of a company's stock options (the Black-Scholes formula uses a company's dividend yield as one of its variables, causing the option's value to decline if the yield is increased). Therefore, if CFOs are considering a material change in dividend policy, they should investigate the potential impact on the company's incentive compensation programs, especially whether the existing employee option agreements address this issue.

SPECIAL DIVIDENDS

Public companies in recent years seldom have announced one-time or "special" dividends, although Microsoft notably paid a $32 billion special dividend in 2004. Special dividends were declared more frequently in the past, but they have generally fallen out of favor with investors, who prefer share repurchases as a vehicle for returning cash to shareholders through a one-time payment. Investors like the reduction in shares outstanding that is achieved through a share repurchase, while they often liken a one-time dividend to a "sugar high" that has no lasting impact on the stock price.

The most common use of special dividends today is in connection with mergers and acquisitions, where the target pays a dividend to shareholders in advance of a stock-for-stock merger. This allows the target's surplus cash to be returned to shareholders, reducing the amount of equity capital that needs to be issued by the acquirer, thereby decreasing the dilution to existing shareholders.

Private companies often declare a one-time dividend to their shareholders. Unlike a public company, a private company isn't expected to maintain a consistent payment, which allows more flexibility in returning cash to its shareholders.

One-time dividends are especially common in connection with a debt refinancing by a leveraged buyout. A portion of the proceeds from the refinancing is paid to the private equity investors, reducing their equity stake in the company and enhancing their return on investment.

DIVIDEND DECLARATIONS

Declarations of dividends require approval from the board of directors. If the quarterly dividend is remaining unchanged, CFOs typically will provide limited or no supporting materials to the board. However, if the recommendation involves a change in the existing dividend rate or a shift in the company's dividend policy, CFOs usually will prepare analytical materials that support the proposed action.

CFOs typically will show the company's history of dividend payments; the percentage of its earnings that have been paid out as dividends each year (its payout ratio); its current dividend yield; its average dividend yield in previous years; and its projections for earnings and free cash flow over the planning horizon.

They will also provide comparisons of the company's dividend policy with other companies in their peer group—either companies in the same industry or else companies that have similar growth rates and asset intensities. The comparisons usually focus on the current yield (annualized dividend as a percentage of share price), the payout ratio (annualized dividend as a percentage of earnings per share or free cash flow per share), and the dividend growth rate (compounded annual increase over time; for example, over five- or ten-year periods).

Finally, they may want to highlight trends in the broader stock market—using either general or industry-specific indexes—and provide an analysis of the company's shareholder base, indicating any preferences for dividends among the major holders.

Dividend Announcement

Declaring a dividend is a material event that usually is communicated through a press release immediately after receiving board approval. Therefore, if the dividend action may come as a surprise to investors, CFOs should be sure that their investor relations and corporate communications people are prepared to field questions. They also may want to provide a heads up to the rating agencies and consider some outreach to major shareholders after the change is announced.

Furthermore, if a company is planning a dividend action that is likely to be positively received, CFOs may want to coordinate board approval with a venue where they can directly communicate the action to investors—such as an investor day presentation, an investor conference, or an earnings conference call.

 REPURCHASE CONSIDERATIONS

Share repurchases are commonly employed by both public and private companies to return cash to their shareholders and manage their shares outstanding. They have a number of advantages compared with dividends, but also some risks in their implementation.

Flexible Payments

The most significant advantage of repurchases compared with dividends is their greater flexibility. They are considered to be less of a long-term commitment and are especially well-suited for redeploying one-time sources of cash such as a divestiture or a refinancing.

This flexibility is more pronounced in an open market program than a cash tender. In an open market program, the company usually maintains an ability to suspend the program due to unforeseen events.

EPS Growth Rate

Share repurchases can accelerate the earnings per share growth rate due to the reduction in shares outstanding—essentially increasing the leverage on the earnings. This higher growth rate can have a positive impact on the company's P/E multiple. For example, if a company is growing its earnings at a 10 percent rate, repurchasing 5 percent of the shares will increase its growth rate to 16 percent if the shares are acquired immediately and to 13 percent if the shares are purchased over the course of the year.

The advantages of repurchasing shares are especially pronounced in a low interest rate environment. The use of cash has a relatively low opportunity cost, especially when compared with the company's cost of equity.

Tax Advantage

Share repurchases formerly had a tax advantage in the United States due to the lower rate on capital gains in comparison with the ordinary income rate that was applied to dividends. However, this difference in personal income tax rates no longer exists—at least until Congress revisits the subject in connection with the expiration of the current tax rules at the end of 2012.

Nevertheless, share repurchases still have a tax advantage compared with dividends: Only the shareholders who sell their stock in a repurchase will experience a taxable event, while a dividend is a taxable event for all taxpaying shareholders.

Positive Signal

It is often argued that announcements of share repurchases are positive signals to investors, indicating that management has a favorable view about the value of the company's stock. As a result, the stock price may increase upon the announcement of a buyback program.

However, the recent track record of many companies has called this presumption into question, with their shares often trading below the average price that was paid in the repurchase programs. Indeed, because share repurchase programs are often initiated when times are good, they may reflect a perverse bias toward buying when share prices are high, not when they're low.

In any event, unless a company repurchases shares regularly on a sustained basis over time, it runs the risk that its timing is inopportune. And as CFOs can appreciate, predicting the future stock price is always a gamble, largely dependent on economic and financial conditions outside the company's control.

Debt Leverage Target

Share repurchases can be flexible vehicles for rebalancing a company's capital structure. For example, if the company has more equity capital than indicated by its debt leverage targets, it can increase its leverage through a repurchase, thus lowering the company's cost of capital. For this reason, CFOs may want to combine a repurchase program with a debt issuance, especially if the financial markets are favorable.

However, if CFOs are too aggressive in rebalancing their capital structure, they run the risk of repurchasing shares and then having to reissue shares in the future. The key is to distinguish between changes in the company's debt leverage that are relatively permanent versus those that are transitory.

Cash Flow Savings

When shares are repurchased, a company avoids the need to pay dividends on those shares going forward. This can result in significant cash flow savings when compounded over time, especially if the company has a relative high yield or a dividend policy that calls for annual increases.

Companies with relatively high yields can realize a positive cash flow arbitrage versus the after-tax earnings on their cash balance or the after-tax cost of their debt. For example, if the company has a dividend yield of 3.0 percent and a marginal tax rate of 35 percent, this equates to a breakeven pre-tax cost of debt of 4.6 percent (3.0%/.65).

Offset to Dilution

A common justification for repurchases is to offset the dilution due to stock issuances, with companies often establishing an explicit goal of not increasing their shares outstanding. The sources of dilution can include:

- *Incentive Compensation:* Shares may be issued as restricted stock and stock options in a company's incentive compensation programs. Restricted stock has two advantages versus options in managing a share repurchase program: It involves fewer potential shares to be repurchased and there is greater certainty concerning the number of shares that will need to be repurchased.
- *Mergers and Acquisitions:* Shares may be issued in a merger or acquisition to achieve a tax-free exchange. A repurchase program can offset these issuances with no effect on either the tax or accounting treatment for the transaction. Often the acquirer will state its intention to repurchase the shares when the transaction is announced, allowing analysts to make pro forma adjustments to both shares outstanding and earnings per share.
- *Employee Purchase Programs:* Employee stock purchase programs formerly represented a potentially significant issuance of shares. However, after the Enron debacle, companies generally stopped encouraging employee stock ownership and the accounting treatment was changed: The maximum discount to avoid an expense was reduced from 15 to 5 percent and any "look back" pricing was deemed to be a stock option that must be expensed. Consequently, these programs are now a relatively minor source of dilution for most companies, and the issuances can be easily offset with share repurchases.
- *Dividend Reinvestment Programs:* Another minor source of dilution can be the company's dividend reinvestment program. However, the issuance of shares through these programs is fairly predictable and can be offset by repurchases.

Private Company Repurchases

Private companies often will repurchase shares from minority shareholders or employees—especially those who have left the company—as a way to provide them with liquidity and to stay below the maximum number of shareholders to remain a private company. The transactions typically involve a valuation of the shares by an objective third party.

However, the need for this type of repurchase program may become less compelling with the advent of secondary markets for private shares—provided that these markets gain traction and that their regulatory issues can be addressed.

In addition, private companies may repurchase equity from their venture capital or private equity investors, using either the proceeds from a refinancing or surplus free cash flow from operations. This is a fairly typical transaction and can enhance the investors' discounted returns on investment.

 ## OPEN MARKET PROGRAMS

Open market programs represent the lion's share of share repurchases. The company announces its intention to repurchase a target dollar amount of shares (or sometimes a target number of shares) over an indefinite time period, although they generally are expected to be accomplished within a one- to two-year time period. This approach communicates the company's intention, while still giving it the flexibility to suspend the program in the event of financial duress or due to acquisitions or other unforeseen strategic actions. Moreover, it facilitates a dollar averaging approach to the repurchases, mitigating the risk that the company is buying shares at the peak of the market.

In implementing an open market program, CFOs will engage an investment bank to act as the company's agent in executing the transactions. They will organize a procedure to provide instructions each day concerning the price and volume parameters. The number of shares that can be repurchased each day is subject to Securities and Exchange Commission (SEC) rules, but block purchases are exempt, giving the CFO considerable flexibility to set the volume targets. The CFO also will partner with the general counsel to ensure that discretionary repurchases are not made during "blackout" periods or if the company possesses material information that has not been publicly disclosed.

Shareholders will expect regular updates concerning the status of the repurchase program (e.g., in connection with earnings announcements or investor presentations). CFOs will want to keep investors well-informed, especially if a decision is made to suspend or terminate a program; otherwise, they can lose credibility in announcing future programs.

Accelerated Share Repurchase Program

Several CFOs in recent years have implemented open market repurchases through an accelerated share repurchase (ASR) program. This allows them to repurchase the shares over time, but to obtain an immediate reduction in shares outstanding and a positive impact to earnings per share from the outset.

In order to receive this accounting treatment, the CFO enters into a contractual commitment with an investment bank to repurchase a stated dollar amount of shares. This contract will commit the company to repurchase a specified number of shares at an estimated cost based on the current market value of the stock, with a "true up" at the end of the program to reflect the actual costs incurred in repurchasing the shares.

The company's shares outstanding are reduced immediately to reflect the estimated shares to be repurchased and the true up is treated as an "option" that is settled through paid-in-capital, thus not impacting the income statement. However, if the true up is paid in shares, it will cause shares outstanding to increase at that time.

The CFO manages an ASR program in the same manner as a conventional open market program, providing parameters to the investment bank concerning the timing of repurchases and the prices to be paid. However, the contractual commitment eliminates the company's flexibility to reduce or discontinue the program. In the event of financial duress, the CFO would have to arrange a separate transaction to reissue shares.

An ASR program can be especially beneficial if a company seeks to offset the loss of earnings from a business that has been divested. Committing the divestiture proceeds to repurchases allows it to match the reduced shares outstanding against the loss of earnings, thus smoothing the impact on earnings per share. It is also a valuable technique in repurchasing shares issued in an acquisition, enabling the transaction to be more accretive or less dilutive from the outset.

Example of ASR Impact

Let's assume that a company has net income of $100 in year 1, $110 in year 2, and $120 in year 3. If it repurchases 10 percent of its 100 shares outstanding, the impact on its earnings per share can be compared as follows:

	Conventional Repurchase			Accelerated Repurchase		
Net Income	$100	$110	$120	$100	$110	$120
Shares Outstanding	100	95	90	100	90	90
Earnings Per Share	$1.00	$1.16	$1.33	$1.00	$1.22	$1.33
Growth Rate	—	16%	15%	—	22%	9%

TENDER OFFERS

If public companies pursue a one-time share repurchase, they typically execute the transaction through a tender offer at a fixed price or at a price that is set through a Dutch auction. In a Dutch auction, the company specifies a minimum and a maximum price and then all of the repurchases are made at the lowest price that achieves the targeted number of shares to be repurchased (subject to the minimum and maximum price).

The advantage of a tender offer is that it allows a major repurchase to be executed relatively quickly, which reduces the market risk inherent in an open market program. However, it exposes the company to the risk that it is repurchasing all of the shares at an inopportune time—possibly at a market peak.

Similar to an ASR program, a tender offer results in an immediate reduction in shares outstanding. Therefore, it is often used when a CFO seeks to offset the dilution from shares issued in an acquisition or to redeploy the proceeds from a major divestiture.

RETAINING STRATEGIC CASH

As an alternative to returning cash to shareholders through dividend payments or share repurchases, CFOs may prefer to retain a portion of their company's free cash flow either as a surplus cash balance or as unused credit lines. This provides more financial flexibility, allowing greater cash resources to be redeployed in the future.

CFOs often refer to this as "strategic" cash to distinguish it from "operating" cash that is needed to run the business. Strategic cash can facilitate acquisitions or investments or can provide a buffer against uncertain economic or financial conditions. It is consistent with the maxim that "cash is king," giving a company more strategic options.

However, retaining strategic cash can be viewed unfavorably by investors, who may be concerned about undisciplined spending and the relatively low return on investment.

Facilitate Acquisitions

CFOs are understandably reluctant to budget for unidentified acquisitions that may or may not be executed in the future. At the same time, they want to maintain flexibility concerning the timing and pricing of the potential transactions—thus allowing the company to be patient and opportunistic in its consideration of alternatives. Having cash on hand is the best insurance that CFOs will be able to respond with alacrity to opportunities and not be subject to the vagaries of the financial markets.

Having ample financial resources can be a significant advantage in negotiations with the seller and can facilitate tactical responses in competition with other potential acquirers. Sellers usually want to be paid in cash, especially if they are marketing a business through a competitive auction. Long-term debt financing can be difficult to arrange quickly and bridge financing can be expensive.

Furthermore, with a large cash balance, CFOs can avoid being reliant on stock or debt issuances to effect potential transactions; often the best acquisition opportunities become available during a market downturn, which very well may be an unfavorable time for the acquirer to issue stock or debt.

Facilitate Investments

Another argument for retaining cash is that it can finance major reinvestments in the business. If funding is not a constraint, a company may be motivated to develop additional business opportunities that will produce shareholder value.

This argument especially applies to companies in capital intensive industries (e.g., energy or telecom) and to companies in research-intensive industries (e.g., high technology or pharmaceutical) that are investing in projects with uncertain long-range payoffs. No CFO wants lack of financial resources to be the constraint that frustrates attractive reinvestment projects.

Respond to Future Events

A third argument for retaining surplus cash is that it provides more flexibility in an uncertain and volatile world. It provides protection against downsides— such as disruptive technologies, economic recessions, and market turmoil—but also offers the opportunity to capture upsides. For example, a market downturn is a great time to repurchase stock or to introduce new marketing campaigns against weakened competitors.

In many ways, retaining cash is akin to an investment strategy where a portion of the portfolio is maintained in liquid investments, thus giving the CFO more diversification of financial resources and more flexibility to respond aggressively to future events.

In addition, multinationals often retain much of their strategic cash in their international subsidiaries. This has tax advantages—avoiding the additional tax on repatriation—and provides flexibility to expand their international business with offshore funds.

Undisciplined Spending

While retaining strategic cash can be a cost-effective way to accommodate potential acquisitions, shareholders may be concerned that the money will not be spent wisely—particularly if the company does not have a track record of making value-enhancing acquisitions. They may fear that if funds are readily available, a company will become undisciplined in its approach to acquisitions—that the cash will "burn a hole in its pocket." Investors usually prefer that any surplus cash be returned to shareholders through dividends or share repurchases—a "bird in the hand."

Unless a company is well-known as a superior acquirer—such as a private equity firm or a company with a documented track record of success—investors will be skeptical that it can redeploy the cash profitably. This skepticism applies equally to acquisitions and long-term investment programs.

If a decision is made to retain surplus cash for strategic purposes, the CFO will need to provide frequent and convincing reassurances to investors that the company is committed to a disciplined approach to acquisitions and investments and that it will review any potential opportunities in comparison with the alternative uses of capital, including paying dividends to shareholders or repurchasing the company's stock.

Low Return on Investment

A second argument against retaining surplus cash is that it produces a meager return on investment, especially in a low interest rate environment. Cash is typically invested in high-quality, short-term investments (such as Treasury notes or top-rated commercial paper)—assuring safety and liquidity, but producing a return that is far below the company's cost of capital.

A few technology companies with very large cash portfolios—notably Microsoft and Google—have recently expanded their investments into new areas such as corporate debt, equities, and derivatives (including commodities). However, these strategies are very controversial, and some shareholders have been vocal in their opposition, advocating that the surplus cash be used instead for dividends or share repurchases.

CASH INVESTMENT POLICIES

Banks and other financial services companies are especially focused on maintaining appropriate investment policies, as are companies who manage customer funds in a fiduciary relationship. However, given the recent experiences in the financial crisis, it's safe to say that virtually all companies—including private companies, governments, and nonprofits—have reviewed and reinforced their investment policies.

Investment Policy Statement

Every company should have a documented investment policy statement that is approved by the board of directors. The format and contents can vary, but it typically should include an overview of the company's cash management objectives, guidelines, and administration.

- **Objectives:** It should describe the cash portfolio, for example, whether it is divided into categories of cash (such as operating cash versus strategic cash) and who manages it—and specify the investment objectives (especially the tradeoff among yield, safety, and liquidity). It also should identify the benchmark for measuring performance (such as a market index).
- **Guidelines:** It should set forth the guidelines for investing the cash—types of investments that are permissible, target maturities, limits against concentration of assets, and credit requirements (such as minimum debt ratings).
- **Administration:** It should specify the administration of the portfolio—the custodian, the record keeping and compliance systems, the authorizations and controls, and any investment or other consultants that have been retained.

Trends

For the most part, companies have instituted conservative guidelines for investing their cash and their boards of directors continue to be risk averse. Generally, they prefer to sacrifice potentially higher returns for the additional safety of prudent investment strategies.

The trends toward approving explicit investment policy statements and establishing conservative investment guidelines are widespread among companies, including nonprofits, but are especially pronounced among state and local governments. Several governmental units have posted their policy statements on the web.

During times of market distress, CFOs will operate even more conservatively than the investment policies allow. For example, knowing the tendency of the rating agencies to lag actual events, they will more closely monitor their counterparty and credit risks and take anticipatory actions to limit their exposures.

PART THREE

Mergers and Acquisitions

CHAPTER SEVEN

Identifying Acquisition Candidates

P ROBABLY THE MOST IMPORTANT determinant of success in an
acquisition program is identifying attractive candidates in the first place.
If a potential transaction does not make strategic and business sense, it's
highly unlikely to create shareholder value—no matter what price is paid or
how well it's executed.

RATIONALE FOR ACQUISITIONS

A threshold question is *Why pursue mergers and acquisitions?* Do they make any
sense as a business strategy? CFOs should ponder this question carefully before
embarking on an acquisition program. The skeptics abound, and CFOs will
need to have a firm grasp of their rationale for pursuing them.

At the outset, they should acknowledge that many academic and market
commentators have argued that acquisitions have a high failure rate, often
destroying shareholder value. Indeed, the empirical evidence indicates that
while acquisitions generally create net value, the benefits obtained by the
acquirer often are outweighed by the premium it has paid to the target's shareholders. Also, the skeptics rightly point out that their execution is fraught with

risks that range from failing to identify potential liabilities, to underestimating the degree of difficulty in melding two disparate cultures, to creating conflicts in distribution channels and customer relationships.

Nevertheless, CFOs should recognize that while strategic transactions admittedly are difficult to execute, this is likewise true with alternative growth strategies—such as investing in research and development or launching new products—and that very few companies have achieved long-term success without using acquisitions to advance their strategic objectives. The fact is that acquisitions often represent a *faster, cheaper, and less risky* alternative to organic expansion.

Therefore, although CFOs are wise to view acquisitions with caution, they should focus their efforts on maximizing the probability of success, rather than eschewing acquisitions altogether. In particular, CFOs can mitigate the risks by following *rigorous business practices* in their review of potential transactions and applying *consistent procedures* in their execution.

Furthermore, they can implement proven strategies for identifying potential targets, including sticking to adjacent spaces, taking a portfolio approach, requiring a business sponsor, and exercising patience and flexibility.[1]

ADJACENT SPACES

The odds of success are much greater when the acquirer pursues adjacencies— *logical extensions* of a company's current business mix that can be taken on incrementally. In contrast, diversifying into a new area often does not create value; these types of transactions are inherently more difficult to execute, and they typically lack sufficient synergies to justify the premium paid to the acquired company. Furthermore, shareholders usually can more efficiently obtain most of the benefits from diversification through the construction of their own investment portfolios—and can achieve this diversification without paying a premium.

Adjacent acquisitions take advantage of a company's *intrinsic strengths*— management knowhow, customer insights, and cultural orientation—and also have the advantage of being *brand consistent*. Furthermore, a company can more easily communicate the strategic rationale for an adjacent acquisition than one that takes the company far afield from its current business mix. When a deal does not require a stretch of the imagination, it is easier to gain buy-in from investors, customers, and employees—which can make a real difference in the transaction's ultimate success.

PORTFOLIO APPROACH

A company is more likely to be a successful acquirer if it has *accumulated experience* in making deals. This argues for several smaller transactions versus a bet-the-company deal, especially if the company's acquisition program is in its nascent stages or if the acquirer is expanding into unfamiliar territory.

Moreover, doing several transactions can produce *more predictable financial results* over time. Diversification offsets the probability that a few of the transactions will go awry and can give acquirers offsetting exposures to acquisition targets that are in differing phases of their growth cycles—with some acquisitions providing immediately attractive returns on investment and others requiring a longer period of gestation to realize their ultimately favorable levels of profitability.

Of course, the counterargument to a portfolio approach is that it is just as hard—if not harder—to execute a small deal as a large one; thus, an acquirer should focus its resources on transactions that have greater upside potential. Certainly this argument has some validity, and doing too many small deals can be a recipe for chaos, especially if the acquirer doesn't enforce stringent guidelines for their integration.

CFOs should seek to find the golden mean, where a company can learn through the process of executing several transactions, but not to become so diffused and unfocused as to negate the discipline that's required for long-term success.

BUSINESS SPONSOR

While CFOs undoubtedly should expect to play a strong leadership role in executing a company's acquisition program, they should not be the driving force for a transaction. Instead, it should be axiomatic that the CEO or a business leader takes *ownership* for the acquisition—including accountability for delivering the business results and projected synergies. This leadership is absolutely imperative and should be one of the key criteria that CFOs use to evaluate whether potential transactions are likely to create rather than destroy shareholder value.

Likewise, although bankers or consultants can be fertile sources of transaction ideas and market intelligence, CFOs should never rely on these outsiders to determine the desirability of a potential transaction or the price to be paid. Instead, the transaction should be proposed and driven by a business sponsor who is fully committed to the strategic and business objectives to be attained and *personally accountable* for the transaction—from start to finish.

Finally, in addition to being accountable, the business sponsor ideally should be *passionate* about the transaction. Doing acquisitions is tough work—especially after the deal closes and the integration begins. Therefore, CFOs should take comfort when a transaction has a sponsor whose passion can overcome the inevitable ebbs and flows of a combination. Conversely, a lack of passion should be a warning flag that however appealing a transaction may look on paper, the execution and follow-through may not go as planned.

PATIENCE AND FLEXIBILITY

Of all the reasons why companies undertake transactions that destroy shareholder value, the most common is that they are *too anxious* to do the deal. Similar to shopping for groceries when you are hungry, you can end up buying too much of the wrong things. For example, if a company is having difficulty with a particular business unit, trying to fix it through an acquisition is seldom the right course of action. The company usually will be much better off to divest the business, or to fix it first before considering an acquisition. Too often, adding an acquisition to a troubled business simply makes it a larger problem.

Similarly, if a company is *too fixated* on pursuing a strategic objective or too narrow in its consideration of potential alternatives, it can end up buying the wrong company or paying too much. Patience is indeed a virtue in considering acquisitions, as is the flexibility to say no. That's why CFOs will often describe their acquisition strategy as "opportunistic," which is a way to signal to investors that the company will be patient in contemplating acquisitions and will not undertake transactions unless all the stars are aligned.

Investment bankers have an expression for this patient and flexible approach to acquisitions: *"Wait for another bus."* CFOs are wise to heed this advice.

STRATEGIC PURPOSE

Although CFOs are ultimately responsible for analyzing the financial valuation of the acquisition candidate and whether it's likely to add shareholder value, they can make an even bigger contribution by ensuring that the transaction makes sense from a non-financial viewpoint. Somewhat paradoxically, CFOs should be obsessed from the outset on the strategic purpose rather than on the financials—making sure that the transaction is driven by business and strategic objectives and not as an exercise in financial engineering.

To this end, rather than focusing initially on the financial attributes of a potential acquisition, the CFO should seek to clarify the strategic rationale—to articulate clearly and persuasively the reasons that the transaction has business logic. To this end, CFOs should be able to answer two overarching questions: *Why are we the most logical acquirer?* and *How will this transaction advance our strategic objectives?*

Only after CFOs can answer these threshold questions convincingly, should they turn to the projected financial impacts of the proposed transaction—to confirm that it makes economic as well as strategic and business sense. This requires stepping back from the specifics of the transaction and focusing on the basic objectives being pursued—in other words, clarifying the underlying strategic rationale for the transaction.

TYPES OF ACQUISITIONS

It usually helps to consider the rationale within the broad categories that describe the types of acquisitions that can be pursued: consolidations, bolt-ons, platforms, and transformations.

Consolidation Transactions

"Consolidations" usually reflect a recurring business pattern whereby an industry matures and then the industry participants seek increased market share and efficiencies through combinations with each other. The consolidations can occur through mergers between major companies (such as the recent experience in the banking and telecom industries) or through a roll-up of smaller companies in a fragmented industry (such as the consolidation trends in the printing and other service industries). Consolidations may reflect cross-border synergies on a global scale, or they may be contained within a specific country or geographical region.

Although consolidations generally have ample potential to produce efficiencies through greater economies of scale, they also can be difficult to execute due to the incompatibility of cultures, information technology systems, or compensation and benefits programs; and they often are accompanied by revenue dis-synergies as customers choose to maintain a diversity of choices among their suppliers. Also, to obtain regulatory approvals, the acquirer may be required to divest some of the operations, thereby losing a portion of the projected benefits from the transaction.

Most important, consolidation transactions often involve excessive premiums that are paid by the acquirer; this may compel the acquirer to make overly aggressive assumptions for the projected benefits in order to justify the price paid to the target's shareholders—making it more likely that the deal won't live up to expectations.

To facilitate consolidations that make economic sense, an acquirer may attempt to accomplish a *"merger of equals"* whereby a relatively low premium is paid to the acquired company's shareholders, typically in a stock-for-stock transaction. However, negotiating these types of transactions can be problematic due to "social" issues: Who is the CEO? Where is the headquarters? What is the company's name? Who are the board members? What are the brand names? Moreover, agreeing to a relatively low premium may induce interlopers to make a competitive offer at a higher price. Furthermore, a merger of equals can create ambiguities in the integration of the companies, causing delays in execution and a failure to realize all of the projected synergies from the combination.

If a company is going to pursue a consolidation transaction, it should have a vision concerning the future dynamics of the industry. And if it believes that industry consolidation is inevitable, it can consider four primary alternatives:

1. **Do not participate in consolidation transactions**: This allows the company to maintain focus on increasing its standalone value, but may make it more difficult to compete effectively as the industry consolidates.
2. **Agree to be acquired at a premium price for shareholders:** This alternative usually maximizes the short-term valuation, but may not be the best long-term alternative for creating shareholder value.
3. **Acquire other industry participants:** This allows the company to strengthen its competitive position, giving it more economies of scale and market clout. This alternative may work out well in the end, but it also may cause some short-term pain for shareholders due to the premiums paid in the acquisitions and the difficulties in realizing projected synergies.
4. **Be a consolidator now and an acquired company later:** This strategy maintains flexibility concerning the ultimate industry configuration and balances some short-term pain with an expectation for an eventual payoff. However, it's a difficult strategy to communicate and execute, and may be considered more of a fallback approach if the company's acquisitions don't create value.

CFOs can help a company sort through the strategic alternatives in an industry consolidation, helping to quantify and sensitize the potential scenarios. In addition, CFOs can provide constructive input concerning the types of transactions to be pursued, while reinforcing the need for discipline in crafting the terms.

Bolt-on Transactions

"Bolt-ons" (also called "tuck-ins") represent the most frequent type of acquisition, usually involving the full and relatively rapid integration of the acquired company within an existing business of the acquirer. Bolt-ons can be motivated by a desire to add the target's customer base, geographic reach, technologies, knowhow, product lines, brand names, or other valuable assets. In most cases, a bolt-on will produce attractive near-term financial returns for the acquirer—provided that a reasonable price is paid for the target.

Although not typically as difficult to integrate as consolidation transactions, a series of bolt-ons can result in unexpected complexities and incremental costs, especially if they lead to a proliferation of disparate information technology systems, varying compensation and benefit programs, conflicting distribution channels, or ambiguous brand identities.

The most successful acquirers in bolt-on transactions tend to employ *consistent and extremely disciplined processes* for integrating the acquired companies and they usually are manifestly ruthless in their identification and realization of cost synergies. For example, they normally impose standardized information technology systems and achieve immediate and total conformity among back office functions such as payroll; benefits; accounts payable; procurement; and email, voice mail, and other communication tools.

Because bolt-ons tend to be motivated primarily by cost synergies, they usually can produce relatively rapid returns on investment—typically being accretive to earnings immediately or within a year or two, and earning a positive accounting return on investment within the near future. They also can be relatively low risk, especially if part of a series of similar transactions.

CFOs should be particularly sensitive to the prices paid for bolt-ons, ensuring that their projected returns are achievable and worth the effort involved in their execution and integration. They usually only make sense if the price is right.

Platform Transactions

"Platforms" refer to transactions that allow the acquiring company to enter a new business or market, typically an adjacency to one of its existing businesses.

As discussed earlier, this focus on adjacencies is usually critical to a platform's ultimate success, in contrast with diversifications into totally unrelated businesses, which are much more problematic.

Often platforms are pursued where industries or technologies are converging, creating either a necessity or an opportunity to expand the acquired company's business or product lines. In this case, the acquirer typically makes the judgment that entering the new space through an acquisition is preferable to a purely organic alternative.

For example, the acquirer may be seeking a new technology, an infrastructure, a management team, a customer base, or a brand identity. In the ideal case, a platform acquisition is encouraged by the acquirer's customers, or at least is readily accepted by the customers as a logical and desirable extension of the acquirer's existing product offerings and brand image.

A platform transaction typically has fewer near-term cost synergies and therefore tends to have a longer financial payback than either a consolidation or a bolt-on transaction. It also can entail more risk exposure due to the acquirer's unfamiliarity with the business space or its greater reliance on the target's management team, who may not be committed to remaining after the noncompete agreements have expired. In particular, if the platform transaction involves a small, entrepreneurial business being acquired by a larger, more mature company, the acquirer should reasonably expect that not all of the management will thrive in their new environment and should plan on some turnover.

A platform can involve a company that operates relatively independently from the acquirer's other businesses—perhaps with *"earnout"* incentives whereby the earnings are shared with the acquired company's management for a defined period. Also, a focus on rapid integration may be less of a priority for a platform than a bolt-on, so as not to impair the acquisition's culture or customer relationships. Usually the primary evaluation metric is revenue growth—at least over the near term—with the acquisition's return on investment not reaching fruition until its growth strategies have achieved their stated aims.

A platform may involve an aggressive plan to consolidate a fragmented industry, usually involving several smaller transactions. This *"roll up"* strategy can generate attractive returns, but requires strong discipline in the prices paid for the transactions and rigorous conformity of systems and processes as these smaller entities come into the fold. It also requires the development of strong management processes; an experienced management team is usually a prerequisite to executing a roll up strategy successfully.

Transformative Transactions

Without question, transformations are the most controversial and the most difficult to pull off. The acquirer is attempting to shift its *center of gravity*, usually to lessen vulnerability to a stagnant or declining business. The existing business often is managed to generate cash flow—which is used to finance the acquisition and expand the new business—or is jettisoned through a divestiture or spinoff.

Pursuing a transformative transaction is like asking the dealer for four cards in a hand of straight poker. It may work out, but it certainly would have been preferable to start with a pair of aces, let alone a full house. To succeed, it takes a highly qualified and courageous CEO, an attractive acquisition or merger opportunity, a reasonable price that is paid, and a lot of luck.

It also requires a supportive shareholder base; investors understandably may be concerned about the potential risk and reward tradeoffs as the company embarks on this high risk alternative. While some transformations have succeeded—such as Westinghouse's conversion into CBS—the business landscape is littered with the carcasses of companies that have not survived the transition.

If considering a transformation, CFOs will be challenged by investors to articulate a compelling rationale—especially a credible answer to the question: Why should the cash flows or divestiture proceeds from an existing business be reinvested in a new business rather than returned to shareholders? In addition, they will need to convince investors that management has the capabilities for executing this high wire strategy and realizing the financial advantages that are contemplated from the transaction.

 NOTE

1. Nolop, Bruce, "Rules to Acquire By" (September 2007, *Harvard Business Review*), pp. 129–132, 134, 136–140.

CHAPTER EIGHT

Evaluating Acquisition Candidates

THE CFO SHOULD WORK CLOSELY with the business sponsor and the deal team in evaluating the candidates for a merger or acquisition. Even if an investment bank or other external financial advisor is engaged, the CFO remains directly responsible for determining the assumptions and projections that will establish the target's valuation. The CFO should ensure objective assessments of the target and apply consistent methodologies in the financial analyses.

 ## VALUATION METHODOLOGIES

CFOs should use a combination of methodologies to determine an estimated valuation for the target. The valuation techniques usually include discounted cash flows, comparable companies, precedent transactions, and a leveraged buyout analysis. If the target is a public company, the valuation will also include a premiums paid analysis.

Discounted Cash Flows

Discounted cash flow analyses are used to compute the net present value of the target, as well as internal rates of return using different assumed prices. CFOs prepare standalone projections for the target, and then overlay the projected net synergies, as well as the estimated costs of execution and integration.

The standalone projections can be based on models prepared by security analysts or other third parties, on internal forecasts provided by the target company (perhaps with adjustments by the acquirer, usually to make them less optimistic), or on estimates prepared by the acquirer using assumptions developed through due diligence (the best alternative). The synergy projections are normally developed by the acquirer, although ideally the target's management will provide some input.

Comparable Companies

A comparable company analysis arrays valuation measures for the target against companies that are deemed similar. The comparison reflects current market valuations and includes performance measures and ratios that are typically used to value companies in that industry (such as multiples of net income, earnings before income, taxes, depreciation and amortization [EBITDA], free cash flow, revenue, or book value). If an acquisition candidate is in diverse businesses, the valuation can be based on a weighted-average composite of values.

In performing this analysis, CFOs should ensure that the current performance data are representative of normalized financial statements. If not, they can adjust the data to eliminate unusual items that may be distorting the comparisons or incorporate alternative time periods; in addition, they can focus on forward looking estimates, such as the forecast for next year's earnings per share.

Precedent Transactions

An analysis of precedent transactions looks at the relevant multiples paid in arms-length acquisitions of companies that are similar to the target. These multiples are normally based on the trailing twelve months prior to the announcement of the transaction.

In addition to analyzing the financial multiples—such as price paid relative to net income or EBITDA—CFOs can also consider non-financial measures such as the price paid per customer, the price paid per barrel of oil, or other performance measures that are relevant for the target's industry.

Leveraged Buyout

Depending on the target's industry—and whether it generates relatively stable earnings and cash flow—a leveraged buyout (LBO) analysis can provide a further data point in valuing the target. An LBO analysis essentially considers the price range that likely could be realized through a private equity transaction.

An LBO analysis normally establishes a floor valuation for the target, but there are also circumstances where a private equity transaction can exceed the price to be paid by a strategic acquirer. The key variables in this analysis are the amount and cost of debt financing that is currently available in the market (usually measured by the multiple of debt to EBITDA) and whether the target's industry is currently out of favor in the stock market (usually evidenced by a low valuation multiple to EBITDA).

Premiums Paid

If the target is a public company, the valuation should include an analysis of premiums paid over the market value in other public transactions. Because it is often unclear when the potential transaction began to affect the target's stock price, it is advisable to perform this analysis using alternative reference dates.

In addition, if the acquirer is paying stock for part or all of the consideration, the CFO should analyze the historical exchange ratios between the two stocks—showing the market premium that is being paid based on average stock prices over both shorter and longer time periods.

Limitations of Methodologies

CFOs should be mindful of the inherent limitations in each of the methodologies. In particular, they should recognize that discounted cash flow valuations are extremely sensitive to the terminal values that are assumed— usually based on an assumed terminal multiple of free cash flow or EBITDA, or on an assumed perpetuity growth rate. For this reason, it can be useful for CFOs to calculate the amount of the target's valuation that is coming from discounted cash flows over a foreseeable time period (say, the next five years) versus the value that is derived from the longer-term assumptions, especially the terminal value.

At the same time, CFOs should be aware that the comparable company and precedent transaction analyses reflect historical and near-term financial results, which may not be indicative of long-term trends. This can cause an acquirer to overpay for a target whose business is likely to decline, possibly due to an unproductive research and development program or a failure to invest in marketing and advertising.

STANDALONE AND SYNERGY VALUES

CFOs should seek to distinguish between the target's standalone value versus the value created through the transaction. This is an important distinction that can highlight the dynamics of the proposed acquisition and provide a benchmark for negotiating the deal terms.

Market versus Intrinsic Value

The standalone valuation uses projections for the target that exclude synergies and the costs of executing and integrating the acquisition. It is an estimate of the target's intrinsic value on a *"fully distributed"* basis—which assumes that the target's common stock is held by public shareholders who do not have a controlling interest and that its market value does not include an acquisition premium.

If the target is a public company, the CFO should either validate or challenge the presumption that its current stock price is a fair representation of its intrinsic value. This recognizes that while the financial markets may be efficient on average over the long run, there definitely are times and circumstances where a given stock may not be appropriately valued by the market.

CFOs should be particularly vigilant in detecting a potential discrepancy between the target's intrinsic and market values when the possibility of a transaction may be baked into the stock price—often due to speculation that the target is in play. In other words, CFOs should make sure that the standalone valuation of the target does not include an acquisition premium—which would be tantamount to double counting the value that the acquirer is bringing to the party.

Value of Synergies

After valuing the target on a standalone basis, CFOs should add the value of the net synergies to be derived from the combination, less the costs of executing and integrating the transaction. The value of the synergies can be estimated using a discounted cash flow analysis or by assuming a market multiple on the annualized contribution from the synergies.

For example, if the annual synergies are estimated to be $40 million of incremental EBITDA and companies in the industry trade at a multiple of five times EBITDA, then the value of the synergies can be estimated at $200 million.

CFOs should then compare the value of the synergies with the estimated premium over standalone value that is being paid to the target's shareholders. For example, if the synergies are estimated to have a net present value of $200 million and the premium over the target's standalone value is estimated to be $100 million, the comparison indicates that half of the net value creation is being paid to the target's shareholders and half is being retained by the acquirer:

$$[\text{Premium to Target} = \$100]/[\text{Value of Synergies} = \$200]$$

$$= 50\% \text{ Paid to Target's Shareholders}$$

$$= 50\% \text{ Retained by Acquirer}$$

If the acquirer is paying common stock rather than cash to the target's shareholders, then additional value is transferred through their continuing ownership interest in the value of synergies retained by the acquirer. For example, if the target's shareholders receive 10 percent of the acquirer's shares outstanding, the calculations are revised as follows:

$$[\text{Target's Ownership} = 10\%] \times [\text{Synergies Retained by Acquirer} = 50\%]$$

$$= 5\% \text{ Additional Value Transferred to Target's} \\ \text{Shareholders}$$

$$= 55\% \text{ Paid to Target's Shareholders}$$

$$= 45\% \text{ Retained by Acquirer}$$

CFOs should be mindful of this ratio throughout the deal negotiations and remain vigilant against the all-too-frequent temptation to offer a price that compensates the target's shareholders for most, if not all, of the value of synergies. Otherwise, even though the transaction creates value, it can be a losing proposition for the acquirer's shareholders.

PRO FORMA ANALYSES

In addition to the valuation analyses, CFOs also will prepare pro forma analyses of the potential acquisition, taking into account not only the standalone projections for the target, but also the estimated net synergies and transaction costs.

Earnings per Share

The most common pro forma analysis is to compute the incremental impact on earnings per share due to the acquisition. This analysis can assume either the financing actually being used for the transaction or, alternatively, it can assume a financing mix that reflects the acquirer's assumptions for its long-run capital structure.

For example, the acquirer may be financing the transaction with debt that has an after-tax cost of 5 percent, while its weighted-average cost of capital is estimated to be 10 percent. In this case, if the acquisition will earn an after-tax return on investment of 8 percent, it will be accretive when using the cost of debt, but dilutive when using the weighted-average cost of capital. The latter is a better theoretical exercise, but using the actual financing shows the financial impact that the stock market will see.

Probably the best solution is to show the pro forma impact both ways. This allows the CFO to make apples-to-apples comparisons among transactions, but also to show the actual impact due to the specific terms of the transaction. This favors paying cash rather than stock—which doesn't make sense from a corporate finance perspective—but reflects the way that the market reacts to transactions.

When analyzing the accretion or dilution, CFOs should focus on two key points. First, they should consider the year-over-year trends; dilution is more tolerable if it is forecast to improve each year and to become accretive in the near future. Second, they should consider the magnitude of the accretion or dilution; a percentage change of greater than 5 percent is a good rule for when the accretion or dilution can be viewed as material.

Return on Investment

The pro forma accounting return on investment can be computed using the acquirer's cost of capital, showing the economic value added (EVA) from the transaction. However, CFOs should recognize that it usually is very difficult for an acquisition to produce positive EVA during the first few years if a premium is paid over the target's book value. The premium causes an increase in the target's invested capital and the write-up of intangibles causes a decrease in the target's earnings due to the amortization charges. Therefore, CFOs may want to exclude the amortization of intangibles in their pro forma EVA analysis.

Moreover, in comparison to a discounted cash flow analysis, an accounting-based EVA analysis does not give as much value to the projected growth in future earnings. If a high growth company is being acquired, it likely will be several years before a conventional EVA analysis will show a positive return on investment. This may create a bias toward acquisition targets that have lower growth rates and quicker realization of synergies.

Nevertheless, if an acquisition is projected never to earn a positive EVA over a foreseeable time horizon, that should be a red flag for CFOs in analyzing the likelihood that the transaction can add shareholder value. In particular, it means that the acquirer is betting on substantial future growth, which should be scrutinized carefully for its reasonableness.

Return on Equity

Another common analysis is to consider the impact on the company's return on equity (net income as a percent of book equity). Normally, this analysis is computed using the actual financing for the transaction—which means that there is no capital charge for an all-cash transaction. It can be a useful analysis if the acquirer will be paying with excess cash or unused debt capacity and will not need to raise additional equity in the future, thus indicating the incremental accounting return on shareholders' invested capital.

Other Pro Forma Analyses

Depending on the type of acquisition, additional pro forma measures may be especially pertinent. For example, if acquiring a high-growth business, the CFO should analyze the pro forma impact on the acquirer's revenue growth rate. In contrast, if acquiring a low growth business, the contribution to the acquirer's EBITDA or free cash flow may be more relevant.

In addition, CFOs should perform pro forma analyses that relate to the strategic objectives for the transaction. For example, they might focus on non-financial measurements, such as the impact on customers or market shares, or show how the transaction will affect the company's business profile, such as the percentage of its revenue in emerging markets.

Stock Price Impact

The pro forma analyses are especially important in cases where the acquirer is issuing stock to the target: They can indicate the potential near-term impact on the acquirer's stock price, which can affect the value of the consideration to be received by the target company's shareholders (as well as the purchase accounting adjustments).

ACQUIRER'S STOCK VALUATION

If the acquirer is issuing stock as part of the consideration, the CFO will want to assess whether its stock price prior to the announcement reflects its intrinsic value. If the stock is judged to be overvalued, this will effectively reduce the consideration paid to the target; if the stock is considered to be undervalued, this will effectively raise the premium being paid, perhaps making the transaction not economically viable.

For example, if the CFO believes that the acquirer's stock price is undervalued by 10 percent, this raises the implicit premium by 10 percent in an all-stock transaction and by 5 percent if half the consideration is being paid in stock.

However, CFOs should recognize that while targets will perform due diligence on the acquirer's stock price, they are highly unlikely to accept a lower premium as a result of their analysis. Instead, they tend to fear an overvalued stock—which can be a good reason not to proceed with the deal—and to consider an undervalued stock as potential upside, but not a reason to accept a lower price.

 RISK CONSIDERATIONS

In evaluating potential transactions, CFOs should explicitly address their implications for enterprise risks—analyzing both positive and negative effects. They should analyze the financial implications under different scenarios and consider the strategic implications in light of the company's business objectives.

Financial Implications

Acquisition analyses typically focus on one or a very limited number of scenarios. A few CFOs have tried to employ Monte Carlo analyses and other sophisticated methodologies, but their greater complexity tends to overwhelm the benefits: It is hard to maintain transparency when the assumptions are varied, to distinguish the relative effects caused by each of the variables, and to apply the standard valuation techniques that are largely based on accumulated experience and heuristics.

Nevertheless, CFOs should consider alternative scenarios in their acquisition analyses, especially when analyzing major transactions. In particular, they should include a downside scenario where several things are assumed to go wrong at the same time. This recognizes that a number of key variables may be correlated and that no matter how well an acquisition is executed, its value can be eroded due to factors outside of the acquirer's control.

At the same time, sensitivity analyses can also reveal positive effects on the acquirer; for example, the company may become less vulnerable to economic or political uncertainties as a result of the combination, or the company may be less reliant on major customers or products. In other words, although diversification should not be the primary motivation for the transaction, it can be one of the benefits that is realized.

Strategic Implications

CFOs should also consider the acquisition's risks from a strategic perspective. For example, the potential benefits from a transaction simply may not be worth the increased risk exposure due to excessive strain on the company's technology infrastructure or the likelihood of too much channel conflict. However, in making this assessment, CFOs should be careful to distinguish between those risks that can be resolved by investors' diversification versus those risks that investors would not want the company to retain.

Conversely, the benefits to the company's risk position—for example, due to the greater diversification of technologies, customer demographics, or brand names—may make the transaction more compelling, perhaps overcoming a relatively modest return on investment. In other words, reducing risk can be one of the strategic motivations to proceed with a transaction in the first place, assuming that the financials can be made to work satisfactorily.

CHAPTER NINE

Executing a Merger or Acquisition

W HEN A COMPANY IS READY TO pursue a potential merger or acquisition, the CFO usually partners with the business sponsor and general counsel in leading a deal team that conducts due diligence, prepares a business plan, establishes the pricing parameters, negotiates the contract terms, and integrates the acquired company.

In addition, the CFO actively coordinates all of the various parties involved in a transaction, both the internal management and the external advisors, who can include investment bankers, lawyers, accountants, tax specialists, consultants, and other participants at various stages of the transaction. This coordination can contribute to a smooth and error-free execution, and can increase the likelihood that the transaction will fulfill the company's business and financial objectives.

 ## DUE DILIGENCE

After entering into discussions concerning a transaction—either through one-on-one negotiations or as part of a competitive auction—the deal team will conduct a thorough due diligence review of the acquisition candidate. To the extent possible, this will include a relatively constant group of staff people who work on all of the acquirer's transactions and who can apply consistent procedures in ensuring that all the bases are covered.

Negotiated Transactions

Due diligence is best accomplished through a methodical, painstaking approach that involves substantial requests for information to be provided by the target. This is one of the reasons that acquirers normally prefer negotiated transactions with a willing seller. If they can reach a meeting of the minds about the desirability of a deal, both parties can invest the substantial time and energy to do a proper review of all the considerations involved—making it more likely that the integration will go smoothly and that neither side will be surprised or disappointed.

Furthermore, if the acquirer is a strategic competitor, the acquisition candidate may feel more comfortable sharing confidential or sensitive information about its products, customers, and other aspects of its business when it is likely to lead to a combination than when it is part of a competitive process with an uncertain ending. In an auction, the seller often fears that a strategic acquirer is simply on a "fishing expedition."

Competitive Transactions

An auction typically involves simultaneous discussions with several potential acquirers through most of a two-stage process—a "preliminary indication of interest" and then a "final bid"—usually with relatively standardized information provided to the auction participants through a data room—which today is typically provided in electronic form—and through well-orchestrated management presentations.

Potential acquirers can submit requests for additional information or for answers to specific questions, but the target's management team is usually stretched due to their need to be responsive to several potential buyers at the same time. Also, the seller does not want to give any impression that there is not a level playing field among the auction participants.

It is only after the auction process has been narrowed to one or a few participants that the acquirer can ascertain some of the most valuable information—such as customer lists or pricing strategies. And because the auction normally imposes strict time constraints, the acquirer can find it challenging to perform a thorough review in the allotted window of opportunity. Moreover, this final phase of an auction is usually termed *"confirmatory"* due diligence, which makes it difficult for the acquirer to expand its scope too aggressively.

Responses to Auction Limitations

Given the stark contrast between negotiated and competitive deal environments, CFOs should take some action steps to increase their odds of success. First, they should seek to pursue negotiated transactions whenever possible— perhaps making a preemptive bid that is contingent upon the seller agreeing to exclusive negotiations. The CFO can argue that a negotiated transaction will be quicker and more certain than an auction, which may be attractive to the target, especially if the acquirer can offer an attractive price that does not include a financing contingency.

Second, CFOs should seek to limit the number of auctions in which the acquirer participates, thus avoiding some of the strain on the company's scarce business and staff resources. Participating in auctions has opportunity costs that should only be incurred if the CFO believes there is a reasonably good probability that a transaction will be consummated. Like most things, acquisitions benefit from greater focus.

Third, CFOs should seek to overcome the inherent limitations to conducting due diligence in a competitive auction. For example, they can:

- *Leverage external information sources*—such as bankers, consultants, accountants, and the Internet—to learn as much as possible about the target (but remaining compliant with the nondisclosure agreement).
- *Organize a swat team* for conducting confirmatory due diligence if the company reaches the final stage of the process (accomplishing as much as possible in a limited amount of time).
- *Include representations and warranties* in the contract (marking up the seller's contract that is submitted with the final bid).

Due Diligence Checklist

Plenty of checklists are available and the mergers and acquisitions specialists within law firms can provide state-of-the-art itemizations of the various areas that need to be covered in a due diligence review. However, CFOs should recognize that while generic checklists can be terrific blueprints—especially for the legal and financial items that need to be covered—they should be supplemented with tailored procedures that reflect the acquirer's specific business and strategic objectives.

CFOs should also take pains to ensure that the due diligence process does not devolve into a rote, "check-the-box" type of exercise. Instead, the primary focus should be on issues that can determine a deal's success or subject the acquirer to material financial, operational, legal, or reputational risks.

Establishing continuity in the due diligence team can go a long way toward obtaining the right level of focus; working with a detailed checklist, an experienced deal team can leverage their accumulated expertise and direct their energies toward the issues of most concern.

Due Diligence Team

Due diligence teams historically have been dominated by financial and legal people, with a primary focus on verifying the assets and liabilities, reviewing the legal and governance documents, and discovering any liabilities or other exposures that are not currently shown in the financial statements. These objectives remain central to the due diligence efforts.

However, much of today's focus is on *business due diligence*, especially learning information about the target that can form the basis for a business plan to integrate the companies effectively and to realize the projected synergies from the transaction. The team should not hesitate to request relatively detailed and sensitive information from the target, including answers that may require opinions and interpretations—and not just data—about customers, competitors, products, and markets, as well as strategies for addressing long-term challenges in the business. The target may resist some of these requests, but they are critical to confirming that the acquisition will indeed make business sense.

In addition, there is greater focus on human resource considerations—such as the compatibility of the *compensation and benefits programs*. The danger is that conforming to the acquirer's programs can make the target's cost structure uncompetitive; however, maintaining separate programs can create administrative costs and headaches, especially if the nonconforming programs continue to proliferate.

Acquirers are also more focused on the *compatibility of the cultures*, which frequently can make or break a successful integration. The horror stories of incompatible cultures are legion—providing cautionary tales for all acquirers and their CFOs.

Technology is another area of increased concern, especially when it is fundamental to the target's business model. Incompatible systems can be a deal killer, as can the need for significant investments to bring the target's infrastructure up to the acquirer's standards. These can be issues that fester if not addressed immediately in the integration plan.

It is also important to review the target's support systems, including the compatibility of *financial reporting* technologies. The proliferation of general ledgers is something to avoid.

Finally, due diligence teams often involve a broad and expanding group of *specialists* who can lend their expertise to the review. For example, human resource specialists may asses the capabilities and potential of the target's management team—helping to determine whether they can play a leadership role in the combined company going forward. Other specialty areas may include accounting procedures (including a review of the target's Sarbanes-Oxley compliance), environmental issues, litigation exposures, tax planning, or regulatory compliance.

Sharing Conclusions

Once the team members have completed their reviews, they should share their conclusions with the rest of the due diligence team and prepare a summary report for the business sponsor—along with any suggestions for strategies to mitigate the issues that have been identified.

CFOs should appreciate that the goal of due diligence is not to produce a riskless transaction, but to foster a common understanding of the relevant facts and to ensure that the acquirer's decision-makers are made aware of all the material risks and opportunities—which then can be considered in negotiating the deal terms and ultimately in deciding whether to proceed with the transaction. It is one thing not to know about the issues, but it is another thing if the acquirer can accept the issues with eyes wide open.

 BUSINESS PLAN

Preparing a detailed business plan is the cornerstone of a successful transaction—the work product that largely determines the target's valuation and dictates the plan for its integration. The plan is shaped by the information gleaned through due diligence and should manifest the acquirer's strategic and business objectives.

While the CFO can provide active support to the business plan's preparation, it is critically important that the business sponsor takes the lead in its development and assumes personal responsibility for its implementation—including the financial projections. To that end, the CFO should strive to reinforce the business sponsor's "ownership" of the transaction.

The business plan should be as detailed as possible, with specific target dates and explicit accountabilities for:

- *Communicating with stakeholders,* including employees, customers, vendors, and regulatory authorities.
- *Realizing cost and other synergies,* including an itemization of the planned headcount reductions.
- *Integrating infrastructure functions,* including IT systems, payroll, benefits administration, telecommunications, and email.
- *Achieving business milestones,* including the proposed actions with respect to brand names, sales reorganizations, and leadership roles.

In each case, the CFO should confirm that designated individuals will be accountable for completing each of the action steps in a timely manner.

 ## FINANCIAL PROJECTIONS

Of course, the business plan should also include detailed financial projections—typically three to five years—that will serve not only as the yardstick for measuring the transaction's performance, but also as guideposts for determining the target's valuation and the price to be offered. The goal should be to produce aggressive, yet realistic projections—similar to the company's methodologies for preparing its long-term financial model.

In addition to the overlay of projected synergies, the target's historical and projected financial statements should reflect the allocations and accounting treatments that will apply after the acquisition. Some typical examples include applying purchase accounting adjustments for intangibles and goodwill, excluding non-recurring items, consolidating tax returns, reflecting revised compensation arrangements, allocating overhead expense, and using constant currencies.

Intangibles

If the acquirer is paying more than the target's book value, the assets will be written up to their fair value, including the value of intangible assets such as customer lists, brand names, patents, and technology systems. These intangibles will be amortized over their estimated useful life, which means that the acquirer will need to have relatively definitive plans for their use.

For example, the value of a brand name can have a perpetual life—and thus not be amortized. However, if the acquirer plans to phase the brand name out over time, the amortization will reflect this shorter life.

Goodwill

As the residual from all of the purchase accounting adjustments, the transaction is likely to show a goodwill asset on the balance sheet. Although not amortized, the goodwill is subject to the risk of a future write-off if its value diminishes. Therefore, CFOs will want to understand this risk and to consider if there are any mitigation strategies to consider.

In addition, the goodwill is usually tax deductible in an asset deal. This should be included in the cash flow projections, but it will not affect net income.

Non-Recurring Items

CFOs may choose to exclude certain non-recurring revenue or expenses from the pro forma financials—both historical results and future projections. For example, they may exclude a positive or negative legal or insurance settlement or a special bonus related to the transaction.

In addition, CFOs typically exclude some deal-related expenses from the business plan projections. For example, they usually exclude expenses—such as investment banking and legal fees—that are not intrinsic to the business.

Tax Status

If the acquisition involves a U.S. private company, it may be organized as an S corporation, where the shareholders are taxed as individuals or a partnership. The financials will need to be adjusted to include a corporate tax expense, reflecting the conversion of the target to a C corporation, which will be included in the acquirer's consolidated tax return.

Compensation Arrangements

If the target is closely held, it may be paying compensation to the owners that will not be continued after the acquisition. The financial statements should be restated to reflect the anticipated compensation arrangements going forward.

Overhead Charges

CFOs should adjust the financials to reflect the allocated and direct overhead expenses that will be borne by the target after the transaction is consummated. They can either include only the acquirer's incremental expenses (which is the best approach in valuing the target) or they can include the fully allocated costs (which is likely the way that the target will be charged going forward).

Constant Currencies

In preparing the pro forma financials, CFOs may choose to adjust the target's historical results to reflect constant foreign exchange rates for its international operations. This can facilitate comparisons of the target's historical and forecasted results.

 ## FINANCING PLAN

Given the fundamental corporate finance principle that separates investment decisions from financing decisions, the CFO's valuation of an acquisition candidate should be largely agnostic to the way that transaction is to be financed. However, the expected financing plan will influence the pro forma analyses, which in turn may affect the acquirer's stock price reaction. Therefore, when evaluating a potential transaction, the CFO will need to reflect the likely financing arrangements in some of the analyses.

In addition, arranging financing is a critical part of executing the transaction. The CFO should develop a short- and long-term financing plan, understand the likely costs, estimate the impact on the company's financial projections, determine whether an offer to the target should include a financing condition, and ensure that the acquisition will not cause the company to violate its debt covenants.

Cash versus Equity

The CFO's first decision is to determine whether the transaction will be paid totally in cash, totally in equity, or through a combination of the two. In most cases, CFOs will prefer to pay cash: It's easier for the seller to value, and it is usually favored by the target's shareholders. In addition, it is typically favored by the acquirer's shareholders, who prefer not to be diluted. And if an acquirer is listed on a U.S. stock exchange, it must receive shareholder approval to issue more than 20 percent of shares outstanding.

Nevertheless, there are good reasons why a CFO may decide to issue equity—usually in the form of common stock, but sometimes as a convertible preferred. First, the acquirer may not be able to retain its debt ratings unless it includes equity in the consideration. Second, the seller may prefer equity to facilitate a tax-free transaction for its shareholders. Third, the seller may desire to share in the perceived upside in the acquirer's stock due to the perceived benefits that will accrue from the transaction or due to a perception that the acquirer's stock may be undervalued.

The issuance of equity is often associated with consolidation transactions, especially in connection with a merger of equals. Equity also is more likely to be used in a negotiated transaction than in an auction process; in an auction, the seller typically prefers the certainty and speed of execution of cash. Nevertheless, equity is occasionally used in competitive auctions, usually if it allows the seller to obtain a higher value. For example, Capital One offered common stock to win a competitive auction for ING's online banking platform, giving ING a 10 percent ownership stake and a board seat.

Short-Term Financing

The CFO's second decision is to determine how the transaction will be financed over the short term. Because the target typically wants to close the transaction quickly and not be subject to a financing contingency, CFOs normally will pay for the acquisition out of surplus cash balances or by tapping existing lines of credit. However, if they do not have sufficient funds available, they may need to arrange short-term bank loans, with the expectation that they will refinance the funding subsequent to closing.

For major transactions, CFOs may obtain "bridge" financing, usually from the banks that are serving as financial advisors for the transaction. The ability of major banks to provide this one-stop shopping has become an important consideration in CFOs' evaluation of their financial advisory relationships.

Long-Term Financing

The CFO's final decision is to determine the long-term financing for the transaction. If stock has been issued to satisfy the seller's desire for a tax-free transaction, the acquirer often will repurchase part or all of the shares in the open market, thus eliminating the dilution from the original issuance. To fund this repurchase, the CFO may need to arrange additional long-term debt financing.

In addition, CFOs will usually issue long-term debt or equity to refinance any short-term financing issued in the transaction. To some extent, the nature of this refinancing may reflect the assets and financial characteristics of the target's business. However, unless the acquisition has caused a material change in the acquirer's overall portfolio, the refinancing plan will largely reflect the CFO's overall objectives with respect to the company's long-term capital structure.

PRICE NEGOTIATIONS

Although the business sponsor should be the decision maker concerning the price to be paid, the CFO can influence the negotiations, helping to ensure pricing discipline and realistic determinations of value.

Point of Indifference

The valuation analyses performed by the acquirer are essential to confirming that the proposed transaction will create shareholder value and establishing the parameters for the price that will be offered. In particular, the CFO should develop a clear-eyed appraisal of the maximum price to be paid.

Especially in the case of a competitive auction, it is important to define in advance this *"point of indifference"* where the transaction no longer makes sense. Otherwise, it is too easy to get swept up by the deal fever that is aroused by the competitive process.

Board Authorization

The board of directors can help enforce pricing discipline. The CFO usually will prepare a decision memorandum or presentation for the board of directors (usually with a prior review by the finance, audit, or executive committee) that contains the background for the transaction; the strategic rationale; the business plan; the financing arrangements; and the various financial analyses, including the valuation analyses and the pro forma impact of the proposed transaction on the acquirer's financial statements.

Because the board members typically have not been intimately involved in the negotiations, they can provide objective feedback not only about whether the transaction makes sense, but also the maximum price that should be authorized. Furthermore, by requiring the company to seek additional approval to raise its offer above the authorized amount, the board is establishing a last line of defense that can help avoid a non-economic transaction. While this approval process gives management less flexibility in responding to fluid deal dynamics, it is a tradeoff that usually pays off over the long run.

Earnouts

Earnouts are often used to bridge a gap between the seller's expectations and the price that the acquirer is willing to pay. However, while earnouts can be an elegant solution in some cases—especially when the target will be run separately and the acquirer wants to retain the management team—they can also create problems in the future.

First, they can retard the speed of integration, making it harder to realize cost synergies. Second, they can lead to disputes over accounting allocations. Third, since the adoption of FAS 141R, contingent consideration is subject to fair value accounting, which creates potential volatility to earnings during the earnout period.

Therefore, CFOs should be wary of their use, try to limit their life, and not let them represent too much of the purchase price (around 10 to 20 percent is a good guidepost for their maximum amount).

Flexibility to Walk Away

It is also important that the acquirer not be wedded to a specific transaction. Similar to the real estate admonition "don't fall in love with the house," if the acquirer is too strongly committed to a specific acquisition candidate, it is very susceptible to overpaying—often under the guise that the target's "*scarcity value*" justifies a higher premium. While paying an extraordinary premium for scarcity value may be valid in rare situations, CFOs should be wary that it's not sophistry—usually advanced by investment bankers to rationalize a higher price than warranted by the valuation analysis.

Because transactions typically involve a substantial investment of time and emotion, it's often very hard to walk away from a deal. Therefore, CFOs should serve as a modulating force, helping to preserve the company's ability to say "no," especially in response to competitive offers or unreasonable demands. Saying no is certainly better than experiencing buyer's remorse after the deal fever subsides.

 ## CONTRACT TERMS

Partnering with the general counsel, the CFO usually plays an active role in negotiating the deal terms—making sure that all of the key issues are considered and providing input with respect to the liability exposures, the contingency arrangements, and the employee agreements.

Liability Exposures

The CFO should seek to limit the acquirer's exposure to liabilities subsequent to the transaction. Constructing the transaction as an acquisition of assets rather than the stock of the target company can be a significant advantage, as it generally limits much of the liability exposure that otherwise would be attendant to the acquisition. However, in many instances, a stock transaction is the only alternative that is possible.

The acquirer can also obtain protections through the representations and warranties provided by the seller—usually through defined procedures for compensating the acquirer for breaches of these assurances. However, they are usually subject to a maximum amount, and, as a practical matter, it may be difficult to collect these reimbursements if the business is acquired from individuals who don't have deep pockets. Furthermore, it is generally impossible to negotiate any post-closing remedies when acquiring the stock of a publicly held company.

The CFO's best protection against liability exposures is maintaining the flexibility to say "no" to the deal. If a transaction is going to expose the acquirer to unacceptable risks, then it is probably better to walk away, especially if the company has alternatives for fulfilling its strategic objectives. This is particularly true of certain risks—such as environmental or consumer safety concerns—that can tarnish a company's reputation as well as expose it to monetary penalties.

Contingency Arrangements

Another key part of the contract is the set of conditions and contingencies that can cause the deal to be abandoned by either party. Although the possibility of unforeseen events may not be top-of-mind in the discussions between the principals, it is enormously important to think through these arrangements carefully in advance. Some of the key questions include:

- **Deadline:** How much time do the parties have to consummate the transaction (the "drop dead" date)?
- **Regulatory Approvals:** What happens if the transaction fails to obtain antitrust or other regulatory approvals (e.g., will the acquirer need to compensate the target through a breakup fee)?
- **Material Adverse Change:** What happens if there is a significant deterioration in the target's business?
- **Force Majeure:** What are the contingencies for major events (such as natural disasters, terrorist attacks or hostilities, or financial market shutdowns) that may occur before closing?

- **Customer Approvals:** Will the customers need to agree to the transaction and what are the price adjustments or other remedies if some of them fail to agree?
- **Financing Condition:** Is the transaction subject to a condition that the acquirer can obtain financing (which is an especially important consideration in the case of a highly leveraged structure)?
- **Stock Price Adjustments:** If common stock is being paid by the acquirer, will there be a "collar" concerning either the maximum and minimum stock price or the maximum and minimum number of shares, and are there stock price levels where either party can walk away from the deal?
- **Alternative Acquirer:** Can the seller continue to shop the business to other potential acquirers and does it owe a breakup fee if the business is sold to an alternative acquirer?

As the contract is being negotiated, it can be tempting for CFOs not to focus on these contingencies, which can seem like remote possibilities. However, as a prudent application of Murphy's Law, it is better to assume that what can go wrong, will go wrong.

Employee Agreements

The parties also will specify the acquirer's obligations to the target's employees. For example, they will compare the salaries and benefits, including healthcare, with their current compensation. If the target's employees will have less favorable arrangements with their new employer, it is usually desirable to communicate these changes up front, avoiding disappointments or misunderstandings after the acquisition is completed.

Similarly, because employee turnover usually increases after closing—both voluntary and involuntary turnover—the agreement should clarify the acquirer's obligations to pay severance or provide career counseling. For example, the acquirer's commitment to pay severance often is based on a "double trigger" that applies if an employee is involuntarily or "constructively" terminated by the acquirer within a specified time frame (typically six months to two years).

If certain employees are considered essential to the acquirer's business plan, the transaction may be subject to them signing employment contracts, including a non-compete provision for a specified period of time (typically six months to three years). In addition, these key employees often will receive bonus incentives that are tied to their continued service.

ACQUISITION INTEGRATION

Of all the steps in an acquisition that can go wrong, integration is probably the one that is most underestimated. To paraphrase a tired cliché, "the devil is in the integration details." Integration skills are often the telltale indicators of companies who successfully execute their acquisition strategies versus acquirers with a propensity to destroy shareholder value.

For example, GE Capital has been known to be an acquirer with superior capabilities in executing transactions. A *Harvard Business Review* article attributed GE Capital's ability to integrate acquisitions to four principles that can be paraphrased as follows:[1]

1. Acquisition integration is a process that begins with due diligence.
2. Integration management is a full-time job.
3. Decisions should be made and implemented as soon as possible.
4. Integration should meld not only the business operations, but also the cultures.

Business Plan Reviews

CFOs should employ the business plan as the primary tool for evaluating a transaction's performance. To that end, CFOs usually institute a regular process for reviewing the progress of the acquisition's actual results against the business plan's expectations—with a focus on completing the integration milestones, delivering the forecasted synergies, achieving the projected financial results, and documenting any lessons learned that can affect the acquirer's approach to future transactions.

Companies usually conduct these reviews quite frequently during the first year after a transaction is consummated and gradually reduce their frequency thereafter. These reviews are critical to creating a culture of excellence in executing acquisitions, providing the foundation for future value-enhancing transactions.

Business Sponsor Involvement

The business sponsor's hands-on involvement is absolutely critical to the successful execution of an acquisition. This applies not only to realizing the business and financial objectives, but also to performing the seemingly mundane tasks of integrating all of the various back office functions that affect the day-to-day activities of employees—including their ability to get things done in their new environment.

In particular, the business sponsor can make a real difference in talent retention, which is often a challenge in the wake of an acquisition. By establishing a good working relationship with the target's management team, the business sponsor can smooth their assimilation into the acquirer's culture and facilitate their adaptation to unfamiliar operating and administrative procedures.

Gatekeeper

Most acquirers find it desirable to establish a gatekeeper for accessing the target after a transaction is announced, with clear ground rules concerning the scope and frequency of visits and information requests. Otherwise, the target's employees can be overwhelmed by a deluge of visits and requests from the acquirer's well-meaning staff people, including members of the CFO's financial organization.

Above all, the acquirer should do everything possible to ease the on boarding of new employees; to eliminate any obstacles to a smooth integration; and to focus resolutely on achieving the acquisition's strategic, business, and financial objectives.

Post-Closing Adjustments

Finally, the CFO should establish rigorous processes for determining the post-closing "true ups"—adjustments to the purchase price that reflect updated financial statements and any indemnities that arise from the representations and warranties. For example, the price in private transactions is often adjusted for the amount of working capital on the target's balance sheet or the seller may need to indemnify the acquirer for an environmental or other type of liability.

The procedures for these adjustments will be spelled out in the sale agreement, including "holdbacks" of a portion of the purchase price, minimum and maximum amounts for the adjustments, deductibles against potential claims, and "flyspecks" that establish a minimum amount for each issue that is raised. The agreement also will include time limits to raise issues, which can create some urgency for the acquirer to complete its post-closing reviews.

CFOs can realize material savings by approaching these adjustments seriously—ensuring that the reconciliations are conducted thoroughly and accurately and often enlisting the help of an outside accounting firm with expertise in this type of analysis.

NOTE

1. Ashkenas, Ronald N., DeMonaco, Lawrence J., Francis, Suzanne C, "Making the Deal Real: How GE Capital Integrates Acquisitions" (January 1998, *Harvard Business Review*), pp. 165–170, 172, 174–178.

CHAPTER TEN

Executing Divestitures and Spinoffs

C FOS SHOULD REGULARLY CONSIDER potential opportunities for selectively pruning a company's business portfolio. This can sharpen the company's strategic focus and generate capital to be redeployed in the business or else returned to shareholders.

 ## DIVESTITURE EVALUATIONS

CFOs should recognize that periodically reviewing the company's portfolio is a healthy exercise that can generate significant shareholder value. Some of the reasons for divesting a business can include:

- **Strategic Fit:** It no longer fits with the company's strategic objectives.
- **Return on Investment:** It is not expected to earn the company's cost of capital.
- **Value of Synergies:** It will have more value to an acquirer who can realize synergies.
- **Risk Implications:** It has risk exposures that the company does not want to retain.

- **Management Focus:** It will not receive sufficient focus from the company's management.

Simply put, a divestiture can make a great deal of strategic sense, especially if the business is likely to receive an attractive valuation in the market. After a divestiture candidate has been identified, CFOs then can perform a financial analysis to confirm that the divestiture makes economic sense—comparing the value to be obtained in the market versus the value to be realized from retaining the business.

Valuation Analysis

In analyzing a divestiture, CFOs should use the same valuation methodologies that are applied to acquisitions. They then should consider the alternatives for accomplishing a divestiture, determine the likely value to be received, estimate the likely time frame for completing a transaction, and assume a tentative use of the proceeds. They also should analyze the pro forma impacts and judge whether the transaction is likely to be positively received by investors.

HIRING INVESTMENT BANKERS

Unless the divestiture is too small or the transaction is likely to be very straightforward, it usually makes sense to hire an investment banker or other financial advisor to confirm that the transaction makes economic sense; to recommend a divestiture process; and, most important of all, to help execute the transaction, which can be quite labor intensive, especially if conducting a competitive auction.

Investment bankers can be very helpful due to their merger and acquisition expertise, their contacts with potential acquirers, and their knowledge of market values. In a sell side assignment, they usually are well worth their admittedly high fees.

They also can provide a *"fairness opinion,"* which may be desired by the board of directors or required by debt covenants. However, some investment banks are reluctant to provide these opinions, so it is good to clarify up front whether this service will be included in the engagement—which may influence the CFO's choice among potential advisors.

The other alternative is to hire an additional firm to provide the fairness opinion, but not to assist with the transaction. This adds some cost, but helps to ensure an independent appraisal that is not influenced by the potential transaction fee.

Compensation Arrangements

CFOs also should consider the way that they want to compensate the investment bankers. They can pay a fixed amount, which lends certainty to the total, or they can pay a sliding scale (normally a percentage of the proceeds), thus creating incentives to perform. Another common alternative is to apply different percentages to varying levels of proceeds, which creates additional incentives to obtain a higher price.

The main disadvantage with incentive arrangements is that they can result in a relatively high fee for the transaction, which may not be indicative of the investment banker's performance (e.g., it may have resulted from a low-ball estimate of the likely price to be received). Furthermore, incentive fees can make it more difficult to consider non-price criteria when comparing alternative bids (e.g., a higher bid may include more liability exposures, or may be contingent on obtaining financing or receiving antitrust approval).

Regardless of the way that the fee arrangements are structured, CFOs should request precedents of fees paid in similar transactions. In addition, they may want to obtain a market check from another investment bank or a law firm to confirm that the proposed fee is consistent with the going rate.

CFOs also should closely scrutinize the way that the divestiture proceeds are calculated. For example, they should understand how cash or working capital will be treated, as well as the acquirer's assumptions of debt or other liabilities. Earnouts or other contingent payments can also create complications that should be clarified in advance.

Finally, CFOs should be vigilant concerning ongoing entanglements. These continuing obligations can include a "tail" that commits the seller to pay the fee if a transaction occurs within a specified time period (usually one to two years) or an agreement to use the investment bank as an advisor on other transactions, such as financings or other merger and acquisition transactions. While it is reasonable to agree to "consider" the bank for future assignments, an iron-clad commitment should be avoided under most circumstances.

 ## AUCTION OR NEGOTIATED

The two basic approaches to a divestiture are to conduct an auction or to negotiate a one-off transaction, although there are several permutations between these two alternatives. For example, the seller can conduct a limited auction, with a handful of selected participants, or it can pursue simultaneous negotiations with a few potential acquirers.

Competitive Auctions

The primary advantage of an auction is that it can create competition among the potential acquirers, usually resulting in a higher price and better contractual terms. However, it is a disruptive process that can be very time consuming for the management of the business being divested, and it is hard to execute an auction quietly in the market. In particular, the business can deteriorate, which can be especially problematic in the event of a failed auction.

If an auction is pursued, the steps usually include preparing an offering memorandum, inviting potential acquirers to participate, negotiating non-disclosure agreements, establishing a data room (often electronic rather than physical), holding information meetings, soliciting preliminary indications of interest, narrowing the bidders, distributing contracts to be marked up by the bidders, seeking final and best pricing, and negotiating a definitive sale agreement with one or two of the bidders.

Negotiated Transactions

In contrast, a negotiated transaction is usually accomplished through more tailored exchanges of information with one or a few potential buyers. It can be a quieter and less disruptive process than an auction, although the seller should recognize that it's still hard to avoid leaks, especially in industries with active grapevines. Nevertheless, a negotiated deal represents less risk to the business.

A negotiated transaction often includes a "letter of intent" that clarifies the key terms, although both parties recognize that it is a non-binding agreement and the terms are often changed due to information learned in due diligence or to reflect changes in the business or the financial markets.

To preserve its negotiating leverage, the seller normally preserves its options to conduct an auction or to retain the business. CFOs should also insist on relatively short windows for "exclusive" negotiations. If the negotiations are going well, the time period can always be extended; but if not, the seller has more flexibility to pursue an alternative path.

Retention Agreements

In either approach, the prospective transaction usually causes considerable anxiety among the divestiture's management team, whose future prospects may be highly uncertain, especially if the business is being sold to a strategic buyer. Therefore, it is usually helpful to establish retention agreements with the management team, including incentive bonuses through the estimated closing date for the transaction.

Furthermore, because of the risk to the business, CFOs generally should not initiate a divestiture process unless there is a good probability that it will result in a completed transaction at a reasonable price. If a transaction is not consummated, it may be difficult to restore the business momentum due to a pall of uncertainty that can affect the management team and perhaps customers as well.

 ## STOCK OR ASSETS

CFOs generally prefer to execute a divestiture through a stock transaction rather than an asset deal. A stock deal makes it much less likely that the seller will retain liability exposures, creating less residual risk subsequent to closing.

Nevertheless, the seller may favor an asset deal if the tax treatment is better or if it is necessary to attract buyers at an attractive price. In this case, the seller will seek to negotiate contractual terms that limit its potential financial exposures to known liabilities, as well as to existing issues that are not known prior to closing.

The acquirer is likely to seek compensation for existing liabilities through the seller's contractual representations and warranties. One of the advantages of divesting through an auction process is that the seller may have more leverage in negotiating the contract terms, including limitations on its exposures to representations and warranties.

 ## FINANCING CONDITIONS

If the seller is conducting an auction where the potential buyers include private equity firms, the transaction may be offered with prepackaged bank financing attached. This "stapled" financing can expedite a transaction and make it more likely to be consummated. However, some shareholders of public companies have challenged this practice, claiming that it compromises the investment banker's objectivity due to the prospect of receiving lucrative financing fees.

Otherwise, the bidders in auctions are expected to arrange their own financing and are asked to describe the financing arrangements in their proposal. In particular, they will state whether their offer is contingent on obtaining financing, which will be one of the criteria used to select the winning bidder. Generally, the best alternative will be a strategic buyer with cash on hand; the next best will be an acquirer with committed bank financing; the least best will be a "highly confident" letter that financing can be obtained.

If the acquirer does not have financing arranged, then the CFO must assess the probability that it can be obtained and factor this contingency into the evaluation of the offer. This may cause the CFO to eliminate a bidder from an auction or to discontinue a negotiated transaction.

Seller Financing

CFOs are sometimes faced with a request to offer seller financing to expedite a divestiture to a third party with limited access to capital. This typically does not become an issue unless the divestiture is not attracting much interest and the possibility of seller financing is the only way that it can get done.

In these instances, CFOs generally recognize that seller financing (typically in the form of subordinated debt or preferred stock) will be illiquid and will have a reasonable probability of not being repaid in full. Moreover, the interest rate may not reflect an arm's length valuation.

Consequently, CFOs will recognize that the fair market value of seller financing may be substantially less than its face value. They usually will establish an appropriate reserve against loss—thus mitigating the company's exposure to a potential write-off in the future.

 MANAGEMENT PARTICIPATION

Another delicate issue concerns the possibility of the divestiture's management team becoming involved in a sale to a private equity buyer. On the one hand, the management team's participation in a transaction can give comfort to the private equity firm and result in a higher offer. On the other hand, their participation involves obvious conflicts of interest—especially if the potential buyers include both strategic and private equity acquirers.

When confronted with this dilemma, CFOs should recognize that there are no foolproof ways to avoid the inherent conflicts, and to manage the issues in the best manner possible—leaning heavily on guidance from the general counsel and often external legal advisors as well. The best approach is to deal openly with the issues and to ensure that everyone is aware of the potential consequences.

 ## TAX-FREE SPINOFFS

In some situations, CFOs may recommend that a divestiture be accomplished through a spinoff rather than a sale transaction. First, a spinoff usually can be accomplished as a tax-free transaction for both the company and its shareholders; this is especially important if the market value of the business substantially exceeds its tax basis. Second, a spinoff preserves the upside for shareholders if the value of the business is currently depressed and is expected to increase in the future. Third, a spinoff typically has less execution risk than a sale transaction.

The primary disadvantage with a spinoff is that it does not produce any cash for the seller. However, this disadvantage can be mitigated if the business raises debt prior to the spinoff and dividends the proceeds to the parent company. Furthermore, additional cash can be raised through a *sponsored spinoff* in which a private equity firm makes a minority equity investment in the company prior to the spinoff.

Another disadvantage to a spinoff is that it does not capture the value of the synergies that can be realized through a sale to a strategic acquirer. In fact, the spinoff will require incremental expenses to operate as a standalone public company.

However, provided that there is no pre-existing agreement, the value of synergies can be realized subsequent to the spinoff if a strategic acquirer makes an offer directly to the spinoff's shareholders. This will be a taxable event for the spinoff's shareholders, but if sufficient time has passed, it should not result in a tax liability to the parent company.

A substantial portion of the parent company's shareholders may not be able to own the spinoff's shares, resulting in considerable churn in the spinoff's shareholder base. For example, index funds usually cannot retain the shares of a spinoff (it usually will not be part of the index) and institutional shareholders may be compelled by their investment policies to sell the shares. However, while this turnover can depress the share price at the outset, spinoffs generally have achieved superior stock market performance after this initial period of adjustment. This outperformance is usually attributed to enhanced management focus after separating from the parent company.

Morris Trust Spinoffs

CFOs formerly could use a Morris Trust structure to achieve favorable tax treatment through a spinoff transaction. This treatment emanated from a court case in 1966 that ruled that if a parent company was acquired immediately subsequent to a spinoff, no tax would be owed by either the parent company or the spinoff's shareholders.

However, this tax treatment was changed by Congress in 1997. The legislation provided that if either the parent company or the spinoff is acquired, then the spinoff is a taxable event to the parent company unless it can be proven that there was no integrated plan and enough time has passed (generally at least six months to two years).

Nevertheless, CFOs can still take advantage of an exception built into the legislation—a *reverse Morris Trust*. This exception applies if the spinoff merges with another company, provided that the spinoff's shareholders own a majority of the combined company's shares. In other words, it is still treated as a tax-free spinoff so long as it is the acquiring company.

The reverse Morris Trust structure was used, for example, in Verizon's spinoff of a portion of its wireless operations into FairPoint Communications and Walt Disney's spinoff of its radio business into Citadel Broadcasting. Most recently Mead-Westvaco used this structure in a transaction with Acco Brands. Consequently, although a reverse Morris Trust requires specific facts and circumstances, it's a proven alternative that CFOs should include in their playbook of divestiture alternatives.

SPLIT-UPS

In a split-up, a company divides itself into two or more publicly held companies. Although it is usually accomplished through a tax-free spinoff, it is more akin to a de-merger than a divestiture.

Split-ups eliminate the conglomerate discount for disparate businesses. Furthermore, the separated businesses often perform better due to enhanced management and shareholder focus. As a result, the announcement of a split-up transaction usually results in at least a short-term increase in a company's stock price. Some recent examples include Fortune Brands, Marathon, ConocoPhillips, and Kraft.

Activist investors may propose a split-up as a way to increase the value of their shareholdings. Therefore, CFOs may want to analyze this alternative in advance of receiving a proposal, gaining an understanding of the pros and cons of the potential transaction. And if makes sense, they may want to advocate a split-up as a way to create shareholder value.

Furthermore, if a company decides to retain disparate businesses, the CFO should seek to maximize the advantages of them being part of the same company; in addition to overhead savings and greater economies of scale, these benefits can include tax savings, lower debt costs, cross-selling between businesses, and any halo effects in the marketplace due to the company's overall reputation and brand image. Furthermore, customers, suppliers, and employees may take comfort in the greater financial strength of the combined entity.

EQUITY CARVE-OUTS

Another alternative is to sell a minority stake in a subsidiary company via an "equity carve-out." In this relatively rare form of transaction, the parent company typically sells up to 20 percent of the shares of a subsidiary, thereby continuing to file a consolidated tax return and preserving the flexibility to execute a tax-free spinoff in the future.

Companies usually pursue equity carve-outs to call the market's attention to a valuable business whose shares will trade at a premium valuation to the parent company's and to offer stock incentives to the subsidiary's management team. For example, EMC sold 10 percent of the shares of its fast-growing VMware subsidiary in 2006—thus highlighting the significant increase in the value of the business since being acquired by EMC and its growing contribution to the parent company's market valuation.

While equity carve-outs can highlight an undervalued business, they require arms-length arrangements with the parent company, which can create administrative complexities and potential conflicts of interest. Furthermore, issuing the shares may cause shareholders to propose a complete separation through a sale or spinoff.

CHAPTER ELEVEN

Responding to Takeover Offers

Without question, responding to a potential takeover offer can be a significant test of the CFO's leadership skills and analytical capabilities. The criticality of this responsibility applies to CFOs of both private and public companies, although they will be much more subject to legal considerations and constraints in a public company context.

Indeed, it has become axiomatic for public company CFOs—along with CEOs and boards of directors—to profess their commitment to maximizing shareholder value, including being open to the possibility of a third-party purchase of the company. This does not mean that companies must solicit an offer or to respond favorably if an offer is received, but in the modern corporate finance environment, it does mean that they must give careful consideration to any bona fide offer, including an objective evaluation of its merits.

 GOVERNANCE POLICIES

CFOs should be well aware of their companies' governance policies, which have become increasingly important considerations among investors. While take-over defenses in the past were often viewed positively as protections against a corporate raider or as vehicles for negotiating a better price, they now are viewed more critically by many investors and the shareholder advisory services (such as Institutional Stockholder Services and Glass Lewis).

For example, many investors advocate that a company's governance policies should include:

- **Independent Chairman:** Separate Chairman and CEO roles, or a Lead Director at minimum.
- **No Staggered Boards:** A single class of directors who are elected each year.
- **One Class of Stock:** Equal voting rights among all shareholders.
- **No Shareholder Rights Plan:** Redemption of existing rights ("poison pill") and no new plan (but boards usually preserve their ability to enact a plan in the future).
- **Majority Director Votes:** Majority vote in favor of a director, or at minimum, director's offer to resign if receives less than a majority vote.
- **No Supermajority Voting:** Majority of outstanding shares to approve a takeover rather than a higher percentage.
- **No State Law Restrictions:** Not subject to state laws that require consideration of other constituencies besides shareholders or that impose other restrictions.
- **Special Meetings:** Ability of shareholder groups to call special meetings.

In addition, shareholders have advocated greater influence over management compensation (*"say on pay"*) and ability to make proposals through proxy statements (*"proxy access"*).

Through a combination of voluntary actions and governmental mandates (e.g., the Dodd-Frank Act), companies have made remarkable strides in their governance policies in recent years. CFOs should be aware of their company's changes—which can be positive factors in their investor relations programs—and be knowledgeable about the governance polices that will establish the context for the board's evaluation of potential proposals.

 ## REVIEWING AN OFFER

Upon receiving a takeover proposal, the board of directors will initiate a process to review the offer and to determine the appropriate response. It may establish a *special committee* of independent directors who will facilitate the review on behalf of the board.

Depending on the nature of the offer and whether it has been made public, the board may choose to enact a *shareholder rights plan (poison pill)* that gives the company more flexibility in the timing of its response. It does not matter if the board previously withdrew a plan; it can institute a new one, provided that it has not made a commitment to the contrary.

In almost all cases, the board will engage financial advisors to assist in its review of the proposal, as well as external counsel who will guide the company through the labyrinth of laws and governance rules that surround a public company's actions under these circumstances. While the board is not under any compulsion to take specific actions, it is subject to fiduciary obligations to its shareholders; thus, the board will be very circumspect and deliberate in performing its responsibilities.

Although the board will make the choice of financial advisors to engage, the CFO may be asked to orchestrate a process to consider the alternatives and to provide input concerning the candidates for this role. Normally, the board will interview advisory candidates through a formal process, including written presentations that outline their qualifications and address the board's criteria. The board typically will review each candidate's *potential conflicts* (especially any business relationships with the other party); its *prior interactions* with the company; its *experience* in similar advisory assignments; and most important, its *proposed approach* to this particular assignment, including the individuals who will form the *advisory team*.

Strategic Plan Projections

After the advisors have been engaged, the CFO plays an important role in providing the information that will inform much of their review of alternatives, which can range from maintaining the current course, to pursuing a sale of the company, to a variety of alternatives in between. To this end, the CFO will organize a process to share information with the financial advisors concerning the company's historical financial performance and its outlook, as indicated by the strategic plan and long-term financial model.

The company's financial advisors will play the primary role in evaluating the takeover offer and will provide objective assessments concerning the offer in comparison with the current plan or other alternatives. However, the financial advisors generally will rely a great deal on assumptions and projections provided by the company. The CFO should ensure that the financial advisors have a thorough understanding of the strategic plan and that they have a sophisticated appreciation for the various assumptions and methodologies that underpin the financial projections.

The CFO will also play a leadership role in analyzing potential alternatives to the strategic plan that are suggested by the financial advisors as a way to unlock shareholder value. For example, the company might evaluate the potential desirability of a divestiture, with the proceeds used to pay a special dividend or to repurchase stock. Another alternative might be a financing transaction—such as an increase in debt leverage—that may create additional value.

 ## CONDUCTING A SALE PROCESS

If the board of directors determines that a sale of the company is in the shareholders' best interest, then the CFO will be an important player in the team that conducts the process for the potential sale transaction. Because the company's consideration of alternatives will be subject to legal and regulatory constraints—notably the *"Revlon"* obligation to obtain the best price for shareholders—the integrity of the process becomes extremely important from this point forward, which creates a necessity for the CFO to operate within this framework.

Subject to the guidance provided by the company's legal and financial advisors, the CFO usually will play an active role in the following tasks:

- Identifying potential acquirers who should be contacted as part of the process.
- Developing historical and projected financial information to be provided to potential acquirers.
- Assembling detailed due diligence materials to be included in the data room.
- Making knowledgeable experts available to answer detailed questions with respect to the company's historical financial results, financial projections, and due diligence materials.
- Meeting with potential acquirers to discuss the company's strategies, financial performance, and financing plans.
- Keeping the rating agencies updated concerning the current status and potential actions.
- Communicating with investors, as appropriate, concerning the sale process.

ACTIVIST SHAREHOLDERS

In the modern financial world, companies may be confronted with activist shareholders who suggest actions that they believe will create shareholder value. In this event, the CFO will help the company to evaluate the proposals, which may have been communicated publicly.

CFOs will work closely with the company's financial advisors in reviewing the alternatives—much in the way that they would in connection with a takeover proposal—and evaluating whether they will create shareholder value in comparison with the company's existing strategic plan. In performing this role, CFOs will objectively analyze the financial implications of the alternatives being considered and elucidate their potential advantages and disadvantages—including any financial or execution risks—so that the board of directors has the best information possible in formulating the company's response.

GOING PRIVATE TRANSACTIONS

A *management buyout* may be considered as an alternative to a takeover proposal from a third party or in connection with reviewing a proposal from an activist shareholder. In addition, the management team may propose a going private transaction as a way to enhance shareholder value.

In each of these potential scenarios, CFOs should recognize the potential conflicts of interest, especially in light of the board's fiduciary duty to maximize the value for shareholders in a change of control transaction. At a certain point, the CFO's role may necessarily shift from a disinterested analyst to an interested participant.

Furthermore, CFOs should recognize that even a relatively informal analysis of a going private transaction can inadvertently trigger market rumors that stimulate speculative trading in the company's stock—perhaps creating pressures for the company to respond through a public statement. Consequently, CFOs should be circumspect about engaging in a dialogue with private equity firms unless they have explicit approval from their CEO and board of directors—and should be especially cautious in providing projections or other confidential information.

Nevertheless, with appropriate guidance, CFOs should be able to navigate the legal and ethical requirements in considering a potential management buyout. In particular, a management buyout may make sense if the company's stock price is judged to be undervalued or if management needs to take actions that are likely to depress the stock price for the foreseeable future.

In these instances, it may be appropriate for the CFO to work with an investment bank in assessing whether the company's cash flow and earnings can produce an offer that is likely to be competitive with other alternatives. If so, then it may be appropriate to initiate a dialogue with one or a few private equity firms.

PART FOUR

IV

Funding

CHAPTER TWELVE

Establishing Capital Structure Objectives

THE CFO'S SKILL IN MANAGING the capital structure can have a material impact on a company's cost of capital and can make the difference between financing strategies that are appropriate for a company versus those that cross the line of prudence. As became abundantly evident in the recent financial crisis, the effectiveness of the CFO's management of the capital structure literally can determine a company's life or death as a going concern—obviously a responsibility that should not be taken lightly.

The capital structure is also fundamental to accomplishing the company's strategic and financial objectives: The financing decisions must be in sync with the investment decisions.

 LEVERAGE TARGETS

One of the most important decisions is the establishment of debt leverage targets, which provide the underpinnings for the company's financing strategies. CFOs usually express their debt leverage targets in three different ways: a cost of capital assumption, company-specific leverage ratios, and a debt ratings objective.

Cost of Capital Assumption

The most fundamental of the leverage targets is the ratio between the market value of a company's equity securities and its total market capitalization. This is the ratio that is used in the capital asset pricing model to determine the company's weighted average cost of capital; it represents the target capital structure for financing the company over the planning horizon (say, the next five to 10 years).

For example, the CFO may assume that the target ratio is 30 percent debt and 70 percent equity. This implies that if the company needs additional financing, the incremental funding will be raised in that proportion of debt and equity. Likewise, if the company generates surplus cash, it implies that 70 percent will be returned to shareholders and 30 percent will be used to pay down debt.

This is a theoretical assumption; the company's actual capital structure at any point in time may differ considerably from this assumed financing mix, especially during periods of volatile stock prices or interest rates. Nevertheless, it is the purest definition of the target that the CFO intends to use in meeting the company's funding requirements.

Company-Specific Ratios

CFOs also express their objectives in terms of leverage ratios that are used by analysts in their industry or that are contained in their debt covenants. For example, they might communicate their debt leverage targets using one or more of the following ratios:

- *Debt to book capitalization,* which is equal to net debt (total debt less cash) as a percent of net debt plus book equity.
- *Debt to EBITDA,* which is equal to total debt divided by EBITDA (earnings before interest, taxes, depreciation, and amortization).
- *Debt to cash flow,* which is equal to total debt divided by cash flow from operations.
- *Interest coverage,* which is equal to EBIT (earnings before interest and taxes) divided by interest expense.
- *Fixed charge coverage,* which is equal to EBIT divided by interest expense, preferred dividends, and an interest component for operating leases.

Highly leveraged companies tend to use debt to EBITDA as their primary ratio, while less leveraged companies tend to use debt to book capitalization.

Furthermore, companies in regulated industries—such as banks—will express their leverage targets as defined by their regulatory requirements (e.g., Tier 1 capital as a percent of assets).

Debt Ratings Objective

Most important, CFOs will also express their leverage targets in terms of their desired debt ratings from the rating agencies. This is normally the way that CFOs communicate their capital structure objectives to both debt and equity investors; the ratings objective is easily understood and preserves some leeway with respect to the company's targets for its cost of capital and company-specific leverage ratios.

 ## LEVERAGE CRITERIA

While the establishment of leverage targets can seem deceptively simple, the manner of their development is actually quite complex, involving a number of factors that can influence the targeted mix between equity and debt in a company's capital structure.

Of course, the primary motivation to use debt is the lower cost of capital. However, this motivation can be countered by other considerations, including the company's strategic plan objectives, its size and maturity, its business profile, its risk tolerance, and its need for financial flexibility. The leverage targets can also be influenced by long-term conditions and trends in the financial markets.

Strategic Plan

The leverage targets normally are highly dependent on the company's business and financial objectives. CFOs should establish targets that provide the financial wherewithal to accomplish the company's strategies, which may imply greater or lesser use of debt.

They should also evaluate the company's need for financial flexibility. Higher debt leverage usually comes with strings attached—especially restrictive covenants—that may be incompatible with accomplishing the company's strategic objectives.

In particular, CFOs should analyze their strategic plan's financial projections—especially the forecasted cash flow from operations in comparison to the company's requirements for capital expenditures, dividends, share repurchases, and acquisitions—as well as the potential volatility in the projections. The leverage targets should be appropriate not only for the base case projections, but also using alternative assumptions, including a downside scenario.

Size and Maturity

The CFO's range of alternatives in setting the leverage targets will be largely influenced by the company's size and maturity. Larger, well-established companies generally will have more access to capital and less risk of insolvency than smaller, start-up companies. Simply put, a large capitalization company has more flexibility in its funding sources—even if it is not too big to fail—and therefore it has greater ability to handle debt.

Smaller, less-established companies tend to have less flexibility to use debt and often must fund their expansion with a higher percentage of equity. Therefore, they usually will employ less debt leverage in their target capital structure.

Business Profile

The ability to employ debt will also be affected by the company's business profile. A company in an asset intensive industry—such as natural resources or real estate—will be more likely to use debt, especially if the assets can serve as collateral for creditors. Companies with greater diversity in their earnings and cash flow streams also can employ more leverage.

In contrast, companies in industries with low asset intensity—such as high technology or professional services—typically have less ability to use debt. This is particularly true for companies that are highly dependent on a product or service that can be threatened by competitors.

The ability to employ debt leverage will also be influenced by the company's operational leverage. In general, CFOs should be more cautious in using debt when earnings and cash flow are volatile.

Furthermore, maintaining a strong credit rating may be important to a company's customer relationships. For example, companies that hold customer cash in a fiduciary capacity must be focused on the strength of their balance sheet.

Risk Tolerance

The leverage target will also reflect the relative appetite and tolerance for financial risk among the company's board of directors, shareholders, and customers, often reflecting the prevailing norms in the company's industry and product lines. CFOs should also be mindful of the capital structures used by competitors, which may indicate that assuming more or less financial risk is necessary to stay competitive.

Moreover, if a company has a history of conservative financial management, it may be problematic to shift too greatly or too quickly—especially if the new policy has not been signaled to investors well in advance of the change.

In contrast, a company may be very comfortable with risk. This is particularly true when companies are owned by private equity investors, who can diversify their risks among a portfolio of investments. They may prefer to employ more debt to lower the cost of capital, accelerate expansion, and capture more of the potential upside.

Market Conditions

Finally, the leverage decision may be influenced by conditions in the financial markets. For example, a company will be less likely to employ debt leverage during market environments where its access to liquidity and long-term debt capital is severely constrained. In general, higher debt levels will be more desirable and feasible in favorable markets than during periods when investors are more risk averse.

However, the leverage target should reflect long-term strategies and CFOs should be careful to distinguish between prolonged and transitory market trends.

RATING AGENCIES

Historically, the two most important rating agencies have been *Standard & Poor's*, which is part of McGraw-Hill, and *Moody's Investors Service*, which is an NYSE-listed public company (after a spinoff from Dun & Bradstreet in 2000). A third major agency that has gained greater prominence and influence in recent years is *Fitch Ratings*, which is owned by Fimalac, a French company.

Three lesser-known agencies are *DBRS* (Dominion Bond Ratings Service), which was formed in 1976 and is based in Toronto, *Egan-Jones Ratings*, a private firm that was founded in Philadelphia in 1994, and *Rapid Ratings*, which was founded in New Zealand in 1991 and brought to the United States in 2007. An additional agency, *Kroll Bond Ratings*, began operations in New York in 2010 with the stated intention of "building a service that restores trust in credit ratings." Each of these newer agencies features a business model that focuses primarily on the users of the information rather than on the issuers.

While it is true that the major rating agencies have lost much of their credibility due to their failure to anticipate the recent financial crisis, they still have considerable clout in the securities markets, largely due to governments, institutions, and companies that use their ratings to define permissible investments in corporate, sovereign, and municipal fixed income securities. They can also sway fixed income investment decisions by individual investors. Moreover, the publicity generated from their changes in ratings can influence the stock prices of the affected companies.

A frequent criticism of the major rating agencies is that their fees are paid by the issuers. To investors, this can represent a conflict of interest, especially when issuers can shop among the agencies to obtain an acceptable rating for their proposed debt issuance. To CFOs, this payment structure can give the agencies too much leverage in raising their fees, usually giving companies little alternative but to pay the higher rate.

 RATINGS CATEGORIES

Although the agencies have slight differences in the definitions of their ratings categories, they are sufficiently similar to facilitate a shorthand communication of a company's ratings target. Generally they can be expressed as triple-A

Debt Rating Categories

Moody's	Standard & Poor's	Fitch
Aaa	AAA	AAA
Aa	AA	AA
A	A	A
Baa	BBB	BBB
Speculative:		
Ba	BB	BB
B	B	B
Caa	CCC	CCC
Ca	CC	CC
C	C	C

(very rare!), double-A, single-A, triple-B, double-B, single-B, and three levels of C-rated debt. Moody's uses slightly different letter combinations (such as Baa instead of BBB) but the categories are substantively the same. Ratings of triple-B and above are "investment grade," while ratings of double-B and below are "speculative."

Each rating category can also include the addition of a plus and minus (or numerals 1 through 3 for Moody's), which affects how many "notches" the ratings are changed. For example, declining from A+ to BBB+ (or from A1 to Baa1) is a three-notch move. The agencies will also communicate their "outlooks," which indicate whether the rating is more likely to improve, remain stable, or decline.

Investment-Grade Alternatives

For most large companies, higher debt ratings are generally more prestigious, which can have a positive impact among customers, suppliers, and employees. For example, ADP is one of the few triple-A companies, undoubtedly giving its customers comfort in outsourcing their payroll services, including the float that is entrusted to ADP in a fiduciary capacity.

However, a company's weighted average cost of capital tends to become lower as it goes down the ratings scale—until it reaches the demarcation between investment grade and speculative debt, where a company's cost and access to capital can be materially affected, especially in difficult financial conditions. Consequently, CFOs of public companies will usually advocate target debt ratings that are mid to lower investment grade—typically in the single-A or triple-B ratings categories.

Investment Grade versus Speculative

The significant difference between investment grade and speculative ratings can be seen clearly in the agencies' definitions. For example, Moody's definitions are:[1]

- **Baa:** "Obligations rated Baa are subject to moderate credit risk. They are considered medium grade and as such may possess certain speculative characteristics."
- **Ba:** "Obligations rated Ba are judged to have speculative elements and are subject to substantial credit risk."

Being classified in the speculative categories generally means:

- **More Risk:** The agencies believe that there is a meaningful risk of a credit default.
- **Fewer Investors:** Many potential investors will be prohibited from purchasing the debt.
- **Less Market Access:** The company's access to the debt markets will be restricted at times.
- **Less Flexibility:** The company's flexibility will be constrained by restrictive debt covenants.
- **High Yield:** The company's public debt securities will be issued in the high-yield market and referred to pejoratively as "junk."

Rationale for Speculative Ratings

Given the negative consequences from a non-investment grade rating, most CFOs strive to achieve and maintain investment grade ratings. So why would a CFO ever advocate a speculative ratings target?

First, in the case of smaller, less-established companies, the cost of attaining an investment grade rating may not be worth it. Indeed, because size and diversification are extremely important attributes in bond ratings, it may be virtually impossible for certain companies to achieve an investment-grade debt rating—even if they have little or no debt. Therefore, if a company needs capital to fulfill its strategic objectives, the high yield market may be its best alternative.

Second, equity investors (especially private equity firms) often prefer the additional upside from the greater debt leverage that may only be possible at the lower ratings categories. They may be especially comfortable with the risk/reward tradeoff when their equity investments are diversified in a larger portfolio and if they also take a position in the debt securities—which may allow them to maintain control of the company in the event of financial duress. Also, private equity investors usually have considerable expertise concerning the leveraged finance market, allowing them to add value through capital structure actions in response to changing market conditions.

 RATING AGENCY DIALOGUES

The CFO will typically maintain regular communications with the rating agencies, updating them concerning any material strategic, business, or financial developments. Provided that they comply with their commitment to maintain confidentiality, the agencies can be treated as "insiders" who can receive non-public information without violating the Fair Disclosure rule or the securities laws.

The ability to share insider information can be especially valuable to CFOs, allowing them to discuss the potential ratings impact from strategic and financial actions that are being contemplated. This can prevent surprises from the agencies, which otherwise can be mercurial in their reactions to material events.

In addition, CFOs typically will meet with each of the agencies annually for a full review of their company's business and financial strategies and to share their current financial projections. These meetings normally include a written presentation, which usually is also provided to the audit committee and perhaps to the full board of directors.

The CFO's meetings with the rating agencies generally produce constructive dialogues, especially if the agency maintains continuity in the team that covers the company. However, the agencies generally will be noncommittal concerning future upgrades or downgrades, which are subject to review by their internal committees.

Furthermore, their ratings actions almost always lag the company's financial performance—on both the downside and the upside—meaning that they usually do not take any actions until the change in a company's status is already reflected in the pricing of its securities in the debt market.

 ## RATINGS CRITERIA

CFOs will also regularly monitor the ratios and metrics that are used by each of the agencies and the credit markets. These credit statistics include debt leverage ratios—such as debt to market and book capitalization, debt to EBITDA and cash flow, and coverage of interest and fixed charges—as well as profitability measures such as operating margins and returns on invested capital.

In reviewing a company's credit statistics, the agencies will consider the stability and trends in the financial ratios, as well as their absolute numbers. Moreover, they will give greater leeway to the credit ratios of larger, more established, and diversified companies, as well as companies with high-quality, stable management. As a result, two companies with the same credit ratios may very well have differing debt ratings, usually reflecting the greater deference that the agencies will give to larger companies.

Although there are more similarities than differences in the rating agencies' approach to their ratings, each of the agencies has distinctive criteria and methodologies. For example, the agencies may differ in their treatment of leases and other off balance sheet rental obligations and in their adjustments for unfunded pension obligations.

Given these differences, CFOs should review their credit statistics with each of the agencies to ascertain how they are calculated. In addition, they should monitor their credit statistics using the agencies' alternative definitions. The agencies are generally willing to discuss the specifics of their ratings criteria and often will provide guidance concerning the improvements necessary to achieve a higher rating. They will also indicate areas of potential concern that could lead to a downgrade.

Nevertheless, while the various credit statistics can be useful indicators in predicting a company's likely debt ratings, CFOs should recognize that they may not be determinative. As noted above, the ratings are heavily influenced by a company's relative size (typically measured by its revenue and assets) and the consistency of its earnings and cash flow, as well as subjective judgments concerning the stability and quality of its management and the rigor of its risk management procedures. In addition, the agencies often have views of industries and businesses that can color their approach to a company's ratings—perhaps reflecting a judgment that the company is a good house in a bad neighborhood.

 INFORMING INVESTORS

Investors usually have a keen interest in a company's rating objectives. At a minimum, most equity as well as debt investors will want to know whether a company intends to maintain or increase its current debt ratings and will seek to learn the circumstances where the company would consider a potential downgrade in its ratings—especially if it would consider a strategic action, such as an acquisition, that would likely take the company from an investment grade to a speculative rating.

Investors will also want to know if the company's debt rating objectives may constrain its capital expenditures, dividend payments, share repurchases, or acquisition strategies. Consequently, CFOs should indicate to investors whether a company's debt rating targets are fixed absolutes that may impact its strategic objectives or whether they are malleable targets that are conditional on the facts and circumstances, including potential acquisition or investment opportunities.

Although CFOs should seek to establish leverage targets that can be expected to last for an indefinite period, they should remain flexible in considering revisions in response to changes in external or company-specific conditions. For this reason, it usually is advisable to express the targets as ranges, providing more room to maneuver and less need for frequent revisions.

 NOTE

1. "Rating Symbols and Definitions" (July 2011, Moody's Investors Service, Inc.), p. 4.

CHAPTER THIRTEEN

Developing Financing Strategies

W ITHIN THE CONTEXT of their leverage targets, CFOs will focus on the target mix of securities in the capital structure. Their over-arching objective is to facilitate the strategic plan objectives, ensuring that the company has adequate financing at a reasonable cost, with limited volatility.

 FINANCING PRINCIPLES

In developing their financing strategies, CFOs will apply core principles to guide their decision making. These principles should include keeping it simple, preserving flexibility, continuing to evolve, and reacting opportunistically.

Keeping It Simple

CFOs should establish a straightforward capital structure that is easily understood and communicated. Common stock and straight debt should be the twin pillars of this capital structure; they are the simplest to execute and, in combination, usually produce the lowest cost of capital. However, convertibles, warrants, and straight preferred stock are legitimate alternatives that—under the right circumstances—can expand a CFO's access to funding or provide lower-cost capital.

As a general rule, CFOs should require complex securities to satisfy a higher burden of proof than plain vanilla alternatives, and they should be cautious in their willingness to serve as a trailblazer for an untested form of financing. Innovation can make sense, but only if the financing technique has been proven in the market and designed to meet clearly stated corporate finance objectives—rather than intended to exploit loopholes in the tax or accounting rules.

Furthermore, CFOs should look out for "hidden costs" embedded in more complex securities and make sure to understand the potential risks, thus avoiding surprises down the road.

Preserving Flexibility

CFOs should also maintain flexibility in their financing strategies. It is usually better to accept a higher cost of financing than to agree to conditions—such as restrictive covenants—that may inhibit a company's business or financial objectives in the future. This is consistent with the CFO's primary objective of advancing the company's strategic plan.

As another example, CFOs should treasure debt call provisions as an especially valuable corporate finance tool. Many CFOs learned this lesson the hard way during the 1980s when they issued 30-year debt that was nonredeemable for life. While eliminating the conventional redemption feature in year 10 provided CFOs with a lower interest rate on the debt, this cost savings was far outweighed by their subsequent inability to redeem this debt—which typically had an interest rate of around 10 percent—during the disinflation era of the 1990s.

Of course, at the time that they entered into these agreements, it seemed inconceivable that interest rates would decline so precipitously. In contrast, the CFOs who paid a higher interest rate for more flexible call provisions looked awfully smart in hindsight.

Continuing to Evolve

CFOs should consider their financing strategies to be constantly evolving. As their company matures and as conditions change in the financial markets, they should review potential strategies for lowering their cost of capital, strengthening their liquidity, or enhancing their long-term flexibility.

In addition to acting proactively from a position of strength, CFOs may also need to respond nimbly to adversity, seeking to preserve the company's credit standing and avoiding threats to the company's strategic plan.

In general, CFOs should always be looking forward and anticipating their capital structure requirements for the future. This involves monitoring their expected cash needs and relating them to the expected conditions in the economy and financial markets.

Reacting Opportunistically

Most important, CFOs should maintain ample flexibility in the execution of their financing strategies, with the latitude to respond quickly to market opportunities. Working with up-to-date market intelligence from their bankers and other external advisors, CFOs can directly and materially impact a company's financing costs through the timing and manner in which they access the capital markets—representing a very tangible example of how CFOs can add significant shareholder value.

For this reason, CFOs should strive to obtain advance agreement from the board of directors concerning their financing strategies and establish streamlined authorizations to implement these strategies in a flexible, opportunistic manner. For example, the board might authorize the chair of the finance or executive committee to approve specific financings within an agreed-upon framework.

 DEBT FINANCING

Straight debt is a primary component of most capital structures. It can be issued privately or publicly, with a wide choice of maturities, structures, and terms.

CFOs must make a number of decisions concerning their debt financing strategies, including the types of debt, the maturity structure, the mix of floating and fixed interest rates, and the possibility of issuing debt in a foreign currency.

Types of Debt

The CFO's first question to answer is, What is the desired mix among the types of debt that can be issued? The basic alternatives are secured debt, senior debt, subordinated debt, and capital leases.

Secured debt is backed by all or a portion of a company's assets (e.g., accounts receivable, inventories, equipment, real estate, fixed assets). The company retains ownership of the assets, but the creditors have preference in bankruptcy.

Senior debt does not have specific collateral ascribed to it. In bankruptcy, unsecured senior debt is generally pari passu with the company's general credit obligations—such as amounts owed to suppliers—and with obligations owed to the company's executives through deferred compensation or non-qualified pension plans.

Subordinated debt can include differentiated levels—such as senior subordinated debt, junior subordinated debt, and mezzanine debt—and is the most vulnerable debt in the event of bankruptcy, although the holders often will receive equity in a Chapter 11 reorganization.

Capital leases are long-term commitments that appear on the company's balance sheet as a form of debt obligation. They can include sale/leaseback transactions where ownership of an asset (e.g., a headquarters building) is sold to a lessor and then leased back to the company. Other examples include entering into capital leases to obtain transportation or industrial equipment or a warehouse facility. Often these financings are motivated by tax considerations.

The CFO's choices among these types of debt will depend mostly on the strength of the company's credit quality and its access to financing. In most cases, the basic tradeoff will be between cost and flexibility. For example, secured financing is generally available at a lower cost than unsecured debt, but can constrain the company's financial flexibility. In contrast, subordinated debt provides more flexibility, but comes at a higher cost; it will also include restrictive covenants that can constrain the company if things do not go as planned. And CFOs of strong credits can enjoy the luxury of having all their needs met through senior unsecured debt—eschewing either secured or subordinated debt altogether—which generally accommodates an attractive blend of both cost and flexibility objectives.

CFOs should seek to develop a long-term game plan around these alternative types of debt, determining the best package to meet the company's funding needs. The danger is that a piecemeal approach can end up costing much more in the form of either greater interest expense or less financial flexibility.

Debt Maturity Structure

Another key question is, What should be the maturity structure for the debt? The first priority is to avoid excessive concentration of maturities, especially within the next one to five years. It is a well-acknowledged truism that companies are more likely to get into financial trouble due to a liquidity shortfall than due to an increase in interest rates. Therefore, CFOs usually seek longer-term maturities that are spread out over time, thereby mitigating a potential liquidity crunch that will require substantial refinancing—perhaps during inhospitable market conditions.

A second priority is to seek an average maturity that relates logically to the company's business horizon (such as a patent approval process for a pharmaceutical company) or to the nature of its assets (such as an investment portfolio for a financial services company).

CFOs will often express their debt maturity objective in terms of its "duration," which is equal to the average life of the present values of the debt's cash flows. Duration indicates not only the average length of time that the debt is outstanding, but also the sensitivity of its market value to changes in interest rates. For example, if a debt security has duration of four years, a 1 percent increase in the market interest rate will cause a 4 percent decrease in its market value.

Another consideration is that longer dated securities usually have a higher interest cost than debt with a shorter maturity—reflecting a positive yield curve—due to the "liquidity preference function" (which states that investors normally demand a higher interest rate for a longer time commitment). For example, during the 2001–2010 time period, the average year-end rate for 10-year Treasuries was 155 basis points above the average rate for 2-year Treasuries.

Fixed versus Floating Rate Debt

A third key question is, What is the desired mix between fixed and floating rate debt? This decision represents a clear tradeoff between risk and reward: Floating rate securities historically have produced lower interest rates over the long term, but introduce greater uncertainty and volatility concerning the company's interest payments in the future.

In answering this question, CFOs should consider the company's financial strength, the stability and predictability of its earnings and cash flows, the nature of its assets, and the company's tolerance for risk. CFOs should include this topic in their review of enterprise risks, and make sure that the CEO and board of directors are comfortable with their strategy.

For CFOs of large companies that have access to the derivatives markets, a popular strategy is to issue long-term fixed rate debt securities and then to enter into interest rate swap agreements that convert the interest expense into a floating rate. In this way, they protect the company's liquidity, but benefit from the cost advantages of floating rate debt. For CFOs of smaller companies that do not have access to the derivatives markets, a similar strategy can be implemented through a bank term loan that features a floating rate.

Finally, while floating rate debt normally is less expensive, CFOs should be ready to seize opportunities to lock in rates at historically low levels. For example, given the extraordinary fiscal and monetary stimulus in the aftermath of the financial crisis, interest costs have been kept artificially low for an extended period—which may make it prudent for CFOs to fix a larger portion of their debt before the eventual return to normalcy.

Foreign Currency Debt

For companies that have major currency translation exposures due to their international operations, CFOs may choose to issue part of their debt in foreign markets, thereby achieving a natural hedge against these exposures. Another alternative is to issue the debt in their home country, but then swap the interest and principal payments into the foreign currency through forward contracts.

However, these strategies will usually only make economic sense if there is a liquid debt market within the foreign country or if there is an active derivatives market in the foreign currency. In addition, while most companies typically will hedge part or all of their "transaction" currency exposures, most do not hedge their "translation" exposures. Because issuing locally denominated debt can be equivalent to hedging a translation exposure, this may be viewed as inconsistent with the company's overall currency management strategies.

Also, while denominating debt in foreign currencies can make economic sense if it creates a hedge against transaction exposures—such as hedging a stream of royalty payments or funding an offshore acquisition—hedging translation exposures can result in a mismatch with cash requirements. For example, if a company is not repatriating its retained earnings from a foreign country and it is paying its foreign-denominated interest with parent company cash, then it is using a cash hedge to offset an accounting exposure.

Finally, employing foreign-denominated debt adds some complexity to the company's financial management, including the need to comply with the rules and documentation requirements for obtaining hedge accounting treatment.

CFOs may conclude that the potential advantages of the hedge are outweighed by the incremental costs and administrative distractions involved.

 ## EQUITY FINANCING

Most equity financing is accomplished through common stock issuances. However, other equity alternatives include convertibles, warrants, and preferred stock.

Common Stock

In public companies, common stock normally is issued as one class that has equal voting rights among all of the shareholders. Therefore, the financing strategies involving common stock are usually quite straightforward: When to issue the stock, how much to issue, and to whom?

A few companies with a legacy of family ownership—especially in the media industry—maintain separate classes of stock with differing voting rights. In addition, dual classes can be used by founders or early investors in private companies as a way to retain control through rounds of financing.

However, most investors object to the dual classes as representing poor corporate governance and the shares with lower voting rights usually will trade at a discount (but they typically have more liquidity than the higher voting shares). Consequently, dual classes are infrequently used in connection with initial public offerings (IPOs) and are restricted to IPOs that enjoy strong investor appetite (e.g., Google).

In theory, companies can also issue classes of stock with differing dividend rates or other differentiated financial policies. Indeed, they can even have separate financial statements, which was the basis for issuances of "*targeted*" or "*tracking*" stock that was intended to highlight the differences between disparate businesses in a single corporate entity.

The progenitor of targeted stock was the Hughes division of General Motors, with several other companies issuing similar securities in the 1980s. For example, Marathon established dual classes to distinguish its exploration and production business from its refining operations.

However, targeted stocks proved to have governance and valuation issues and most have since been redeemed. Today it is generally considered preferable to establish a separate stock by spinning off one of the businesses or by issuing a minority interest through an initial public offering (an "equity carve out").

Convertibles

Convertible debt and convertible preferred securities are hybrids that contain elements of both equity and fixed income securities. They can be attractive to issuers if they expand the size of their financings or facilitate funding from an alternative source of capital, such as a private equity firm. Moreover, they are less dilutive to shares outstanding than common stock and their interest or dividend costs are less than would be required for a fixed income alternative.

Investors typically view convertibles as giving them a minimum return, plus the upside represented by a call option on the company's stock. Alternatively, if convertibles pay no or very low interest or dividends, investors may view them primarily as an equity security that contains an embedded put option whose strike price is equal to the face value of the debt or preferred.

From the issuer's perspective, the biggest disadvantage with convertibles is that they usually are constructed in a "heads you win, tails I lose" manner. If the company does better than expected, it issues common stock to the investor at a bargain price. In contrast, if the company encounters financial difficulties, it must continue to pay the interest or dividend and, more important, must pay the principal at maturity. Moreover, if the convertible securities are publicly held, they can add complexity to the CFO's future financing decisions, as savvy investors may concoct trading strategies that take advantage of inefficiencies among markets. Finally, investors in convertibles usually do not pay the full intrinsic value of the options, especially if they have negotiating leverage in a difficult market environment.

Nevertheless, convertibles can make sense in some situations. First, they can facilitate an investment by a venture capital or private equity firm. In this case, the convertible usually does not pay interest or dividends, and the protection of principal in the capital structure hierarchy may induce the investor to commit funds to the company. Second, in some market environments, investors may have such a strong appetite for convertibles that the terms of the securities are quite favorable to the issuer. Finally, banks and other regulated companies may issue convertible securities that can qualify as a lower cost source of regulatory capital.

If CFOs are considering the issuance of convertibles, they will be well-advised to determine the separate valuations of the equity, options, and fixed income components of the securities—thus understanding their intrinsic value in comparison to the proceeds being raised. Also, they should carefully review the accounting and tax treatment—which can be quite complicated and strongly influenced by the manner in which the securities are constructed.

Warrants

Warrants are long-term call options issued by a company, either as stand-alone securities, or more likely, as an inducement to a lender to provide long-term subordinated debt financing. If a company cannot afford to pay the level of interest expense that would be required for a market rate transaction, warrants represent a vehicle for bridging this value gap. For example, warrants are often included with mezzanine debt financings and are usually detachable from the debt instrument.

As with convertibles, CFOs should be sure to understand the intrinsic value of the warrants—which can be determined by a Black-Scholes or a binomial decision tree analysis—and that they thoroughly explore the accounting and tax treatment.

Preferred Stock

Straight preferred stock is subordinate to unsecured debt in the capital structure, but it has a liquidation preference that ranks above common stock. It can either be perpetual or have a stated maturity, often 10 years. Its dividend payments are usually cumulative, which means that any unpaid preferred dividends must be paid before dividends are paid to common shareholders. In addition, preferred stock holders normally are granted board seats if a specified number of dividend payments are missed.

For the most part, CFOs consider preferred stock to be a relatively expensive fixed income security, largely because the dividend payments are not tax deductible—although clever tax lawyers have designed some exceptions to this general rule through complex configurations. Nevertheless, issuing straight preferred stock can make sense in certain circumstances:

- If the issuer is *not expected to be a taxpayer* for the foreseeable future (usually due to tax loss carry forwards) and thus can't take advantage of the interest deduction on debt.
- If the preferred stock is sold to a corporate investor who will sufficiently compensate the issuer for the *dividends received deduction* (generally 70 percent of preferred dividends are excluded from the taxable income of a U. S. corporation, or 80 percent if the corporate investor owns more than 20 percent of the issuer's common stock).
- If the preferred stock is sold to individual investors who can benefit from the *lower federal tax rate* on dividends compared with ordinary income rates.

For example, the issuer can offer preferred stock with a $25 par value that is designed to appeal to retail investors.

- If the issuance of preferred stock is a *condition to obtaining subordinated debt financing*. For example, if a lender is insisting on a greater equity cushion, issuing preferred stock can be a less costly method of satisfying this condition than issuing common stock.

- If the preferred stock is *treated as regulatory capital* that is less expensive than common stock. For example, banks have issued trust preferred stock as a way to obtain inexpensive Tier 1 capital. (However, this regulatory treatment is being phased out.)

Auction Preferred

In the past, many companies and governmental entities in the United States issued auction preferred stock, which featured a floating dividend rate that was reset through a series of scheduled auctions. It was marketed to corporations and individuals as a short-term investment option to invest their surplus cash at favorable after-tax rates of return.

However, the auction preferred market experienced a dramatic meltdown during the financial crisis, with issuers unable to refinance the preferred and investors being stuck with relatively illiquid and much devalued securities. It is highly unlikely that this market will reopen in the foreseeable future.

OFF BALANCE SHEET FINANCING

Off balance sheet financing may only appear in the footnotes, but it represents a financial commitment that CFOs should consider as part of their capital structure. Indeed, banks and rating agencies will explicitly consider these commitments in their credit assessments.

Therefore, CFOs should compare these arrangements with other financing alternatives and because they typically have higher costs than alternative funding sources, they should only be advocated where they are satisfying a legitimate business purpose—such as enhancing operational flexibility or facilitating a joint venture partnership.

Special Purpose Entities

Although the promulgation of new accounting rules (notably FIN 46) has dramatically curtailed the use of the exotic and controversial off balance sheet financing vehicles of days past (such as Enron's infamous Raptors), CFOs should be ever vigilant in safeguarding the company against the potential abuses of newly designed structures. In particular, CFOs should ensure that any structures proposed by investment banks or other advisors have valid business purposes and are not intended simply to circumvent accounting, regulatory, or legal constraints.

Nevertheless, a company's participation in a joint venture or other form of business partnership can make sense as a vehicle for sharing costs and risks between two or more parties, as well as a legitimate way to utilize tax benefits (such as net operating losses).

Depending on which party has the greater ownership interest, the joint venture may not be reflected on the company's balance sheet. Thus, even though it is off balance sheet financing, this accounting treatment is the result—not the motivation—for the venture: it fulfills a valid business purpose that was facilitated by the financial structure.

Likewise, securitizations can be a good method for freeing up debt capacity—provided that they truly represent a transfer of risk to the third party. CFOs should focus on the recourse arrangements, in particular, to ensure that the transaction fulfills valid business objectives.

Operating Lease Rentals

Operating leases are another example of an off balance sheet financing alternative that can make business sense. By renting rather than owning an asset, the CFO is making a conscious decision to incur higher long-term financing costs in exchange for greater operational flexibility. For example, renting office space can reduce a company's real estate costs: It facilitates reconfigurations of the company's real estate footprint to reflect changes in space requirements and shifts its expense base toward more variable rather than fixed cost commitments.

As other examples, renting warehouse space can provide more flexibility in a company's supply chain and customer servicing arrangements, and renting office or industrial equipment can allow the company to adapt easily to meet new requirements or to take advantage of new technologies or product improvements.

Industry Norms

For some industries, off balance sheet arrangements are an integral part of the companies' business models. Some examples include:

- *Transportation companies* may lease much of their equipment, such as airplanes or trucks. They often can obtain a lower cost of financing than through conventional debt and they can gain greater long-term flexibility in adjusting their fleet for volume requirements.
- *Natural resource and commodity companies* often use take-or-pay or requirements contracts that lock in product sales or supply arrangements over a long-term planning horizon.
- *Retail companies* usually lease their stores, giving them more flexibility to close down underperforming locations.
- *Oil and gas companies* use operating leases for drilling rigs and other equipment, giving them greater flexibility to shift the locus of their exploration and production activities.

CFOs generally should be comfortable with these industry practices that have evolved over time and recognize that deviating too greatly from the accepted norms could put their companies at a competitive disadvantage.

Outsourcing Contracts

Off balance sheet financing arrangements can be embedded in outsourcing contracts. For example, companies can request that the outsourcing provider incur certain costs—such as severance payments to laid-off employees or rentals for dedicated facilities—and then recover these costs over the life of the outsourcing contract. These may be justifiable business arrangements, but CFOs should recognize that they implicitly represent a form of financing, which should be compared with other financing alternatives.

Impact on Management Compensation

Finally, CFOs should be cognizant of the potential impact of off balance sheet structures on bonus plans or other incentive compensation. Business leaders are appropriately motivated to maximize their performance against agreed-upon targets, but sometimes the definitions for these targets can distort decision making. For example, if a company charges a cost of capital on its net assets, a business division may achieve higher profitability through an operating lease; in this case, the higher profit is due to the rentals being less that the ascribed cost of capital.

The bottom line is that CFOs should ensure that any off balance sheet arrangements make business sense and, if necessary, recommend potential modifications to the performance criteria for incentive compensation. Given the goal of motivating good business decisions, the CFO can help define the scorecard that creates the right behavioral incentives.

 ## DEBT COVENANTS

Debt covenants can be important considerations in the CFO's capital structure decisions, possibly impinging on a company's ability to pursue its strategic objectives. In some cases, a CFO may strongly prefer to avoid restrictive covenants as much as possible, even if it entails a more expensive cost of capital.

Alternatively, CFOs may choose to accept the covenants as a justifiable condition to gaining more access to debt capital at better rates. And especially for small companies or start-ups, restrictive covenants may be required to tap the debt markets in any form.

By design, covenants come into play when something does not go as planned, which may be the very time when CFOs need the most flexibility in meeting their funding needs. This does not mean that it never makes sense to agree to potentially onerous covenants—the company may have no viable alternative—but it does mean that CFOs should carefully consider the tradeoffs involved, including contingencies that may seem improbable at the present time.

Maintenance Covenants

Maintenance covenants apply at all times and are most associated with bank financing. Some examples include:

- **Leverage ratio:** Maximum debt to EBITDA.
- **Interest coverage ratio:** Minimum EBITDA to interest expense.
- **Fixed charge coverage ratio:** Minimum EBITDA to sum of interest expense, preferred dividends, and interest component of rentals.
- **Shareholders' equity:** Minimum book value of equity.
- **Debt ratings:** Minimum debt ratings, or else interest rates that fluctuate with changes in the debt ratings.
- **Capital expenditures:** Maximum amount of capital expenditures per year.
- **Material adverse change:** No material change in the borrower's financial condition.
- **Business activities:** No major change in the borrower's business description.

Incurrence Covenants

Incurrence covenants constrain specific actions and are normally associated with high yield financings and syndicated bank loans. Some typical examples include:

- **Additional debt:** Prohibits new debt financings by the parent company or subsidiaries unless specified leverage or coverage ratios are met on a pro forma basis.
- **Restricted payments:** Prohibits dividends, share repurchases, or equity investments unless leverage or coverage tests are met and amount to less than a specified percentage of net income.
- **Negative pledge:** Restricts the pledging of assets as collateral in secured financings.
- **Asset sales:** Prohibits asset sales unless "fair value" is received and restricts the use of proceeds.
- **Affiliate transactions:** Requires "arms length" or "fair value" terms for any transactions with affiliated companies.

Change of Control Provision

Another important consideration is, What happens in the event of a proposed change of control? For example, the covenants may provide that a merger or consolidation is permitted only if the acquiring company can comply with financial tests, including the borrower's debt incurrence ratios. Another alternative is to require that the credit rating of the new company is equal to, or better than, the acquired company's.

For high yield securities, the indenture usually specifies that in the event of a change of control, the debt holders can have their securities repurchased at a price of 101 percent of their par value. This option can be especially valuable to holders of debt securities that are trading at a substantial discount to face value: It effectively transfers value to the debt holders from the shareholders, who otherwise likely could have received a higher price for their stock.

Covenant Negotiations

Depending on the volatility of a company's financial results and its need to maintain financial flexibility, CFOs may seek to limit their use of financing alternatives that involve certain incurrence or maintenance tests; or more likely, they may attempt to negotiate covenants that provide the most flexibility to pursue the company's business and financial strategies.

To a very great extent, the CFO's negotiating leverage will be a function of the company's debt ratings, with higher rated credits enjoying fewer and looser covenants. In contrast, if a company is rated below investment grade, the company generally will have little latitude to obtain a covenant package that differs from the prevailing standards in the bank loan or high yield debt markets.

The types and terms of the required covenants tend to ebb and flow with market conditions; thus, the CFO's negotiating leverage generally will be greater when the financing markets are vibrant than during periods when market conditions are weak. This is another advantage of entering the capital markets on an opportunistic basis, creating the possibility to negotiate a less restrictive covenant package. Moreover, in favorable market environments, CFOs may have more freedom in defining the covenant terms (e.g., by establishing a higher debt leverage ratio or a lower interest coverage ratio than normally would be possible).

DEBT REFINANCINGS

A debt refinancing can be motivated by a decline in market interest rates, by improvements in the company's financial results, or by more favorable conditions in the financial markets—as evidenced by a greater amount of debt leverage that can be financed on a given amount of earnings or by covenants or other terms that are superior to the company's existing arrangements. By executing a refinancing, CFOs can:

- Lower the annual interest expense.
- Increase the amount of debt financing.
- Extend the debt maturity structure.
- Obtain less restrictive covenants.

Of course, refinancings will be facilitated by call provisions that allow the company to redeem the existing debt at set prices. Otherwise, much of the advantages of a refinancing will be offset by the premium required to purchase the existing debt—because its market value will have increased as a result of the lower interest rate environment.

Nevertheless, even if the debt is not callable, CFOs may determine that the extension of the maturity or the improvement in the covenant package is worth the incremental cost. In this case, they can repurchase the debt through the open market or else exchange a new issue of debt for the existing debt. Alternatively, they can arrange the new financing on favorable terms and hold it as cash until the existing debt matures—essentially prefunding their future financing requirements.

Private Equity Refinancings

Private equity firms often use debt refinancings to restructure the capital structures of their portfolio companies, with the proceeds often used to reduce their equity investments. Given their relatively high cost of equity, the private equity firms can execute refinancings that decidedly improve their returns on investment.

Consequently, they typically try to increase a company's earnings quickly—and thereby the amount of debt leverage that it can support—and aggressively take advantage of opportunities to refinance debt in response to market opportunities that may be prove to be fleeting.

Example of Debt Refinancing

Let's assume that Company XYZ was acquired by a private equity firm in year 1 and that due to higher earnings and improved market conditions, it can refinance the debt in year 2. By using the proceeds to pay a dividend, the private equity firm can substantially reduce its equity investment and thereby enhance its return.

	Year 1	Year 2
EBITDA	$100	$125
Debt to EBITDA	3.5	4.0
Total Debt	$350	$500
Equity Investment	*$200*	*$50*
Total Capital	$550	$550

DEBT FOR EQUITY SWAPS

For CFOs that want to lessen their debt burden, a debt for equity swap is a proven and well-accepted technique. In this transaction, a company typically issues shares of its common stock in exchange for its existing debt securities. The debt holder often can obtain a higher price for the debt than otherwise available in the open market and provided that the equity shares are reasonably liquid, can convert the shares into cash.

At the same time, the company usually obtains equity at a better all-in price than would be available through a new issuance—saving the underwriting costs and pricing discounts associated with an equity offering—and books a profit if the debt is purchased at a discount from its face value. This can be a source of regulatory capital for banks or other regulated companies.

While debt for equity swaps usually are negotiated as one-off transactions with debt holders, CFOs also can swap equity through an exchange offer made to all debt holders. These exchanges are subject to Securities and Exchange Commission (SEC) requirements—such as the length of time that the offering needs to be outstanding—and may be subject to a shareholder vote. However, they can be an efficient vehicle for transforming a company's capital structure in a relatively short period of time.

A major debt for equity exchange can be especially important for a CFO who needs to perform radical surgery on a company's capital structure within a finite time period. It also can help reassure investors that the transaction fully satisfies the company's capital requirements, thus avoiding the uncertainty and progressive dilution that can accompany a long drawn-out series of smaller transactions.

Fiduciary Obligations

Major debt for equity exchanges can be very dilutive to existing shareholders, effectively transferring value to the debt holders. This can cause consternation for boards of directors who generally are charged with a fiduciary obligation to preserve and enhance shareholder value. However, the courts have ruled that at a certain point the company enters the "zone of insolvency" in which the board's obligations generally shift to preserving value for creditors and other stakeholders.

Rating Agency Reaction

In what can seem like "Alice in Wonderland" logic, the rating agencies will treat a major debt for equity recapitalization as requiring an automatic debt downgrade, even if the company's credit position is strengthened materially. The agencies reason that since their debt ratings reflect the probability that debt will be repaid as scheduled at its face value, any deviations from this expectation necessitates a lower rating.

Their treatment may seem counterintuitive, if not illogical. However, despite the lower ratings, the debt markets will reward the improved credit standing with higher valuations for the company's remaining debt. As another counterintuitive result, this higher market value for the remaining debt will result in a charge to net income for companies that mark their debt to market pursuant to FAS 159.

 BANKRUPTCY

Although every CFO dreads the possibility, events may conspire to necessitate consideration of a bankruptcy filing. In this case, the CFO should seek to preserve as much value as possible, avoiding the dissipation that can occur as a result of prolonged uncertainty and a protracted consideration of alternatives.

Bringing in financial experts in advance of a potential filing—along with the hiring of experienced bankruptcy counsel—usually is a wise step that can preserve value for the stakeholders. This is an area where specialized expertise and accumulated experience are essential to making the right decisions under pressure.

Depending on the circumstances and reflecting the advice received from the company's advisors, CFOs facing a potential bankruptcy dilemma generally can consider the following four primary alternatives:

1. **Recapitalization:** Avoid a bankruptcy filing, attempting to arrange a recapitalization with the support of the company's creditors. This usually involves exchanging the existing debt for a new debt issue or equity.
2. **Prepackaged Plan:** Arrange a prepackaged bankruptcy whereby the creditors and other stakeholders have agreed to a new capital structure that is effected through a court-enforced bankruptcy judgment under Chapter 11.
3. **Chapter 11 Filing:** Enter into a Chapter 11 bankruptcy filing that preserves the company's ability to operate post-bankruptcy as a going concern, usually with most or all of the equity going to the debt holders and other creditors. This allows the company to obtain debtor in possession (DIP) financing.

4. **Chapter 7 Filing:** Enter into a Chapter 7 bankruptcy filing that liquidates the company, with the proceeds usually going primarily or exclusively to debt holders and other creditors.

Determining the best course of action necessarily will reflect a careful comparison of the pros and cons of the alternatives. The CFO typically will partner with the financial and legal advisors in this analysis, and with their advice, will take preparatory actions to preserve value and maximize the company's flexibility.

CHAPTER FOURTEEN

Ensuring Short-Term Liquidity

I N EXECUTING THEIR CAPITAL STRUCTURE STRATEGIES, CFOs should be hyper-vigilant in ensuring that the company maintains adequate and reliable access to liquidity. They should seek to guarantee the availability of cash under almost all circumstances—including unforeseen or even unprecedented dislocations in the financial markets.

To satisfy their needs for liquidity, CFOs may advocate maintaining a larger cash balance than needed to run the business. They should also develop contingency plans to obtain short-term funding in the event of either exogenous forces that can curtail access to the capital markets or company-specific issues that can cause sudden and unpredictable requirements for cash.

BANK LINES

For almost all companies—including nonprofits—their planning for liquidity typically involves arranging lines of credit from banks or other financial services companies. The short-term sources of credit can take various forms, such as banker's acceptances, warehouse financing, floor planning, and credit cards. Larger companies with strong credit ratings can also tap the commercial paper market, which can provide short-term unsecured financing at attractive rates.

However, as the mainstays of their financial planning, CFOs typically will arrange *revolving credit lines* that can fund the company's operating activities and back up their other funding sources, such as commercial paper financings. These lines can be unsecured or secured by assets such as receivables and inventories.

Banking Relationships

Given the importance of bank credit commitments in meeting their liquidity needs, CFOs appreciate the need to cultivate strong relationships with their banks—keeping them informed about the company's financial results, sharing short- and long-term financial projections, generally avoiding surprises, and establishing personal bonds based on mutual trust and respect for one another. However, one of the harsh lessons from the financial crisis is that CFOs should not rely too much on either personal or institutional relationships with their banks.

As evidenced during the crisis, if banks are dealing with their own liquidity and survival issues, they inevitably will be rationing their customers' access to credit—and will be doing so based on cold-hearted assessments of the customer's profitability to the bank and its perceived ability to repay any loans. Relationships simply are not going to outweigh the banks' objective judgments concerning the commercial arrangements. Or as Donald Trump would say, it's business, not personal.

In addition, CFOs should be sure to diversify their banking relationships, thus affording access to credit from alternative sources and making them less vulnerable to a particular bank's financial condition and lending policies.

Contractual Commitments

CFOs should establish contractual commitments from their banks that are as iron-clad as possible, providing financing in almost any conceivable—or even seemingly inconceivable—circumstances. In particular, the CFO should ensure that the company's general counsel carefully reviews the credit facilities to confirm their validity in times of duress. Otherwise, if the bank's commitment has too many exclusions, the facility may be inoperable at the very time when it's needed most.

Achieving greater certainty of receiving funding may require the CFO to pay a higher commitment fee to the bank, but this trade-off probably is worth making in a volatile world.

At the same time, CFOs may want to establish commitments with more than one bank, thereby securing access to credit from alternative sources and more flexibility to switch services if a bank encounters difficulties.

CASH PLANNING

Another critical task for CFOs is to institute rigorous cash planning practices, including regular forecasts of their projected short- and long-term liquidity requirements. This means analyzing and managing both expected and potential cash uses, including:

- **Seasonality of Revenue:** Projecting the seasonality of the sales cycles and calculating the time required to convert these sales into cash.
- **Inventory Levels:** Given the forecasted sales cycles, estimating the requirements for work-in-process and finished goods inventory.
- **Trade Payables:** Estimating the flows of trade payables given the inventory requirements.
- **Major Payables:** Anticipating major cash outlays such as tax payments, management and employee bonuses, pension fund contributions, dividend payments, share repurchases, interest payments, or litigation settlements.
- **Capital Expenditures:** Forecasting the spending plans for major capital expenditures.
- **Debt Maturities:** Planning for the maturities of debt securities and perhaps arranging new financings in advance of the scheduled maturities.
- **Strategic Transactions:** Considering cash sources and uses from pending acquisitions or divestitures, including any contingent payments such as earnouts.
- **Cash Repatriations:** Estimating potential dividends or other cash payments from international subsidiaries.

In addition to preparing baseline cash forecasts, CFOs should consider the sensitivities of their cash flows to sales levels that are much higher or lower than forecasted. They should also supplement their regular cash planning exercises from time to time with contingency plans that prepare for a potential liquidity crisis.

CONTINGENCY PLANNING

While it is virtually impossible to anticipate every possible scenario or set of circumstances, some advance contingency planning is likely to be a valuable exercise for CFOs to pursue, helping them to understand their various options in an emergency and—it is hoped—instilling confidence in their ability to manage through a liquidity shortfall.

In particular, CFOs should stress test their cash requirements for either business issues—such as a disruption in supplier arrangements—or system-wide issues—such as a financial market shutdown—that can cause an unforeseen cash shortfall.

Mitigation Strategies

To a large extent, CFOs' risk assessments will reflect their company's business profile and relative credit strength. Their company's characteristics will also greatly influence their choices among mitigation strategies.

CFOs of large, creditworthy companies typically will confirm that they are not too reliant on sources of short-term funding—such as commercial paper—that are vulnerable to market dislocations. Furthermore, they will seek to ensure that they have sufficient back-up credit facilities—even if it results in higher annual commitment fees. They will also monitor their counterparty exposures in swaps or other derivative contracts.

CFOs of smaller, less creditworthy companies will consider various methods of offsetting their liquidity risks, ranging from maintaining "rainy day" funds; to obtaining additional credit lines; to identifying possible short-term cash preservation strategies, such as factoring of receivables, suspending payments to suppliers or employees, or deferring investments in fixed assets.

Bank CFOs usually will have access to funding through repurchase agreements and the Federal Reserve's discount window (or a similar arrangement for non-U.S. banks). Consequently, their primary focus may be to ensure that the bank is complying with all of its regulatory requirements—thereby continuing its access to the governmental facilities—and that its reputation remains beyond reproach—thus ensuring continuity in its customer deposits. They will also closely monitor their exposure to counterparty arrangements that can become vulnerable due to contagion from failures by other institutions.

As a best practice, CFOs should consider, in advance, all of their potential levers to avert a liquidity crisis that otherwise could cause irreparable damage to their company's reputation and credit standing—or even threaten its viability as a going concern. This planning exercise may reinforce their comfort with their status quo arrangements, but it also may indicate supplemental actions—such as increasing bank credit facilities—that should be pursued with alacrity.

LIQUIDITY RATIOS

As one of their ongoing responsibilities, CFOs routinely monitor various liquidity ratios to determine the status of their company's cash position and to measure their progress against working capital objectives. Liquidity ratios can provide early warnings of issues and can highlight areas where corrective actions should be taken. Examples include:

- **Current Ratio**: Current assets divided by current liabilities.
- **Quick (Acid-Test) Ratio:** Cash and equivalents plus accounts receivable divided by current liabilities.
- **Working Capital Ratio:** Cash and equivalents plus accounts receivable and inventory less payables divided by revenue.
- **Days of Sales Outstanding:** Accounts receivable divided by average daily revenue.
- **Inventory Turnover:** Cost of goods sold divided by inventory (on a first in first out [FIFO] basis).
- **Days of Payables Outstanding:** Trade payables divided by average daily purchases.

 ## WORKING CAPITAL STRATEGIES

Besides monitoring the ratios, CFOs can make meaningful impacts through their working capital strategies, which can reduce costs and serve as valuable weapons in their arsenal of liquidity protections.

Management Incentives

The most important tool in working capital management is to establish incentives for the business leaders to focus on cash flows. Too often bonus plans are based solely on accounting criteria (such as net operating profit after tax) and do not incorporate explicit targets for cash flow management.

By including cash flow objectives in the incentive plans—either a free cash flow target or a specific target for working capital—CFOs can enlist the full cooperation and support of the business units.

Accounts Payable

Because accounts payable systems are often automated to pay suppliers at designated time intervals, they may be paying some bills earlier than necessary.

CFOs may be able to preserve cash by applying more discretion in varying the payment schedules, distinguishing between the criticality of suppliers and their tolerances for days past due. And, of course, there is the age-old practice of disbursing checks from remote locations.

Paying suppliers early to receive a price discount can be a good economic decision, but only if the size of the discount exceeds the company's cost of debt and the company has sufficient liquidity to make the payments. CFOs should recognize that procurement departments may be motivated to obtain these discounts—which typically count toward their cost savings objectives—and confirm that they make economic sense. In any event, the discounts may need to be foregone if the company needs the liquidity.

Accounts Receivable

The personal involvement of CFOs can often make a big difference in collecting accounts receivable that are past due. They can directly encourage customers to make more timely payments, which in addition to reducing days of sales outstanding, can lower bad debt reserves and write-offs. They can also outsource collections for a contingent fee.

In addition, CFOs can institute automated payment systems with customers, thereby facilitating prompt payments and reducing billing discrepancies. Another strategy is regularly to review lockbox configurations because postal services are constantly changing their delivery routes.

In a mirror image of their analysis of purchasing discounts, CFOs can help determine whether a company should offer discounts to customers for early payments. This can be an economically viable alternative so long as the cost of the discount paid is less than the company's after-tax cost of capital for that period. It also should be considered if the company is strapped for cash.

Sales Commissions

Another technique is to base the payments of sales commissions on the receipt of payments from customers, rather than when the sales are booked. This gives sales people a stake in collections and credit decisions, although it can be argued that it may divert them from making additional sales.

Inventories

CFOs can analyze whether the inventories of finished goods can be reduced or even eliminated for slower moving items. They can help weigh the financial trade-offs between the cash freed up from eliminating an item versus the potential for lost revenue.

They can also propose greater use of just-in-time arrangements with suppliers, thus reducing work-in-process inventories. Given their role in enterprise risk management, CFOs are well-positioned to assess the cash flow benefits in relation to the risks of supply chain disruptions and can help ensure that there are appropriate back-up arrangements.

Spare Parts

CFOs can analyze the possibility of discontinuing spare parts for obsolete or low volume products. Also, they can review whether spare parts storage can be consolidated into fewer facilities.

Cash Management

By centralizing a company's banking arrangements into one or a few banks, CFOs can establish more efficient systems for collecting and investing cash flows each day. In addition, they can establish policies for investing surplus cash that ensures immediate access to a portion of the funds in the event of an emergency. This typically involves sacrificing some yield for the enhanced liquidity.

 TRAPPED CASH

For U.S. companies with international operations, access to non-U.S. cash balances may be constrained by tax considerations. Given that the United States has a global rather than a territorial tax system and because most international income is taxed at lower rates than 35 percent, CFOs normally have an incentive not to repatriate cash; if they certify that they do not intend to dividend the retained earnings, they are not subject to incremental U.S. tax.

This tax constraint can cause cash to be "trapped" overseas, perhaps making it difficult for CFOs to fund the parent company's interest and dividend payments. Thus, CFOs should maintain a good understanding of their foreign tax credit position and know how much cash could be repatriated to the United States with little or no tax cost. In addition, they should have a rough idea of the maximum amount of cash that could be repatriated quickly, if necessary, and a ballpark estimate of the incremental tax cost that would be incurred.

CHAPTER FIFTEEN

Obtaining Long-Term Financing

A LTHOUGH IT IS BETTER TO HAVE too much than too little capital, this margin of safety comes with a price. Therefore, it is always a delicate balance between the desire to be well-capitalized versus the fear of being over-capitalized.

In striking the right balance, CFOs will consider not only the amount of capital that should be raised, but also the variety of sources from which it can be obtained. Each funding alternative has its unique blend of advantages and disadvantages, which CFOs will factor into their capital structure equation.

VENTURE CAPITAL

For start-ups and young companies, financing traditionally has come from equity investors who are seeking significant upside in exchange for a material risk of loss. Depending on the stage of a company's development and the amount of capital required, these investors can range from "angels" (private individuals) to large venture capital firms (institutions).

Venture capital is usually the most expensive funding and can be difficult to obtain in size; thus, venture capital financing normally is approached with the twin goals of minimizing the amount raised and delaying the funding until it is absolutely required. However, its availability is also the most uncertain, subject not only to the quality of business plans presented, but also to the conditions in the venture capital market, which can fluctuate materially.

Venture capital is typically raised in stages, which allows the investors at each stage to have more information about the progress to date and the future prospects for the business. This usually results in a lower cost of capital (less dilutive) than the funding raised in the previous stages, but it is still likely to be materially dilutive to the founders and earlier investors.

In addition to providing funding, venture capital investors can usually offer their management skills and wealth of experience to a fledgling business, often serving on the company's board of directors. They can also be a good sounding board for decisions related to the future of the business—such as whether projects should be abandoned, expanded, or deferred.

Corporate Venture Funds

As an alternative to the venture capital firms—which typically are funded by pension funds and other institutional investors—some corporations have established venture capital arms that are targeted at specific industries. The sponsors of these corporate funds are usually seeking advantages in addition to the financial returns—such as windows into new technologies, as well as opportunities for commercial or strategic relationships.

Consequently, if CFOs consider financing from this source, they should clarify the fund's expectations and recognize that the ongoing relationship may complicate the company's potential strategies in the future. For example, it could constrain the company's flexibility to enter certain business lines; to launch an initial public offering; or to sell itself to an alternative corporate acquirer.

 PRIVATE EQUITY

For more established companies, private equity firms can provide additional capital in the form of common stock, convertible preferred, or mezzanine debt. Private equity financing is generally less expensive than funding from venture capital sources and much greater amounts of capital are available from private equity sources in comparison with the venture capital markets. However, the hurdles for obtaining it are higher—usually requiring a track record of performance and growth. It's also higher cost financing than public market equity.

In general, funding from a private equity firm can be a very attractive alternative for a private company that has moved beyond the venture capital stage, but is not yet ready to go public. Also, private companies can benefit from the managerial skills of private equity investors, whose expertise can help them to expand their business, institute management processes, and prepare for an eventual public offering.

In addition, they often can help companies obtain debt financing, perhaps tapping the markets for syndicated bank loans or high yield debt. Moreover, in some cases the private equity firms can provide subordinated debt financing directly from funds that they have raised for this purpose.

Private equity firms also provide capital to public companies through private investments in public equities (PIPEs). This product provides additional equity capital at a premium rate of return—typically a discount of 10 to 20 percent from the market price—in exchange for a stable source of long-term funds and a relationship with a savvy institutional investor whose imprimatur can provide comfort concerning the company's financial condition and business strategies.

PIPEs are especially well-suited for relatively small capitalization companies that need additional equity funding to support their growth strategies. The biggest disadvantages are the dilution to existing shareholders and any contractual commitments that may constrain a CFO's financing flexibility in certain circumstances.

Sovereign Wealth Funds

It is estimated that sovereign wealth funds had $4.2 trillion of assets at the end of 2010 (up 11 percent from the end of 2009) and that another $6.8 trillion of assets were held in other sovereign investment vehicles, such as pension reserve funds and development funds.[1] Given expectations that these sovereign wealth funds will continue to grow in size and influence, and in light of their stated intentions to expand their private equity portfolios, they may represent an attractive source of funding in the future—including minority or majority equity stakes in developed country companies and private equity investments in emerging market companies.

 INITIAL PUBLIC OFFERING

When companies have achieved a certain size and maturity, they can consider an initial public offering (IPO). This is a seminal step in the life of a company, which is usually prompted by investors' desire to obtain liquidity, the need for additional capital to expand the business, or by constraints concerning the maximum number of shareholders without being subject to SEC disclosure requirements (generally a maximum of 500).

Underwriters

In going public, the CFO usually will interview potential underwriters (a "bake-off" or "beauty contest") and then select one or a few lead managers to orchestrate the process, which in the United States is subject to the Securities Act of 1933, as well as the requirements of the exchange on which the shares are to be listed. The underwriting fee ("spread") will be negotiated as well, although most CFOs of smaller and less well-known companies will have little say concerning the amount paid to the investment bankers, who usually will quote a standard fee of 7 percent for an initial public offering (IPO) in the United States.

Exchange Listing

The CFO will also lead a process for choosing the exchange on which the shares will be listed. The majority of trading now occurs in third-party electronic markets; thus, the choice among exchanges will largely reflect a comparison of their fees, brand image, and services. Also, their listing requirements differ, which may be a consideration in some instances, as well as the governance rules that apply to their listed companies.

Deal Dynamics

In consultation with the company, the underwriters will determine the number of shares to be issued, the range of potential prices for the shares, and the number of shares that are to be sold by the company ("primary" shares) versus the shares, if any, that are to be sold by existing shareholders ("secondary" shares). The underwriters and their counsel will also work with the company in preparing the disclosure documents, as well as the marketing materials that will be used in connection with a "road show" for investors. These are time-consuming processes that give the management team its first taste of life as a public company.

The underwriters will also help the company to determine if and when the offering should proceed, because the investor appetite and market pricing for IPO shares can be notoriously fickle—with an IPO "window" that can shut precipitously for an unpredictable duration.

In launching the offering, the underwriters will seek to have an oversubscribed offering—exercising the *"green shoe"* option to issue up to 15 percent more shares—and to see the shares trade at a premium from their initial offering price. The traditional guidepost is that the shares should trade at a 15 percent premium, but the actual results can deviate wildly from this target, especially for high-technology companies that are perceived as "hot" issues in the market.

Reverse Mergers

As an alternative to a conventional IPO, a private company can execute a reverse merger whereby it combines with an existing public company (which typically is a shell company with little or no capitalization). The private company's shareholders will end up owning the large majority of the shares and controlling the board of directors of the combined company.

The advantages of a reverse merger include the savings of time and money from avoiding the SEC registration process and the payment of underwriting fees. However, a comprehensive disclosure document must be filed with the SEC via a Form 8-K. Another advantage of a reverse merger is that it can reduce the amount of dilution to existing shareholders because new shares are not sold to the public at the time of the merger.

The primary disadvantage of reverse mergers is that they are considered suspect by many investors due to their limited disclosure, their lack of a marketing period, and their limited liquidity. In June 2011 the SEC issued a statement that warned investors about the possibility for fraud or other abuses in connection with reverse mergers. In addition, CFOs should be aware of potentially assuming liabilities through the merger with the shell company.

Special Purpose Acquisition Companies

Another alternative is to go public through a merger or sale to a special purpose acquisition company (SPAC). A SPAC raises equity through an underwritten offering in the public markets for the purpose of acquiring private businesses. SPACs are essentially shell companies that usually have relatively free range (a "blank check") concerning their investments in targeted industries.

Although a number of SPACs were established in the United States during the past decade, they have not enjoyed a solid track record of success. Many have dissolved without completing a transaction (they have a two-year window to complete a merger or acquisition before being forced to dissolve). It is unclear whether they will be viable alternatives for private companies in the future and, in any event, only well-received transactions are likely to receive the requisite approval from a SPAC's shareholders.

In recent years, SPACs have been established outside the United States, including in Europe and China. Therefore, they may become a more popular alternative in the future, especially in markets where the availability of equity financing is limited.

 ## SUBSEQUENT EQUITY OFFERINGS

After going public, companies and their major shareholders have a number of alternatives for raising additional equity. These alternatives include secondary offerings, follow-on offerings, at-the-market issuances, and rights offerings.

Secondary Offerings

In executing an IPO, the underwriters will generally require the company's management team and major shareholders to agree not to sell their shares for a period of time (the "*lock-up*")—usually 180 days. When this time period expires, the shareholders can sell their shares in the market, often through a registered public offering. These secondary offerings are subject to the same kind of market judgments that go into the timing for IPOs, plus they have the added complication that insiders are selling their shares, which may arouse some concerns among potential investors.

Generally, secondary offerings are better received when the sellers are professional investors such as venture capital or private equity firms than when the founders or members of management are reducing their ownership stake. The stock market generally wants the management team to be fully committed to the company and to maintain substantial "skin in the game."

Follow-On Offerings

After a company has gone public, it can sell additional primary shares through follow-on offerings, although the timing is subject to the same kinds of lock-up restrictions that apply to secondary sales. Unlike a secondary offering, a follow-on offering raises equity that is retained by the company, with the proceeds typically used to repay debt or to fund an expansion of a company's business—thus reinforcing the company's growth story and justifying the dilution of existing shareholders.

Follow-on issuances are usually achieved through an underwritten distribution in which investment banks orchestrate the offering of shares during a defined marketing period, including investor presentations and perhaps a road show. However, depending on investor demand, they can also be accomplished quickly with a very limited marketing effort.

At-the-Market Offerings

As an alternative to underwritten offerings, CFOs can issue additional shares in the open market through an "at-the-market" (ATM) offering. This technique is generally limited to companies that are fairly well-established and that have substantial liquidity in their stock.

In an ATM offering (also called a "dribble out") the issuer announces a target amount to be raised and files a registration statement with the SEC that allows the shares to be sold each day, provided that the company is not subject to a "black out" period and otherwise does not possess material information not disclosed to the public.

The company typically engages an investment bank that acts as its agent in selling the shares into the market, usually based on instructions from the company each day to issue a targeted amount of the volume of trades that day. The shares can be sold through electronic markets that aggregate buying and selling activity or through blocks of stock that are sold directly to institutions. The objective is to sell the shares without materially impacting the average price at which the shares trade.

Rights Offerings

Another alternative for raising additional equity is a rights offering. Although relatively rare in the United States, rights offerings are frequently used in non-U.S. markets and are often preferred or even required by the non-U.S. regulatory authorities.

In a rights offering, shareholders are issued warrants to buy additional shares at a fixed price that represents a discount from the market price prior to the offering. The shareholders then can choose either to sell the warrants to other investors or else to exercise the warrants for additional shares, presumably profiting from the discounted price.

The biggest advantage of a rights offering is that existing shareholders are not diluted, which can be an especially important consideration if the size of the issuance is large compared with the existing market capitalization. In addition, a rights offering can be advantageous in accomplishing a financing when a company is undergoing financial difficulties or if market conditions are unfavorable.

The principal arguments against rights offerings are that they can be disruptive to the market for the company's stock, and the company may receive less favorable pricing than through an underwritten offering that is marketed to new investors.

 ## TERM LOANS

Term loans are the work horses of the credit markets, providing funding for companies of various sizes for manifold purposes. The maturities usually range from one to 10 years and can either be secured or unsecured, depending on the quality of the credit and the use of proceeds. The interest rate usually floats over LIBOR (London Interbank Offered Rate) at either a fixed spread or one that varies based on the borrower's current credit ratings. Banks are the primary sources of term loans, but commercial finance companies can offer them as well, often to finance real estate or equipment purchases.

 ## SYNDICATED BANK LOANS

In a syndicated bank loan, an arranger (usually a relationship bank of the borrower) negotiates a bank term loan that then is syndicated among other banks and financial institutions, such as special financing vehicles that hold collateralized debt obligations (CDOs). These financings are especially common for leveraged buyouts, often in conjunction with issuances of high yield debt securities. Syndicated bank loans can be traded privately among the banks and institutional investors and are not subject to SEC registration requirements.

 ## INVESTMENT GRADE SECURITIES

Large, SEC-registered companies with investment grade debt ratings have considerable flexibility in arranging long-term debt financings in the public markets. Generally, they can enter the debt market quickly, typically obtaining their targeted amounts within a single day. Also, underwriters will compete to issue the debt, giving issuers the opportunity to compare proposals from a small group of banks. The underwriters typically will compete on the basis of their relationship with the issuer; the advisory services that they have provided concerning the proposed offering or other matters; and the proposed all-in interest rate for the debt, reflecting both the coupon and the underwriting commission.

The pricing on the debt reflects a fixed interest rate that is based on a spread over Treasuries—reflecting the market's assessment of the credit quality of the issue in comparison with other securities in the market. While this assessment may be partially influenced by the issuer's debt ratings, the participants in the debt market will independently determine their own credit judgments; it's not uncommon for the debt pricing to deviate considerably between two issuers with identical debt ratings.

HIGH YIELD SECURITIES

For non-investment grade issuers, the high yield market can be a fertile source of larger long-term debt financings. This market can be tapped by public companies, but also by private companies that register their debt with the SEC and comply with the ongoing disclosure requirements. The offering is made initially to "qualified institutional buyers" under Rule 144a and then the issuer has a year to file the securities with the SEC.

High yield debt has a lower cost of capital than equity alternatives—especially if the issuer can use the tax deduction for interest payments. Also, the offering does not dilute the existing shareholders—which can be an especially important consideration in closely held companies where the founders desire to maintain a controlling interest. Moreover, the issuer often has the option to pay in kind, which can make it a better substitute for equity than other fixed income alternatives. Finally, high yield financing can be arranged in large size over a wide spectrum of potential maturities, making it an especially flexible vehicle for implementing the CFO's capital structure strategies.

However, the high yield markets are not always receptive to lower rated speculative credits and the spread required above Treasuries can vary considerably, depending upon the market's assessment of the economic outlook and the perceived risk of default on the debt. In addition, the interest payments are subject to Internal Revenue Service restrictions concerning the level of interest rates that are tax deductible.

While high yield debt offers significant cost and other advantages compared with other long-term funding alternatives, CFOs should recognize that the relatively high interest expense can be a drain on cash—possibly exposing the company to a risk of default or even bankruptcy. Therefore, they will want to be confident that the company can comfortably service its debt obligations and comply with the debt covenants, especially if they have other financing options.

 ## STRATEGIC ALLIANCES

In some cases, CFOs may want to consider funding from a company that wants to establish a strategic alliance. This funding normally is in the form of common stock (usually less than 20 percent of shares outstanding) but convertible or preferred stock alternatives also can be negotiated. Strategic alliances can be found in almost any industry, but are more typically associated with technology, pharmaceutical, media, and financial services companies.

Motivations

Providing funding through a strategic alliance can be motivated by a number of considerations, including:

- To obtain insights and knowhow concerning a technology or business model.
- To facilitate commercial arrangements such as research or marketing partnerships.
- To gain an inside track for acquiring or distributing a company's products.
- To establish a preferred position with respect to the potential acquisition of the company.

From the issuer's perspective, the terms can represent attractive financing in comparison with other alternatives and may permit long-term funding to be obtained in size during difficult market conditions—when alternative financing sources may be unavailable. Morgan Stanley's ability to obtain equity financing from Mitsubishi UFJ Financial during the financial crisis is a case in point.

Considerations

However, depending on the motivations of the strategic investor and the strings attached to the alliance, this financing alternative can reduce the issuer's flexibility in the marketplace. Furthermore, the exit strategy for the alliance can be problematic; the strategic partner may desire to achieve future liquidity for its investment, perhaps requiring the issuer to repurchase the securities or compelling an initial public offering. These exit arrangements can result in financing difficulties for the company and may cause disputes to arise concerning the valuation of the securities.

Furthermore, the strategic partner may desire a preferred position in the event of the sale of the company, possibly through a right of first refusal or an option to match a third-party price. This can limit the company's flexibility and perhaps dissuade other potential acquirers from pursuing a transaction.

Given the potential complications, if CFOs pursue a strategic alliance, they will want to understand their partner's motivations and objectives and to make the appropriate tradeoffs between negotiating the most attractive financing terms versus preserving their financial and strategic options.

Moreover, they should work closely with their general counsel and external advisors in crafting financing terms that anticipate the various contingencies that may surface in the future. They should recognize that strategic alliances usually have a finite life, with five to seven years being a reasonable assumption for the typical life expectancy.

 NOTE

1. "Sovereign Wealth Funds" (April 2011, The City UK), www.thecityuk.com, Pages 1 and 3.

PART FIVE

V

Performance

CHAPTER SIXTEEN

Driving Business Performance

C FOS ARE PLAYING EXPANDED ROLES in driving business performance. Not content with being the scorekeeper, they are actively partnering with the CEO and business leaders in generating organic revenue growth and managing the company's cost structure.

 ORGANIC REVENUE GROWTH

As any CFO can attest, it is much easier to increase profitability if a company is growing its revenue. If dealing with a stagnant or declining revenue base, CFOs start each year with the challenge of reducing costs just to stay even with the prior year. It is a treadmill that becomes almost impossible to sustain, especially when the ability to shrink headcount is constrained by costly severance payments.

Therefore, contrary to their out-of-date image as impediments to growth, today's CFOs are focused as much on the revenue side as the expense side of the income statement. Indeed, several recent surveys have identified *"generating revenue growth"* as their number one priority in the current environment.

This does not mean that CFOs should embrace growth strategies that are undisciplined or unprofitable; however, it does recognize that the question is not whether to grow, but *how to grow,* and that the CFO should foster growth initiatives that are meaningful, profitable, cost-effective, and consistent with the company's risk parameters.

They can pursue a number of potential strategies to achieve this goal, including prioritization of focus, use of financial tools, partnering with the business leaders, and interactions with customers.

Prioritization

CFOs can help prioritize the growth strategies, concentrating in areas that match the company's core competencies and historical track record. They can increase the probability of success by focusing the company on what it does best.

Through their leadership roles in strategy, capital allocation, and mergers and acquisitions, CFOs can direct resources to the product lines and geographies where the growth potential is highest—both in the size of the revenue opportunity and the expected return on investment—and discourage efforts that are either too small to move the needle or not sufficiently profitable to justify the management focus. In other words, *accomplishing more by doing less.*

CFOs can also help to determine whether an organic growth strategy can be augmented or replaced by the targeted acquisition of a technology, infrastructure, or skill base. This can accelerate the fulfillment of the growth strategy and, just as important, free up internal resources to focus on other organic growth strategies.

Financial Tools

CFOs can use their financial tools to encourage growth strategies. This includes analyzing what needs to be done and providing the resources to do it. For example, if the strategic plan calls for a specified growth rate, they can help to quantify the potential sources of this growth. This can be especially enlightening if it highlights gaps between the aspirations and the realities—indicating that the company needs to increase its efforts to generate growth and focus on the business strategies that have the most potential to close the gaps.

In addition, they can help analyze whether the growth strategies have sufficient resources to succeed. It's much better to have a few well-funded growth initiatives than to dissipate the resources over several underfunded projects that have relatively low probabilities of success.

As part of their annual budget, CFOs can establish an unallocated pool of resources to be used—at the CEO's discretion—in funding growth opportunities that may arise during the year. In a fast moving world, the company's ability to move swiftly should not be constrained by either resource or budgetary constraints.

In addition, CFOs can influence the company's appetite for new products by the cost accounting procedures used to evaluate their profitability. For example, a cost accounting system that emphasizes economic contribution margins is likely to be more favorable for new products than one which applies full costing from the outset.

Above all, CFOs should emphasize economic benefits rather than accounting impacts when evaluating growth initiatives. They will need to consider the net income ramifications when determining the priorities for projects, but this should be the final and not the first way to evaluate them. A project should not be killed prematurely.

Partnering

CFOs can adopt a mindset as facilitators of growth. Rather than reinforcing the hoary stereotype that they are knee-jerk naysayers to a business unit's creativity and ambitions, CFOs can emphasize their role in encouraging rather than retarding the proposed growth strategies. Functioning as a facilitator of growth is consistent with becoming more of a strategic partner with the business leaders—a role that is being enthusiastically embraced by enlightened CFOs.

Staying close to the business is fundamental to adding value. As described by one CFO, this can include a number of things:[1]

> First, be very connected to the business people in the company and be on top of where the business is moving or can move to. Having a finance group that is well connected and embedded in the business is the key to this.
>
> Second, be connected to other external sources that provide objective input to shape the company's strategy.
>
> And third, engage in a constant debate on possible scenarios and prepare the company to either take advantage of those or make defensive moves.

Given their analytical capabilities and their company-wide exposure to potential opportunities, CFOs are unusually—perhaps uniquely—well-positioned to play a major role in identifying, prioritizing, and executing growth strategies. If the business leaders know that the CFO is committed to growth, they are more likely to work with the CFO productively in making things happen.

To draw the obligatory sports analogy, the CFO can be the *"point guard"* for growth—driving the ball down the court, seeing the potential plays, and finding the player with an open shot. While seldom directly responsible for generating organic growth, CFOs certainly can provide their fair share of assists.

Customer Relationships

CFOs can have a direct impact on a company's revenue through their interaction with customers. This focus on the customer is especially important for CFOs of *business-to-business* companies that market their products and services to CFOs or other C-suite officers. From their experience as customers for enterprise products, they can render useful input to marketing programs, bringing their unique perspectives to the company's sales strategies. In addition, CFOs often will assume responsibility for managing their company's overall relationships with specified major customers.

Furthermore, CFOs frequently make presentations to customer groups about their company's strategies and financial statements, often participating in customer convocations, including advisory group meetings. Another role is to provide reassurances to existing and potential customers concerning their company's financial health and its sustained commitment to a business or product line—reassurances that were much appreciated during the throes of the recent financial crisis.

In *business-to-consumer* companies, CFOs also take an active interest in their company's customer relationships, although in this case their involvement is usually more indirect, such as listening to sales or customer service calls or monitoring customer complaints. This can enable them to stay engaged in the business and can provide essential contextual information for considering potential investments in technologies, marketing programs, or people.

Although CFOs differ in the amount of time that they spend with customers, they share a common belief that staying close to customers is an important part of their job. Likewise, they feel that having first-hand exposure to areas with high growth potential—such as emerging economies—can provide crucial insights toward formulating, executing, and communicating their company's strategic objectives.

 ## COST REDUCTION STRATEGIES

Cost cutting, of course, is a role that traditionally has been associated with the CFO position, and it's a role that has been growing in importance due to the declining number of companies that have chief operating officers. CFOs should partner with the CEO and the business leaders in driving down expenses—thereby increasing profit margins and generating funds to support revenue growth strategies.

In addition, CFOs typically play a leadership role in developing and executing action plans to cope with near-term downturns in revenue forecasts or to respond to cyclical or systemic declines in a company's business outlook. Given the more volatile financial world in recent years, this also has been a role that has grown in importance.

CFOs can employ a variety of proven tools for reducing a company's cost base. The trick is to select the right combination of tools for the particular challenges at hand.

Assigning Targets

Probably the most common tool—often used in connection with budgeting and forecasting—is to establish cost reduction targets that are then allocated to the business unit and staff leaders to define and execute. To be successful, this approach usually requires strong top-down support from the CEO, although the CFO also plays a leadership role in developing and communicating the action plans and ensuring that they are executed in a timely and effective manner.

This approach has the benefit of being relatively easy to administer—provided that there is cooperation from the business leaders—and can be implemented relatively quickly; therefore it is especially well-suited for rapid responses to unforeseen business downturns or financial difficulties. It also has the virtue of leaving the specific decisions in the hands of the business leaders, who usually are in the best position to make the tough choices and who typically appreciate the respect for their autonomy.

The main disadvantage is that assigning targets is necessarily arbitrary and may not reflect the best prioritization throughout the company. Almost inevitably, someone will loudly denounce this approach as using a "meat axe rather than a scalpel."

Another potential disadvantage is that if used too often, this approach can cause business leaders to defer cost reduction actions until their targets have been assigned, thus making it easier to fulfill their mandates. This can foster a reactive rather than a proactive culture.

Reorganizing Functions

Another approach is to analyze specific functions across the company, then to drive savings through the implementation of shared services, outsourcing arrangements, and organizational efficiencies—often with guidance from industry benchmarking statistics that are obtained from consulting firms or other third-party sources. This approach is especially effective for analyzing functions that are widely dispersed throughout the company, such as information technology, finance, human resources, legal, facilities, and procurement activities.

The first step in this approach is to develop a company-wide summary of the costs, which often represents the first time that the costs have been accumulated in a comprehensive total. This calculation can be eye-opening, which, by itself, can reveal opportunities for significant cost reductions. However, CFOs typically go to the next phase, which is to assign responsibilities for reducing the function's total costs through programs and action steps that cross geographical and organizational boundaries.

An issue that arises with this approach is whether to change the budgeting procedures. The main alternatives are:

- **Decentralize and Allocate:** Continue to budget the costs within the respective business units or staff departments and record any savings as they occur.
- **Centralize and Allocate:** Budget the costs within a centralized cost center, but allocate the cost savings to the business units and staff departments at the end of the period.
- **Centralize and Retain:** Budget the costs within a centralized cost center and retain any savings in the cost center—making it less likely that they get spent.

It is probably safe to say that there is no right answer for this budgeting dilemma, with CFOs choosing the system that works best for their purposes. The potential savings usually are sufficient to justify some flexibility in approach, and the process of allocating the savings certainly shouldn't get in the way of taking decisive actions.

The other general observation about this approach is that the *governance arrangements* are important in driving its success; it usually takes a combination of a strong project leader, support from the top, and some type of oversight committee that represents the business units and staff departments that are affected.

Expense Categories

Another common approach is to analyze expense categories that are relatively small in each cost center, but which can add up to large savings opportunities when aggregated across the company. In this approach, certain expense categories are identified as fruitful areas to attack, and then to assign responsibilities for attacking them. Often these responsibilities are lodged with procurement people, but a CFO may prefer to assign someone from the finance organization who has skills in managing projects and motivating changes in behavior.

For example, many companies have been able to make significant reductions in their document management costs by establishing company-wide rules for printing and storing documents and records. Other common examples include expenses for mobile devices, personal computers, travel, and temporary workers.

In implementing this approach, CFOs typically take the following steps:

Step 1. *Aggregate spending* in the expense category across the company (or perhaps throughout the U.S. or another geographic region).

Step 2. *Centralize procurement* of the expense category, usually with a single vendor or two, which are chosen through a competitive process.

Step 3. *Develop procedures* and rules for determining when the expense can be incurred (such as centralized versus personal printing, or limits on document storage periods).

Step 4. *Impose requirements* that everyone must follow the company's procedures and use the designated vendors.

Typically, these projects have relatively small impact in each cost center, but result in material savings in aggregate. However, the savings require the active cooperation and participation by people throughout the company, which may be difficult to achieve due to their desire to maintain autonomy and existing relationships. Therefore, this approach also requires strong support from the top.

Furthermore, implementing this type of program often requires an investment in technology systems for accumulating the data and monitoring the expenses. Consequently, it is usually a longer-term effort and not something that can be instituted quickly in response to a near-term expense target.

Healthcare Costs

Within U.S. companies, CFOs are finding it especially fruitful to attack healthcare costs, which is a spending category that has been growing at an alarmingly rapid rate. Especially in an environment where it is difficult to pass through price increases, a double-digit annual escalation of costs is simply unsustainable for most companies.

In response, CFOs are partnering with their human resource leaders to rein in healthcare costs as best they can. To date, they have focused primarily on:

- Transferring more of the costs to employees, using industry benchmarks for the percentage of costs borne by employers versus the costs paid by employees.
- Using health maintenance organizations and other managed care programs to lower the costs per employee, including a greater use of generic prescriptions.
- Creating incentives for employees to choose less expensive programs with alternative modules for their particular needs.
- Imposing a surcharge if an employee's spouse enrolls in the company's program rather than obtaining coverage through the spouse's employer.

These efforts generally have enabled costs to grow at a lower rate than the overall healthcare inflation rate, but still at a much faster rate than the overall consumer price index. Therefore, additional steps are being pursued, including greater emphasis on measures that prevent the need for healthcare in the first place. These steps can include:

- Establishing medical clinics, prescription drug outlets, and wellness centers at company sites.

- Imposing surcharges on smokers, or providing subsidies for cessation of smoking or for participation in wellness activities, such as exercise programs.
- Lowering the copayments on prescription drugs, thus reducing the probability of an employee incurring a debilitating illness.

Despite all of these efforts, CFOs may feel like they are putting fingers in the dikes to retard the growth in healthcare costs, which are rising inexorably in the United States. Therefore, companies are factoring relative healthcare costs into their global employment strategies, with an advantage to locating employees in countries that provide healthcare through governmental programs. They also are considering healthcare costs in outsourcing decisions.

Compensation Expense

Compensation is another expense category that falls primarily under the domain of the chief human resource officer, but that CFOs should influence, especially in people-intensive businesses. For example, in recent years many companies have frozen or even reduced salaries and have suspended some benefits programs, such as their 401(k) matches for employees in the United States.

However, *performance management* should be the primary tool for controlling compensation costs in most companies. By linking pay to performance, companies can counteract the notion that annual merit increases are an entitlement and can relate pay increases to an employee's annual performance appraisal. In addition, companies should conform their pay practices to conditions in the labor market—compensating employees according to their worth as determined by the market for equivalent skills and responsibilities.

Hiring Freeze

Hiring freezes are frequently used to gain rapid reductions in head counts and compensation costs. However, while these programs can work well as a short-term response to profit pressures, they are a relatively inefficient method for shrinking the work force.

Using this approach, the headcount reductions are largely dependent upon the rate of voluntary turnover—which may decline dramatically if there is an overall rise in unemployment in the economy—and in the areas where there is turnover, key positions may remain unfilled. Therefore, hiring freezes typically are accompanied by a process for granting *exceptions*, especially for revenue-producing positions.

Indeed, many of the benefits of a hiring freeze can be obtained simply by increasing the *bureaucracy* involved in filling or adding a position. The most common example is to require that additions to headcount must receive specific approval from business leaders, the CFO, or the CEO—depending on the level of the position being added. This simple requirement can have a pronounced effect on the speed at which positions are added or filled, resulting in material cost savings.

Another technique is to assume, for budgeting purposes, that there will be an estimated level of turnover each year, and rather than assuming the positions will be filled immediately, to budget for an assumed number of months that will be required to fill the position. This deters managers from hiring in advance of their needs and imposes additional discipline in the hiring process.

Finally, it has been argued that one of the benefits of installing human resource software is that it makes it harder to fill positions due to the steps that need to be followed to comply with the system. While this certainly is not the stated purpose for this software, there is merit in the argument that rigid system requirements can cause managers to move more slowly and perhaps more thoughtfully in their headcount decisions. And a relatively small addition in the time required to fill a position can have a significant impact if applied on a company-wide basis.

Restructuring Program

CFOs can also establish a major restructuring program that is focused on reducing headcount. This can be a major source of cost savings—both the direct compensation expense and the indirect expenses (such as facilities and travel) that are associated with the headcount.

Announcing a restructuring program has two major advantages:

1. If it is big enough, the analysts and investors typically will view the severance and restructuring expenses as *one-time costs* that do not affect the company's long-term run rate. However, this requires CFOs to use this technique judiciously because if restructurings become too common, they will be construed as an ongoing *cost of doing business*, irrespective of the size of the program.
2. Announcing a company-wide program can *remove much of the stigma*, allowing managers to reassure employees that they are not being singled

out. Some areas can be excluded from the program—usually customer-facing positions—but if the program is generally widespread throughout the company, it arguably will encounter less resistance from the people affected.

With the announcement of a restructuring program, the CFO and management team usually can achieve the target reduction in headcount through a systematic review of the company's functions and organizational structure, with the goal of eliminating duplicate or unnecessary activities and streamlining the organization (e.g., by establishing a global rather than a matrix chain of command or by enlarging spans of control and eliminating layers of management).

Often CFOs will work with outside consultants in implementing a restructuring program; the consultants can bring specialized expertise in identifying cost reduction opportunities and can provide discipline and objectivity to the process, mitigating some of the inherent difficulties in eliminating the positions of long-time colleagues.

Scenario Analysis

CFOs also have achieved success through their use of contingency or scenario planning. For example, the CFO can lead an exercise to identify cost savings that could be implemented, if necessary, in response to an unforeseen decline in revenue. If this type of planning is done in advance—often in connection with the preparation of a company's budget or long-term financial projections—the company can act more quickly and decisively in the event that the contingency does occur.

Another example is for the CFO to lead an analytical review of the company's cost base with the same kind of rigor and discipline that would be used by a private equity firm in connection with a management buyout. Consistent with the oft-cited objective to *"spend the company's money as if it's your own,"* this analysis can reveal activities that are "nice to have" versus those that are "mission critical."

Quality Programs

Dating back to the work by W. Edwards Deming in post-war Japan, *Total Quality Management (TQM)* programs have allowed companies to achieve significant and continuous long-term savings through the application of scientifically based programs to revamp processes. TQM programs are generally based on statistical tools that facilitate fact-based decision making and a commitment to continuous improvement throughout the company.

In recent decades, the most well-known programs have been "Six Sigma," which was popularized by Motorola in the 1980s, and "Lean Manufacturing," which evolved from developments in the automotive industry and was publicly embraced by General Electric in the 1990s. In both cases, the programs focus on an analysis of processes and the use of data to streamline the work flow.

Six Sigma seeks to reduce defects to 3.4 per million opportunities. It uses the DMAIC (define, measure, analyze, improve, and control) principles in projects that focus on specific processes or designs. This program typically uses trained facilitators (called "green belts" or "black belts") who work with a project sponsor to produce quantifiable results.

Lean Manufacturing focuses primarily on eliminating waste, which generally relates to any activity or cost that is not valued by the customer. Despite the name, it is not confined to manufacturing operations and can be used to improve any process that involves products or services used by either external or internal customers. It seeks to create processes that are efficient and consistently repeatable throughout a chain of value creation activities.

TQM programs have been shown to produce significant benefits and are valuable arrows in the CFO's quiver of cost-cutting techniques. However, unless properly circumscribed, these programs can become a permanent cost center, offsetting some of the benefits that are generated. Therefore, the best practice is to embed these tools and ways of thinking throughout the company, so that fact-based decision making and continuous improvements become second nature among all of the employees instead of a one-off program.

Continuous Improvements

Even without a formal TQM program, most CFOs believe that it is central to their job description to inculcate a culture of continuous improvement throughout their companies, including their financial organizations. This is particularly true for CFOs in low-margin industries, but cost consciousness is arguably an appropriate mindset for all CFOs. If their primary focus is growth, their efforts to free up costs can fund additional growth strategies or make existing strategies more viable due to the higher margins that can be earned on a new product or service.

Given the fierce competition that exists in most industries, it is axiomatic that CFOs never get complacent—that they openly embrace new technologies, constantly institute new ways of doing things, and ruthlessly jettison those activities and functions that are no longer essential.

FIXED VERSUS VARIABLE COSTS

CFOs are focusing not just on the aggregate size of their company's cost base, but also on its composition—notably the mix between fixed and variable costs. Depending on the characteristics of a company's assets—as well as the volatility of its revenue, earnings, and cash flows—the CFO should establish an appropriate balance of fixed and variable costs, thereby smoothing the company's financial results over a business cycle.

In considering the costs, CFOs typically view employees as largely a fixed cost—at least over the near-term planning horizon. Given the costs of recruiting and training the work force and recognizing the severance and other costs inherent to most work force reductions, CFOs should closely monitor headcounts and consider outsourcing or other contract arrangements—thereby increasing their flexibility in responding to uncertain and possibly volatile business conditions.

Likewise, they should have a point of view concerning the components of the compensation program, especially the mix of fixed versus variable compensation. This mix should reflect and reinforce the company's strategic plan objectives.

For example, using temporary workers can provide much more flexibility than hiring permanent employees and can save considerable costs in a downturn, including severance payments and higher unemployment insurance premiums. Therefore, CFOs may want to target a percentage of the work force that should come from temporary or part-time employees.

In preparing their long-term financial projections, CFOs often will perform sensitivity analyses, including upside and downside business cases. They can gain important insights through these analyses from observing the impact due to costs that are constant versus those that fluctuate. In particular, they can focus on the breakeven rates for earnings and cash flow.

These analyses often can highlight the advantage of moving toward more of a variable cost base, especially given the level of uncertainty that seems to be endemic in the twenty-first century.

 ## NOTE

1. Hund-Mejean, Martina, CFO of MasterCard, in an interview with Avital Louria Hahn of CFO magazine (October 1, 2008, CFO Publishing LLC).

CHAPTER SEVENTEEN

Providing Planning and Analysis

C FOS CAN.ALSO DRIVE BUSINESS performance through the planning and analysis functions that are provided by the financial organization, including budgets and forecasts, which usually are the primary management tools that the CEO and business leaders use to set direction and monitor performance.

In addition, CFOs typically define and monitor performance metrics, measure business performance, and provide business analysis.

 ## BUDGETS

The company's strategic objectives and long-term financial model provide the framework for crafting the annual budget. The CFO is charged with translating this framework into the detailed preparation of each of the line items in the annual budget, including their distribution among manifold profit and cost centers.

It is typically a time-consuming and laborious job, but well worth the effort. It is fundamental to the CFO's playbook, providing direction for the company and serving as an indispensable tool for making tough choices among competing priorities.

Bottoms-Up, Iterative Process

In most companies, the budget is primarily developed through a bottoms-up approach, with the profit and cost centers responsible for preparing their initial estimates for the coming fiscal year. They typically start with a forecast for the current year—which usually has several months to go—consider recent trends, and estimate a "business-as-usual" run rate for the next year.

The next step is to overlay their plans for strategic and business initiatives, as well as their expectations for productivity improvements. This preliminary assessment also includes a tentative estimate of the capital needed to achieve their proposed plans. Thus, the preliminary budget typically is a combination of extrapolating trends and estimating discretionary actions for the next year.

The financial organization then consolidates the numbers into a comprehensive summary, which forms the basis for a series of iterative revisions—typically achieved through review meetings with various levels of management. To facilitate these reviews, it is usually desirable for the CFO to provide as much guidance as possible concerning the targets that the company is striving to achieve.

Eventually, a consensus is formed and, after adding revenue and expense contingencies, the CFO presents the proposed budget to the board of directors for approval. After approval, the budget is then further allocated among the profit and cost centers and divided into quarterly and monthly components.

Benefits of Long-Term Model

Although a company's long-term financial projections typically are driven by top-down formulas rather than bottoms-up calculations, they nevertheless can facilitate the preparation of the annual budget—providing a good starting point for the more detailed and accounting-driven approaches that are used in preparing the budget.

Furthermore, CFOs often find that their long-term financial models can be an effective check and balance against the bottoms-up assumptions that are produced by the budget process; they can help to identify assumptions that may not be realistic or that may be inconsistent with historical relationships. The long-term projections also can indicate either over-optimistic or over-pessimistic biases in the proposed budgets.

Most important, maintaining a long-term financial model can help CFOs instill a culture of continuous adaptation to changes in business and market conditions—rather than being fixated on an annual budget cycle. This helps to perpetuate a culture of rolling forecasts whereby the company is continuously assessing and reacting to its environment, giving the CFO a valuable tool in updating business plans and driving financial performance.

Budget Philosophies

Companies can vary considerably in their approach to projections, with some choosing to establish "*stretch*" targets and others choosing to establish targets that are expected to be met or exceeded each year. Whatever the approach, it is important that CFOs understand the underlying philosophy that prevails throughout the company's culture and that they calibrate the budget projections to avoid communicating plans that are either impossible to achieve or else not sufficiently challenging.

In particular, CFOs should establish "*contingencies*" or "*challenges*," depending on whether the company tends to use aggressive or conservative assumptions. These top-down adjustments can be especially important in setting targets for incentive compensation—to ensure that the management team is incentivized appropriately.

Furthermore, to the extent that CFOs include top-down adjustments in their budget projections, they should make them fully transparent to the management team and board of directors—so that there's no confusion concerning the manner in which the projections have been constructed.

Budget Challenges

Although the budget process is inherently time-consuming—involving substantial give-and- takes among the participants—it is usually a relatively harmonious process. However, the budget preparations also typically feature some challenges that can be particularly vexing to CFOs, including:

Challenge 1: Allowing sufficient time for preparing the budget's financial schedules, but not having the underlying assumptions become too far out of date. Because the budget process typically stretches over several months, the original assumptions may be obsolete by the time that final decisions are being made. For example, the business forecasts will have been updated and there will have been changes to exogenous variables such as foreign exchange and interest rates.

The CFO's typical response is to determine which variables will be updated for the various iterations and to "true up" certain assumptions at the very end of the process.

Challenge 2: The propensity of the business units and staff departments to "low ball" their current year forecasts. Because the budget is often compared with the current year forecast—showing the year-over-year percentage changes—the business leaders may be reluctant to update their forecasts after the budget process begins. In particular, they may want to preserve "cushions" for potential expenses or revenue shortfalls in the current year and not to raise expectations for improved results in the budget year.

In response to this gamesmanship, CFOs can encourage accurate forecasts, while also providing reassurances that this will not result in unrealistic expectations for the next year's budget.

Challenge 3: The tendency to extrapolate trends rather than to consider new priorities and areas of focus. If the business leaders perceive that the budgeting process is primarily the responsibility of the financial organization, it can become a mechanical exercise—with too much emphasis on recent accounting trends rather than on a thoughtful review of growth plans from strategic and business perspectives. Furthermore, the costs may reflect trend lines rather than a zero-based budgeting approach.

To address this issue, CFOs can encourage the personal and active involvement of the CEO and business leaders from the beginning of the budget process, emphasizing their critical role in determining the key assumptions and financial targets.

Challenge 4: Becoming overly preoccupied with intra-company allocations that don't affect the overall financial results. A common frustration is that profit and cost centers may be more focused on negotiating the intra-company allocations of revenues and expenses than on generating income from external sources. While some scrutiny of allocations is healthy, it can easily cross the line into dysfunctional behavior.

In response, CFOs should discourage the preoccupation (and squabbles) regarding allocations. For example, they can advocate a simple, formulaic approach to the allocations and reinforce among the finance professionals that they should be primarily concerned with actions that grow the pie—such as actual cost reductions in shared services—rather than on the size of their slice.

 ## FORECASTS

Forecasts are indispensable tools for managing the business. They highlight where the business is on track or off track, indicate issues that may require remedial actions, and guide management's communications with the board of directors and shareholders. Without timely and reliable forecasts, management would be sailing blindly through some tempestuous waters, especially given the volatility in the financial markets.

The first question is *how often* to produce the forecasts? And the second question is *how detailed* should the forecasts be? For most CFOs, there is a tradeoff between the frequency of the forecasts and their level of details.

Most companies opt for monthly reports, although some of the months may consist of a limited *"flash"* forecast that focuses solely on revenue and operating profit rather than on a full-scale forecast that contains all of the income statement line items. It can be argued that monthly forecasts may be excessive—especially if much of the company's revenue is recorded in the last month of the quarter—and flash forecasts can provide a reasonable compromise for some of the periods.

Another issue concerns the timing of the forecasts, with CEOs and business leaders typically wanting to receive information that is fully up-to-date as of the day they receive the report. However, this usually doesn't allow the finance professionals time to analyze the results and to recommend any corrective actions. Automating and simplifying the forecasting methodologies can mitigate the *speed versus analysis* issue, but there likely will always be a trade-off between the two objectives—a trade-off that seems to come with the territory.

The best practice is to get the results out in a summary format and to be ready with details—unless it is a flash forecast—in response to questions. Another best practice is for CFOs to design forecasts that call attention to material variances from the budget—thereby facilitating quick responses—and to highlight the external as well as the company-specific factors that are significantly affecting the results.

It is also helpful for CFOs to indicate the major changes from the prior forecast, thus providing a snapshot of whether conditions are trending better or worse. Many CFOs choose to color code this type of reporting.

Risks and Opportunities

Forecasts typically represent point estimates rather than a range of potential results. Therefore, a best practice is for CFOs to summarize risks and opportunities that can affect the estimates. The *risks* typically can include potential revenue shortfalls, expense contingencies, or unfavorable movements in external variables such as currencies, while the *opportunities* are the converse, such as revenue upsides, expense reductions, and favorable currency movements.

Some CFOs strive to have the risks *equal* the opportunities, thus having the net impact consistent with the official forecast. The other alternative is to have unequal risks and opportunities, thereby indicating whether there is an *asymmetric* probability that the actual results will exceed or fall short of the official forecast.

Rolling Quarterly Forecasts

As another best practice, CFOs will regularly prepare rolling forecasts for the next four quarters. The advantages from this approach include:

- It reinforces the discipline of continuously revising assumptions and expectations in response to changing conditions.
- It highlights seasonal or special conditions that apply to an upcoming quarter, causing it to veer from the trend lines.
- It indicates the need for action steps in anticipation of potential shortfalls or other issues in the foreseeable future.
- It facilitates the preparation of budgets, which can use the current rolling forecast as a starting point for analysis.

However, most companies are oriented toward an annual budgeting process and do not apply the same kind of rigor to their rolling forecasts, which easily can degenerate into mere extrapolations. Therefore, it is important for CFOs to emphasize the need for careful review of the assumptions, although recognizing that they may reflect more top down estimates than used in budget preparations.

 CASH FLOWS

Traditionally, most companies have been focused primarily on income statement projections in their budgeting and forecasting activities. This can result in a disconnect with their shareholders, who typically are highly interested in cash flow and balance sheet results.

The owners of private companies—especially start-ups or highly leveraged businesses—are usually focused on cash flow due to their relatively high cost of capital and perhaps their limited access to short-term liquidity. And the shareholders of public companies usually use free cash flow as an important indicator in their stock price valuations.

The typical explanation for a lesser focus on cash flow and balance sheet data is the lack of systems that can produce timely information. This may be a legitimate concern. However, if at all possible, CFOs should seek to improve their cash flow and balance sheet reporting and to require cash flows in their regular forecasts. In addition, the best practice is to include cash flow projections in the annual budgets, as well as to link them with incentive compensation objectives.

In particular, business units should regularly budget and forecast their working capital and capital expenditure requirements.

Working Capital

By including working capital as a regular part of their budgeting and forecasting systems, CFOs can encourage greater management focus on potential action steps to enhance free cash flow. Otherwise, working capital projections can become an afterthought, perhaps extrapolated from recent trend lines, rather than line items that receive regular scrutiny.

At a minimum, every forecast and budget should specifically include targets for accounts receivable, trade payables, and inventory.

Capital Expenditures

Likewise, capital expenditures should be budgeted and forecasted regularly. First, this will ensure that project sponsors are focused on the total cash flow impact of their projects rather than on the amounts that are reflected in the income statement during the period. The cash outflow represents the true economic cost, irrespective of how much is capitalized versus the amount that is expensed.

Second, capital expenditures are often an area where the actual cash spending falls short of the budgeted amounts—usually due to projects taking longer to implement than originally estimated. Project sponsors may be reluctant to forecast these shortfalls, fearing that they will be giving up the possibility of using the money as planned.

If CFOs can encourage good faith assessments of the actual spending rates, this can result in better cash flow projections, which in turn can facilitate better capital allocation decisions.

 PERFORMANCE METRICS

Having established the company's strategic objectives and formulated a long-term financial model, CFOs should partner with the CEO and management team to determine the key financial and operational metrics that the financial organization will monitor on a regular basis. Depending on the metric, these key performance indicators typically will be updated and reviewed on a daily, weekly, monthly, or quarterly basis.

In this way, the CFO can help ensure that the company is not only focusing on its current results, but also on the factors that will drive its results in the future—indicating areas where the company is performing well and creating an early warning system for potential problems. Also, the simple process of choosing and monitoring metrics will greatly influence behavior—presumably reinforcing the company's strategic priorities.

Number of Metrics

While there is no magic number concerning the number of metrics, the goal should be to identify the key performance indicators in a *"dashboard"* or *"score-card"* that is regularly reviewed in management meetings. Generally, it is better to have fewer rather than more metrics, but to make more detailed metrics available as back-up information.

The fewer the metrics, the more likely they will be treated as a top priority. Furthermore, having fewer metrics helps center the management reviews on potential responses to the information rather than on a recitation of data. The CFO should seek to identify the trends indicated by the metrics, determine what are likely to be the underlying causes for these trends, and recommend action steps to be analyzed and then implemented—preferably as soon as practicable.

In most cases, companies will have a *hierarchy* of metrics that are used for alternative purposes. At the top of the hierarchy are metrics used by the board of directors in their review of executive compensation. The next level is metrics that are regularly reviewed by the CEO and the management team. And then there are the more specific and usually more numerous metrics that are monitored by the various business units and staff departments. The levels of metrics in this hierarchy should be linked to each other, as well as to the company's strategic objectives and long-term financial model.

Dashboard Format

In designing their dashboard formats, some companies prefer graphs, while others prefer numerical data, or a combination of the two. Whatever the format, the important point is that the dashboard should be easily read and composed of metrics that the management team can directly influence. In other words, they should primarily reflect the key drivers of the company's business model— such as the acquisition, retention, and satisfaction of customers; revenue and product mix per customer; fixed and variable cost ratios; or employee head- counts—and not focused on exogenous variables that are outside of manage- ment's sphere of influence.

Many companies like to use a green/yellow/red color code to highlight the status of the metrics against previously agreed benchmarks or targets. This is particularly useful when companies use a large number of metrics and need a vehicle for easily identifying the outliers.

CFOs should also be flexible with respect to the formats for ad hoc reports. The goal should be to communicate simply and effectively—based on the target audience and the purpose for the report—and to avoid an excess of superfluous information.

Financial Metrics

Of course, financial metrics typically will form the core of the dashboard. How- ever, CFOs should resist the temptation to include a vast number of financial metrics—essentially replicating the financial statements. Instead, they should focus on the key drivers of the stock price.

The CFO should selectively focus on the most salient measurements, with the knowledge that more detailed information is available to expand the analy- sis of financial results. In particular, they should include metrics that are used in the CEO's incentive compensation and the metrics that have been identified as performance drivers in the strategic plan.

Non-Financial Metrics

CFOs should also focus on non-financial metrics that are the underlying drivers of financial performance. Because of the intrinsic differences among industries and in light of the variety of business strategies that may be pursued, these non-financial metrics can reflect a wide gamut of possibilities. Some examples include:

Operational Metrics
- Safety incidents or lost-time workplace accidents
- Waste percentages or other quality measures
- Capacity utilization or production statistics
- Network down times or service failures
- Sustainability metrics and ratings

Customer Metrics
- Number of customers or accounts
- Customer satisfaction surveys
- Number of products per customer
- Revenue per customer or account

Employee Metrics
- Revenue per employee
- Total or change in headcount
- Scores in "engagement" surveys
- Voluntary turnover percentages
- Diversity percentages or totals
- Percentage of temporary employees

Innovation Metrics
- Patents or copyrights received
- Number of new products launched
- Ratings from industry analysts

Marketing Metrics
- Market shares for key products
- Brand awareness surveys
- Unique visitors to website

Continuity

CFOs should encourage continuity in the performance metrics that are included in the company's dashboard, with the bulk of the metrics being consistent from one year to the next. This reinforces a focus on long-term as well as short-term action plans.

They also should seek clarity and consistency in the definitions of the metrics. This will limit any ambiguity in measuring the company's progress against its targets.

 ## BUSINESS UNIT METRICS

The performance metrics for the business units usually will reflect subsets of the corporate metrics and specific metrics that apply uniquely to them. In other words, their performance metrics will be a combination that represents both the company's overall strategic objectives and their particular business strategies.

In evaluating business unit financial performance, CFOs normally use *net operating profit after-tax (NOPAT)* as the primary measurement. Many CFOs also add a capital charge based on the business unit's net assets to compute its *economic profit* or *economic value added (EVA)*. The capital charge is normally equal to the company's weighted-average cost of capital.

EVA is a concept that was popularized by the consulting firm Stern Stewart. In addition to applying a cost of capital to the business unit results, CFOs using EVA also may adjust the results to reflect the long-term economics of certain expenditures. For example, they may capitalize and amortize research and development spending or marketing and advertising investments.

In some industries, CFOs evaluate the business units by their *EBITDA*, especially if cash generation is a primary determinant of shareholder value. Increasingly, CFOs also are measuring *free cash flow*, which highlights which business units are generating cash versus the business units that are net consumers of cash.

CFOs typically exclude the effects of currency movements in measuring business unit results and may exclude the impact of new acquisitions and divestitures, as well as certain expenses such as restructuring charges, litigation settlements, or significant asset write-offs that are deemed to be corporate, rather than business unit, decisions.

The CFO's challenges are to ensure that the business unit measures are incentivizing management in positive ways, that the measures are consistently applied throughout the company's operations, and that the methodologies support the company's overarching goal of creating shareholder value. They also should use measures that are easily understood by the business leaders, who may have limited backgrounds in finance and accounting.

PERFORMANCE REPORTS

The typical routine in most companies is for the financial organization to produce monthly reports that show how the business performance compares with the budget and the most recent forecast. In producing these reports, the primary emphasis usually is on timely reporting rather than on thorough analysis; receiving the information quickly is normally the business leaders' first priority, with the analysis to follow.

The reports usually consist of the actual financial results for each profit and cost center, along with a simple variance analysis for each line item against the budget, forecast, and prior period (usually the same month in the prior year). The reports typically will also show the quarter-to-date and year-to-date comparisons.

These reports are normally fairly detailed; thus CFOs typically will design a method for highlighting the material variances—often through a color-coded scheme. This facilitates prompt identification of key issues, usually leading to requests for additional data and analysis concerning the factors that underlie the variances. The paramount objective is to determine whether any shortfalls are caused by factors under management's control and to take action steps to rectify the issues.

In addition, the reports usually will include an update of the company's performance metrics. And as a best practice, they will show the company's progress against the targets that have been established for incentive compensation.

Essential FP&A Qualities

In a briefing paper published in 2011 by the American Productivity & Quality Center (APQC) Mary Driscoll listed "The Seven Essential Qualities of a Winning Financial Planning and Analysis Professional"[a]:

1. Deep knowledge of accounting and performance management
2. Strong grasp of business strategy, functions, markets, and risks
3. Mastery of systems, analytical tools, and data management
4. Can design reports and self-service tools business managers will use
5. Versatile and polished communication skills
6. Customer service orientation
7. Insatiable desire to solve business puzzles

[a]*www.apqc.org*

BUSINESS ANALYSIS

In addition to the business support that is regularly provided through budgets, forecasts, and performance reports, CFOs will become involved with specific business issues—usually involving potential action steps to increase revenue or reduce costs.

To a large extent, CFOs typically will be responding to requests that are made by the business units or reacting to issues or opportunities that have arisen through the performance reports. In addition, they can initiate activities in support of the business objectives. For example, they can focus resources, review cost accounting assumptions, and sponsor "deep dive" reviews.

Focused Resources

In essence, CFOs have the mandate to serve their business clients effectively and efficiently—producing information and analysis that is easily understood, focused on the essential facts, and presented in a manner that can lead to concrete action steps. Put simply, an analysis is only worthwhile if it is valued and used by the CFO's business clients; otherwise, it can become a report that is generated routinely, but which has limited utility in comparison with alternative priorities for the financial organization.

Consistent with this mandate, CFOs should strive to eliminate unnecessary reports. An effective technique used by many CFOs is to suspend the production of some reports on a regular basis, thus ascertaining whether there is sufficient demand to have them reinstated. Often the reports are not missed at all.

The systematic process of culling unnecessary reports is particularly effective when there has been a change in leadership within a business unit. Each leader will tend to focus on different performance metrics and unless the financial organization makes a concerted effort to eliminate some of the old reports, it will be challenged to meet both the old and the new reporting requirements—leaving little time to perform value added business analysis.

Likewise, the financial organization needs to be judicious in agreeing to tailor reports for the particular preferences of each line manager. CFOs should encourage as much standardization as possible; otherwise, the financial organization can be overwhelmed by requests for bespoke formats, which can cause quality and productivity to deteriorate.

In other words, providing good client service doesn't mean that CFOs need to comply with every business unit request. Instead, it is generally healthy to encourage creative tension between the providers and the users of the analytical information.

The bottom line is that CFOs can provide more and better business support if they can redirect and concentrate existing resources.

Cost Accounting

Of course, cost accounting is fundamental to much business analysis, especially the calculation of profitability by product line or customer. CFOs should periodically review the assumptions that drive these calculations—including the allocations of revenue and costs among products and customers—and ensure that they are providing fair representations of the marginal economics.

Because extremely detailed assumptions often are hard-wired into their cost accounting systems, CFOs may want to take a conceptual, rather than a detailed approach from time to time—reviewing the way the formulas are constructed. In some cases, it may be useful for the CFO to make some back-of-the envelope calculations that are admittedly less precise than the computer-generated reports, but which may offer business insights due to the simplified approach and the focus on a few key variables.

Deep Dives

As a final example, CFOs can sponsor a deep dive review of a particular topic, giving finance professionals the chance to analyze a high impact issue and testing their potential to add greater value to the company's business objectives. Unfortunately, these opportunities may not arise naturally due to the exigencies of daily responsibilities. Therefore, CFOs will often need to take proactive steps to help make this happen.

For example, the CFO can partner with a business leader in sponsoring reviews of product line profit margins, cost comparisons against competitor benchmarks, pricing strategies for different customer segments, or potential investments in marketing or sales incentive programs. This gives the finance professionals a chance to step back from their daily routines and to make a value enhancing contribution to the business strategies.

In some cases, CFOs may want to engage consultants to assist with a deep dive; they can provide impetus to the project, offer fresh perspectives, bring specialized expertise, and share best practices from their other clients. However, CFOs usually will want to explicitly define the extent of their engagement—avoiding scope creep—and center the project on specific business issues rather than on broad industry studies.

CHAPTER EIGHTEEN

Managing Financial Risks and Taxes

C FOS CAN DIRECTLY IMPACT THE COMPANY'S financial performance through their management of financial risks and taxes. In managing these key functions, they are pursuing the twin goals of lowering costs and reducing volatility.

Both of these objectives can add shareholder value, but they often entail tradeoffs that the CFO must weigh carefully.

 ## INSURANCE

Purchasing third-party insurance is one of the most common mitigation strategies employed by companies against their enterprise risk exposures. Managing the insurance program is normally within the purview of the CFO, who is responsible for recommending the types and amounts of insurance to acquire and the amount of risk to be retained through self-insurance and deductibles. In addition, the CFO normally will partner with the general counsel in negotiating the terms for the policies that are purchased.

Types of Insurance

For most companies, the insurance policies typically will include:

- **Property and Casualty:** Protection against physical loss and business interruption.
- **Liability:** Protection for product, auto, and other liability exposures.
- **Workers Compensation:** Coverage that meets state law or other mandates.
- **Group Life, Health, and Disability:** Coverage for employees in their benefits package.
- **Directors and Officers:** Protection for the company as well as individual directors and officers (Side A coverage) against shareholder claims and other lawsuits.
- **Umbrella:** Excess coverage above the limits in the other insurance policies.

Depending on a company's business profile, it also may acquire *errors and omissions* insurance or a *surety bond,* as well as policies for specialized purposes such as *aviation, marine,* or *boiler and machinery* insurance.

Insurance Brokers

Because purchasing insurance requires highly specialized expertise, CFOs typically will engage insurance brokers, who can recommend programs based on current conditions in the market and help them obtain competitive rates and terms. The brokers also will assist in major insurance claims.

Working with their insurance broker, CFOs will determine the best combination of self-insurance versus third-party protection. They then will obtain the insurance policies, with their choice of insurer typically based on the amount of coverage and price that is quoted, the insurer's reputation in the marketplace, the insurer's financial strength, the company's prior experience with the insurer, and the proposed terms.

The policy terms can be especially important, such as the coverage that is excluded and the way that damages are calculated. For example, property insurance might exclude claims due to damage from mildew; casualty insurance might exclude floods, earthquakes, terrorism, and other perils; and business interruption insurance might not reimburse the company for allocated overhead costs.

Captive Insurance Companies

CFOs also will determine strategies for administering the risk exposures that are retained by the company, including the most cost-effective way to manage claims. Also, many CFOs believe that self-insurance results in greater focus on reducing the number of claims and lowering the costs per claim.

Depending on the size and scope of their program, CFOs often can save costs by establishing a captive insurance company. They are frequently based in Bermuda, which has a well-developed infrastructure for providing outsourcing services to captives. A captive can also be established in the United States, with many located in Vermont due to state government support and an established infrastructure.

Tax savings are usually important considerations in deciding whether to establish a captive and where it should be located.

Reduction of Losses

As a best practice, CFOs will sponsor programs to reduce losses. These programs can result in cost savings for the risks retained through self-insurance or deductibles, and lower premiums for the risks covered by insurance policies. Some examples include:

- *Safety programs* to reduce lost time incidents and workers compensation costs.
- *Preventive maintenance programs* to reduce property claims for manufacturing or other facilities.
- *Reviews of facility locations* to highlight potential casualty risks and consider possible reconfigurations, including backup arrangements.
- *Disaster recovery plans* to mitigate the potential loss from business interruption.
- *Product quality programs* to reduce the risk of liability claims.
- *Employee training programs* to reduce the risk of errors and omissions.
- *Limits of liability* that are established through customer contracts.
- *Corporate governance policies* that reduce the risks of shareholder lawsuits.

By setting company-wide goals for reducing losses, CFOs can make a notable difference in their cost of risk. It is a major cost category for most companies and worthy of special focus by the CFO and the management team.

This should also be a priority for the company's enterprise risk management program.

Cultivation of Insurers

CFOs can influence both the availability and cost of their insurance by keeping their brokers and insurers informed about the company's financial condition and the steps that the company has taken to reduce risks. For example, the CFO can describe the company's efforts to reduce incidents, such as the implementation of product quality programs that can affect its liability exposure.

Cultivating active communications with insurers can be especially important for companies that are experiencing financial difficulties. CFOs can reassure them that the company is taking steps to address the financial issues and that it fully intends to sustain good management standards and procedures going forward. Otherwise, the insurers may be concerned that the company will neglect its maintenance or other preventive programs.

INTEREST RATES

Managing the company's exposure to fluctuating interest rates is central to the CFO's capital structure strategies; the CFO seeks to strike the right balance between obtaining low-cost capital and exposing the company to interest rate risk. On the one hand, fixed rate debt normally is more costly than floating rate debt. On the other hand, it is less risky, especially during times of market turbulence, which seem to be occurring more frequently and with greater severity.

CFOs should perform sensitivity analyses to determine the company's interest rate expense under various economic and business scenarios—identifying the potential impacts, not only to the company's income and cash flows, but also to its credit statistics and debt ratings. In performing these sensitivity analyses, the CFO will want to take into account any correlations between interest rate conditions (especially the shape of the yield curve) and their company's business outlook.

For example, if a company is in an economically sensitive business—such as an industrial or commodity business—this may work as a natural hedge against higher interest rates, with the greater revenue and profit in a growth environment offsetting the higher interest expense.

Conversely, a company's business outlook may be inversely correlated with the level of interest rates, meaning that a rise in rates will adversely affect the company, not only in higher interest expense, but also through lower operating income. The revenue of home builders, for example, is negatively impacted by higher rates, indicating that they should be cautious in using floating rate financing.

In addition, if a company has limited ability to pass through price increases, it will be more vulnerable to inflation, which is usually correlated with higher interest rates. However, if the company has pricing power, the CFO can be more comfortable in employing floating rate debt.

 ## CURRENCIES

Currency exposure is another financial risk that is managed by the CFO. This includes transaction exposures, which impact a company's cash flow, and translation exposures, which impact the accounting results due to the translation of revenue, expenses, and balance sheet items that are denominated in foreign currencies.

Hedging Policies

As a general observation, most CFOs will consider hedging transaction exposures but will not hedge translation exposures. They reason that hedging should be focused on *economic* exposures, which generally are defined to be cash rather than accounting results.

For example, they may enter into forward contracts for part or all of their forecasted cross-border revenues and expenses, usually through a centralized treasury function that nets the currency exposures throughout a global company. They also may hedge payments that are scheduled to be made in a foreign currency in the near future (e.g., a cross-border acquisition). Also, companies that receive substantial royalties from foreign locations may hedge their forecasted cash receipts or they may hedge a dividend payment that is anticipated from an international subsidiary.

CFOs also will establish policies for how much of their transaction exposures will be hedged under normal circumstances. These policies can include:

- Hedging 100 percent of the net exposures.
- Hedging a portion of the net exposures (say, 50 percent).
- Not hedging unless an exposure is material or unusual.

They usually will analyze their currency risks on a company-wide basis; they will offset the pluses and minuses for each currency and then analyze the net exposures under alternative scenarios. Although a currency exposure may be material to an individual country or business unit, its net impact may not be material to the company as a whole, in which case hedging strategies may not be warranted.

Hedging Transactions

If CFOs decide to hedge their transaction exposures, the best practice is to centralize the implementation within the corporate treasury group. Often the company will work with a bank to establish a netting system through which the exposures are offset against each other, with only the residue risks being hedged through a *forward* contract, a *swap*, an *option*, or a combination of a swap and an option (a *swaption*).

The most common hedging transaction is a forward contract, which is the purchase or sale of the currency on a future date that matches the estimated timing of the cash inflow or outflow. It can be accomplished through an over the counter transaction with a bank or through a futures contract on an exchange (such as the Chicago Mercantile Exchange).

Netting can substantially reduce the cost and complexity of hedging strategies; it can be implemented unilaterally (within a single company) or in conjunction with other companies (through a bilateral or multilateral netting system).

As an alternative, hedging can also be accomplished by investing excess cash in the currency or borrowing in the currency through a short-term credit line.

In most companies, the hedging activities are conducted as a risk mitigation strategy and not as a profit center. Normally, they will not enter into a futures transaction unless there is an underlying transaction that is being hedged—and they will prohibit *speculation* on currency movements.

However, CFOs may consider currency outlooks in the execution of their hedging strategies. For example, they may decide to hedge only a portion of their exposures or they may decide to use an option rather than a forward contract.

Long-Term Planning

While CFOs usually do not hedge their translation exposures, they will consider these exposures in their long-term business planning. For example, a decision where to locate a processing center or a research facility may be partially motivated by the outlook for the local currency.

Generally, it is better to locate cost centers in a country with a depreciating currency. However, if the cash will be trapped in a local currency due to tax or other constraints, then the depreciating currency can be a disadvantage due to the declining value of the cash.

Moreover, any investments in fixed assets in a country with a weak currency will decline in value over time, which will be reflected in *other comprehensive income.* This reduces shareholders' equity, but does not affect net income or cash flow.

 ## COMMODITIES

For many CFOs, raw materials can represent a significant component of their cost structure and a major exposure to cyclical and systemic risks. This raises the question whether they should seek to manage this exposure.

Formerly, companies often hedged their raw material pricing through vertical integration. However, as part of the move toward more pure play investments, companies generally have been deemphasizing ownership of their raw materials. For example, media companies have divested their newsprint plants, and DuPont abandoned its strategy of backward integration into oil (through its spinoff of Conoco).

The strategic bias today is not to integrate operations that involve different financial characteristics and that require different management skills. Also, investors can diversify their exposures to commodities through their investment portfolio. Therefore, companies tend not to own their raw material suppliers, but regularly provide information to investors concerning the size and nature of their exposures, including the sensitivity of their profits to commodity price movements.

Hedging Strategies

For commodities with active futures markets—such as oil, farm products, and metals—CFOs may consider hedging part or all of their exposures through forwards or options. They typically will consider not only their expectations for future price movements, but also the relative costs of the contracts. For example, they will consider the shape of the forward curve—whether the future price is greater than the spot price (*contango*) or lower than the spot price (*backwardation*). In addition, the relative cost of options will reflect the market's expectations for volatility.

CFOs will also consider whether competitors are hedging their exposures. For example, a transportation company may place itself in a competitive disadvantage if it is the only company that hedges its exposure to the price of oil. If oil prices escalate, the CFO is a hero, but if the price declines sharply, the company may not be able to match competitors' pricing strategies. As an alternative to hedging through the futures markets, CFOs may pursue hedging strategies through long-term contracts with their suppliers. For example, they can specify fixed prices or can establish floors and ceilings, or perhaps construct a formula that shares the impact from market price changes between the parties to the agreement.

In any event, it is probably a good idea for CFOs to let investors know the parameters of the company's hedging strategies so that they can build this variable into their earnings model.

 ## INFLATION

Although relatively quiescent in recent decades, inflation historically has been a significant financial risk for most companies, with the possibility of destroying considerable value and creating troublesome management challenges. The 1970s were a particularly vexing period for CFOs in the United States due to the combination of high inflation and a sluggish economy—causing "*stagflation*" to become part of their lexicon and high on their list of chronic worries. Moreover, if operations are located in countries with histories of hyper inflation, CFOs need to be continuously on guard against value erosion.

Given the expansionary fiscal and monetary strategies being implemented throughout Europe and the United States, there is at least a reasonable chance of an acceleration of inflationary pressures—perhaps not to the same degree as in the past, but certainly at higher levels than being experienced currently. And emerging countries will be challenged to sustain their high growth rates without igniting wage pressures and other root causes of inflation.

Possible Strategies

In response, CFOs undoubtedly will be analyzing their company's potential exposures to inflation—determining the potential impacts on revenue and costs, including wages. After analyzing their exposure to inflation scenarios, they then can consider what responses might be appropriate—either in anticipation of a potential issue or as a contingency if inflation resurfaces in the future.

These action steps can include structural changes to the company's business model, such as its pricing formulas, its payment terms, its supply chain arrangements, or the location of its facilities. CFOs also can explore alternative work force strategies, such as modifications to the compensation packages, more or less use of outsourcing arrangements, or more investments in automation and other labor saving technologies.

In addition, many CFOs are taking advantage of historically low interest rates to obtain long-term debt at fixed rates, either to refinance existing debt or to obtain new debt financing—thus providing some protection against the possibility that inflation will cause interest rates to rise in the future. Given the massive fiscal deficits, locking in fixed rates seems like a good bet and a prudent hedge against a revival of inflation in the future.

 ## PENSION FUND

For companies with legacy pension plans that pay defined benefits, the volatility of interest rates and stock prices can represent a significant financial exposure: If their unfunded liabilities increase, this equates to a debt obligation that must be repaid over time.

The liabilities in the pension plan will increase with a decline in interest rates and the assets will decrease in tandem with the stock market: exactly the conditions that prevailed during the financial crisis, causing a surge in unfunded liabilities. This was a wakeup call to many CFOs, highlighting a financial exposure that they would like to mitigate or even eliminate. They generally are considering two strategies: shifting to defined contributions and matching assets and liabilities.

Shifting to Defined Contributions

The first mitigation strategy is to shift the benefit plans to defined contribution payments. This can involve the substitution of greater 401(k) matching or other defined contribution arrangements for all new hires and freezing pension fund accruals for existing employees, perhaps with a grandfather provision to allow the accumulation of additional benefits for a set number of years or through a formula based on the ages of the employees.

However, while these structural changes can gradually reduce the accumulation of liabilities over time, they do not address the legacy obligations, which represent the bulk of most companies' exposure. Furthermore, the changes will be unpopular among existing employees, perhaps creating morale or even retention issues. Therefore, CFOs should be mindful of the potential impact on their company's human resource strategies, including their employee value proposition.

Matching Assets and Liabilities

The second mitigation strategy—which can address both legacy and new pension fund exposures—is to achieve greater matching of assets and liabilities. This strategy involves funding the pension funds with securities that *match the duration* of the liabilities owed to pensioners. This generally means increasing the assets that are held as debt rather than equity securities and increasing the average maturity and duration of the debt securities.

In addition to reducing the volatility of the company's earnings, matching the duration also ameliorates the risk of having to inject additional contributions in the future. Thus, it has cash flow as well as accounting advantages.

However, implementation of this second strategy has a practical constraint: The rate of return assumption that is used in the calculation of unfunded liabilities is based on the mix of assets held in the portfolio. Because equities are assumed to have higher returns than debt, the shift to more debt will cause a decline in the assumed rate of return, thus increasing the unfunded liabilities and the reported pension expense (but not affecting cash flow).

Given this constraint, CFOs generally are reconciled to a *gradual* shift in their pension fund assets, considering any increases in stock values or interest rates as opportunities to rebalance a portion of their portfolios. In addition, they are making voluntary contributions to the pension fund, thus providing more flexibility to modify the portfolio's composition without increasing the net amount of unfunded liabilities.

TAX PLANNING

Another way that CFOs can directly drive financial performance is through tax planning, which can dramatically impact a company's effective tax rate and net income, as well as generate substantial free cash flow through tax credits and deferrals.

Of course, tax planning professionals are the consummate examples of people who require highly specialized expertise; and unless CFOs have come up through the tax function, they are unlikely to add much value in the identification and analysis of potential tax planning strategies. Nevertheless, CFOs can make positive contributions through their oversight of the tax responsibilities.

Policies and Objectives

CFOs can provide overall leadership to the company's tax function, establishing policies and objectives that seek to strike the right balance between risk and reward. For example, tax strategies may produce demonstrable near-term benefits, but may involve exposures to unfavorable tax audits or may constrain the company's future flexibility due to the legal structures that are required for implementation.

In the current environment, CFOs need to communicate their philosophy concerning aggressive tax planning initiatives. For example, to what extent is the company willing to consider complex strategies that have not been specifically approved by the tax authorities, but which are supported by opinions from law firms? Or, what is the company's attitude toward the location of activities in offshore jurisdictions strictly for tax avoidance purposes?

Because tax planning decisions can have political and business ramifications—especially for companies that do much of their business with governmental entities—it is essential that these considerations be factored into the tax planning equation.

The bottom line is that CFOs should nurture and encourage creativity among tax professionals, while also providing guidance and context for using their skill sets in the best way possible.

Curbs on Complexity

CFOs can also help to moderate the natural tendency of tax planning strategies to become excessively complex. Over the years, most companies tend to overlay tax strategies that respond to specific circumstances and opportunities. Especially for long-established multinationals, these strategies tend to build upon one another, resulting in an organization chart for tax entities that becomes mind-bogglingly complicated—with boxes and lines crisscrossing each other like an Etch-A-Sketch gone wild.

Unfortunately, the complexities of these "spaghetti" charts have a cost, not only in the fees paid to audit the various legal entities, but more significantly, in the control issues that can arise from the proliferation of reporting requirements. This control risk is particularly pronounced if a company has experienced turnover in the tax function or has failed to document the transactions adequately. In response, CFOs should:

- **Document:** Request that all of the entities and reporting requirements be documented, including an explanation of the reasons for each entity's existence.
- **Eliminate:** Initiate periodic reviews of the tax entities to determine if some can be eliminated or if their ownership structures can be simplified.
- **Constrain:** Exercise caution in the establishment of additional entities (e.g., in connection with an acquisition) with a relatively high burden of proof to add more complexity.

Complexity can also make it difficult to get answers to seemingly simple questions. By aptitude and training, tax professionals often are very detail-oriented and reluctant to offer imprecise conclusions. However, this preference to perform a complete analysis—with full consideration of all the possible permutations—can impede broader decision making (e.g., a decision whether to repatriate cash from a foreign location).

In response, CFOs can encourage tax professionals to provide *"ballpark"* answers—with the details to come later—and reassure them that there will be no recriminations if their initial estimates are subsequently revised.

Holistic Analyses

In a similar vein, CFOs can help ensure that tax decisions reflect a full range of considerations, not just the likely tax impact. For example, tax profession-als may conclude that cash should not be repatriated from a foreign location because it would have a net tax cost. However, a more holistic analysis might conclude that because of the differential between the company's cost of capital versus what is being earned on the trapped cash, it may be desirable to absorb the tax cost and return the cash to shareholders.

The CFO is in a good position to know when there are competing consid-erations in a decision and can help ensure that all of these considerations are vetted in the analysis of alternatives. In addition, CFOs can encourage active coordination among the tax, treasury, controller, and financial planning func-tions in their review of tax planning strategies.

Net Operating Losses

CFOs can also play a leadership role in preserving and maximizing the value of tax assets, such as net operating losses (NOLs) that can shelter future income.

Although the tax rules in the United States specify that a company has 20 years to utilize its NOLs, from a practical perspective these tax assets will be subject to a valuation allowance if they are not expected to be utilized in a more foreseeable time period. Therefore, given this potential accounting issue and considering the time value of money, CFOs will want to consider strategies for accelerating their usage. Making more pre-tax income is the best strategy, but transactional strategies also should be considered.

For example, the availability of NOLs may make a divestiture more desir-able than otherwise: The company likely will be able to offset any gain on the sale and the buyer likely will pay a higher price due to a write-up of the tax basis of the assets being sold. Moreover, even in the case of a stock deal, the sale can be characterized as an asset transaction for tax purposes (a *Section 338(h)(10) election*).

In addition, CFOs can consider leasing transactions—including sale/leasebacks—or joint venture arrangements that utilize the NOLs. They also can consider prepaying debt to reduce interest expense and perhaps record a taxable gain on the transaction.

Another potential issue with NOLs is the restriction on their use in the event of a change of control (*a Section 382 transaction*). This applies to a sale of the company, but it also can be triggered if a majority ownership stake is accumulated by 5 percent holders during a three year period. If this provision becomes applicable, then the annual use of the NOLs becomes subject to a ceiling that is based generally on the prevailing municipal bond rate and the company's market value at the time of the ownership change. This is one more reason why it is desirable to use NOLs as soon as possible.

Transfer Pricing

With the differences in tax rates throughout the world, much value can be created by recording profits in lower tax countries. Therefore, CFOs typically will focus on transfer pricing among the locations.

The basic standard is that the transfer pricing should reflect a market rate. In some cases, the goods or services will have a market value that can be verified objectively, but more likely the value will be estimated, involving some subjectivity.

From time to time, the CFO should initiate a review of the company's transfer pricing policies —identifying opportunities where the pricing should be changed. This review should involve the business units involved since any changes in the transfer pricing for tax purposes generally should be reflected in the accounting assumptions as well.

Deductions and Credits

With all of the complexities of national tax codes throughout the world—as well as all of the state and local tax jurisdictions in the United States—it is difficult to keep track of the plethora of incentive programs that may apply to a company's activities. And with the various attempts to stimulate the economy, new opportunities keep arising.

There is real money to be harvested from these programs (e.g., subsidies for hiring new workers, for investing in research and development, or for taking environmentally friendly actions). However, taking advantage of these programs often requires extensive investigation and documentation, and the data typically is not easily retrieved from the company's information technology systems.

CFOs can sponsor projects to capture the potential rewards, ensuring that someone is personally accountable and that there are sufficient resources committed. Also, they can establish targets for realizing benefits and enlist additional internal support (e.g., from the human resources and information technology departments).

In some cases, CFOs may decide to hire a third-party firm that will invest the resources and apply the expertise to obtain the tax benefits. They usually will provide these services in exchange for a share of the proceeds.

Tax Compliance

While CFOs definitely should take advantage of any potential benefits from the tax codes, they should also ensure that the company is fully compliant with its obligations to collect taxes. This is especially true with respect to state taxes in the United States.

Given their financial woes, states are imposing new taxes—such as sales taxes on online sales—and are employing third-party firms to audit compliance with respect to a wide range of taxes and fees. For example, companies are being audited with respect to their escheatment practices.

Also, cross-border transfer pricing is becoming subject to more scrutiny. Thus, as CFOs review their transfer prices, they should also ensure that the company is complying with the requirements for calculating and documenting the pricing.

Tax Reform

Finally, CFOs should be contemplating the ramifications of potential changes in the tax rules. This is especially timely given the possibility of corporate tax reform in the United States. For example, what would be the impact if the United States changes to a territorial rather than a global tax system? Or what would be the ramifications if reforms are enacted to eliminate various deductions in exchange for a lower tax rate?

Understanding the company's sensitivity to the various possibilities in tax reform can help CFOs to consider potential action steps. They also will be more prepared to address investor questions concerning the direction and magnitude of the potential impacts.

PART SIX

VI

Accounting and Controls

CHAPTER NINETEEN

Establishing Accounting Processes

A DISTINCTIVE CHARACTERISTIC OF THE CFO role is the natural rhythm that results from the schedule for producing financial reports. Typically, the financial organization is producing financial statements on a monthly, quarterly, and annual basis, along with comparisons against prior periods, budgets, and forecasts.

FINANCIAL REPORTING

For CFOs, the regularity of the financial reporting schedule is both a curse and a blessing. On the one hand, the relentless reporting requirements represent a series of challenges, with more downside than upside for the typical CFO. The financial organization performs repetitive and laborious reviews and reconciliations involving a multitude of schedules and balances, while often coping with system or staffing limitations.

On the other hand, the reporting schedule ensures that CFOs stay up-to-date on the company's current financial condition and facilitates informed communications with the CEO, the management team, the board of directors, and investors. It also provides the basis for in-depth reviews of financial trends and affords the opportunity to make mid-course corrections.

Accurate and Timely

The CFO's paramount objective in establishing financial reporting processes is to produce *accurate* financial statements in a *timely* manner. In many companies, accomplishing this objective requires heroic acts by controllers and financial managers as they endure rituals of long hours and often frenetic activity to produce reliable financial reports within a rigidly compressed time frame.

Given the regularity of the reporting schedule, companies may have a tendency to take their processes for granted. However, they can be quite complex, usually involving numerous judgments, substantial data manipulation, and intensive coordination among a number of people in disparate roles and possibly remote locations.

There are many opportunities for things to go wrong—including the possibility of a restatement of prior results, which is every CFO's worst nightmare, especially in today's unforgiving environment. To err may be human, but it is certainly not good accounting or reporting.

Closing Cycle

CFOs are of two minds concerning the desirability of shortening the closing cycle. They fear that reducing the time period can be counterproductive, increasing the odds of errors and reworks. However, they also recognize that imposing a shorter time frame can actually be beneficial to the integrity of a company's financial reporting—providing the impetus to reengineer procedures and justifying greater investments in technology tools.

Change is good, but it is also hard, especially in the midst of reporting deadlines that are arriving with relentless regularity. Therefore, a CFO usually must provide strong top down support in order to implement improvements in the reporting processes.

And they must take some risks. Otherwise, inertia is likely to sustain the status quo.

Automation

In driving improved processes, automation can be the CFO's best friend. Automation of accounting processes prevents errors from occurring in the first place, significantly increases the odds of catching errors that do occur, and produces timelier reporting. In contrast, if a report is being prepared offline on an Excel spreadsheet, there's a good chance that something can go wrong—if not immediately, then possibly when there is staff turnover or if functions are shifted to a new location. The CFO's core principle should be clear: Wherever possible, processes should be automated, eliminating the need for human intervention and the risk of human error. CFOs should continuously reinforce this objective throughout their financial organizations and should insist on information technology controls that can reliably support the automated processes.

Technology Tools

Going hand in hand with automation is the value to be obtained from technology tools. These tools can include comprehensive enterprise resource planning software that links the financial functions throughout the company, including controls that can prevent errors from occurring. They can also include software that consolidates financial reporting from disparate systems, improves accounts payable and procurement processes, or performs specific tasks, such as tax reporting.

Implementing these tools typically is extremely difficult—with the need to undo the manual processes and compensatory habits that have been ingrained over time—and their cost can often be hard to justify by the usual measures such as return on investment. However, most CFOs have concluded that automating their processes and adding new software tools are justified by the potential benefits to be derived—especially the reduction of risk in a challenging financial reporting environment.

In driving these improvements, their watchwords are *"incrementally"* and *"continuously."*

Documentation

One of the positive outcomes from Sarbanes-Oxley (yes, there are some benefits!) is the greater emphasis on documenting financial procedures and judgments. This documentation has helped to ensure consistency of methodologies and has facilitated the transfer of knowledge among finance professionals, especially in the face of employee turnover and relocations of functions.

Having gone through the initial rigors of complying with Sarbanes-Oxley, CFOs are now reinforcing this best practice by thoroughly documenting all of their processes—not just the ones subject to annual testing—and discouraging any reliance on employee knowhow in their work flows. For all CFOs, the lesson should be clear: Although time consuming and tedious, documentation is well worth the effort.

Checks and Balances

Of course, no matter how automated and technologically advanced, a company's processes are still going to be subject to some human error and will be vulnerable to their weakest links. Therefore, CFOs must rely on their controllers and financial managers to build in procedures to review work products at various stages of their development. This is one of the chief benefits of investing in automation and technology tools; it allows more time for reviews to be performed, shifting the emphasis from data production to thoughtful analysis.

Of course, it is better to do it right the first time, but catching an error certainly is the second best alternative. Given the CFO's goal of error-free accuracy, it is comforting to know that there are some additional procedures to double check the results.

A few other observations about instituting checks and balances are:

- **Common Sense:** It helps to reserve some time for review and reflection, whereby the accounting professionals can consider the reasonableness and logic of the numbers, applying common sense judgments to the reported results.
- **Technology Tools:** The investment in technology tools can facilitate the detection of errors (e.g., they typically can detect mismatched or duplicate entries).
- **Chart of Accounts:** A standardized and simplified chart of accounts can help to avoid inconsistent treatment of accounting entries.
- **Centers of Excellence:** Having regional or company-wide accounting functions in the same location can foster timely communications (e.g., they can facilitate intercompany reconciliations).
- **External Auditors:** Do not rely on the external auditors to catch errors; while CFOs can take some comfort that the external auditors will review and sample test for material errors, they should recognize that the company retains the primary responsibility for producing accurate financial reports.

Good People

It is worth emphasizing that good people are fundamental to timely and accurate reporting processes; attracting and retaining high-quality, well-trained accounting professionals should be a top-of-mind priority for most CFOs. Turnover generally has lessened in recent years due to the slowdown in the economy, but the wars for financial talent are likely to resume as the economy recovers. Indeed, the quest for a well-trained and motivated work force has been a primary impetus for CFOs to consider outsourcing some of their accounting and processing functions.

Accounting firms traditionally have been the predominant breeding grounds for financial talent, reflecting their superb training programs and their on-the-ground exposures to a variety of companies and geographies. However, given the proliferation of regulatory measures and new accounting rules, the accounting firms—as well as the burgeoning regulatory agencies—have been expanding their staffing needs, creating greater competition for experienced accountants. Eventually, this imbalance should rectify itself, but staffing may represent a challenge for some time to come.

Tax Accounting

Tax accounting is an area that deserves special focus. In many companies—especially those with multinational locations—much of the emphasis has been on sophisticated tax planning. However, with the advent of the Sarbanes-Oxley requirements and the adoption of new accounting standards for tax disclosures, the financial reporting responsibilities within tax departments have become much more important. This has created management challenges and has caused stress in accounting systems that may be inadequate for the tasks at hand.

In response, CFOs have been improving the management processes in their tax departments, with more focus on automation, standardization, and documentation. They have also been enhancing the speed and accuracy of their tax information flows—including more timely information from international locations. In many cases, CFOs have invested in new software tools to expedite their tax accounting processes, resulting in dramatically improved capabilities to meet the higher standards now required.

 SEC FILINGS

For public companies, the reporting schedules provide the raw material for complying with the numerous regulatory requirements, including the inexorable promulgation of new or revised governmental and accounting rules. And for both public and private companies, they provide the vehicles for vibrant communications with investors, who have seemingly inexhaustible appetites for more information and analysis.

Companies that are registered under the Securities Exchange Act of 1934 (the 1934 Act) center their reporting schedules around the timing and disclosure requirements imposed by the Securities and Exchange Commission (SEC). The most important are the 10-K, 10-Q, and 8-K filings, as well as the DEF14A annual proxy filing.

CFOs should partner closely with the general counsel and the company's legal team—as well as any outside counsel who are retained for SEC matters—in ensuring that they are fully aware of the current requirements and allowing adequate time to prepare and review the contents of the filings.

Disclosure Requirements

Large registered companies must file 10-Qs with the SEC within 40 days after the end of each fiscal quarter (within 45 days for smaller companies) and the 10-K within 60 days after the end of their fiscal year (within 75 or 90 days for smaller companies). These deadlines have been accelerated in recent years, giving CFOs less leeway in completing their financial statements, securing the necessary sign offs from their external auditors and legal advisors, and receiving the requisite approval from the audit committee.

Generally, companies will impose *"blackout periods"* that begin midway through the third month of each quarter and last through the earnings announcement. These blackout periods restrict transactions in the company's stock by "insiders," who include executive officers, the board of directors, and owners of greater than 10 percent of the company's shares. However, transactions can still be made pursuant to a 10b-5(1) program through which stock is purchased or sold automatically, according to a predetermined schedule.

In addition, companies are required to file 8-Ks within four business days after specified events, such as a financial announcement, a strategic transaction, a major contract signing or completion, or a change in an executive officer or member of the board of directors. This requirement is supplementary to a company's general requirement under 10b-5 of the 1934 Act to disclose material information to the market.

XBRL Mandate

Since 1993, the SEC has required electronic filings to be made through "EDGAR," its Electronic Data Gathering, Analysis, and Retrieval system. However, the SEC plans to supplement EDGAR with uses of interactive data and eventually replace EDGAR with the Interactive Data Electronic Applications (IDEA) system.

As part of this initiative, the SEC now requires filings to be made using eXtensible Business Reporting Language (XBRL) software. This software facilitates the extraction of information from the filings and makes it easier for stock market analysts to make comparisons among companies.

XBRL provides a computer-readable identifier for each item of data. According to the SEC's announcement of the new mandate, interactive data using the XBRL language "can create new ways for investors, analysts, and others to retrieve and use financial information in documents filed with us. For example, users of financial information will be able to download it directly into spreadsheets, analyze it using commercial off-the-shelf software, or use it within investment models in other software formats."[1]

Plain English

In addition to shortening the time frames for filings, the SEC has been requiring additional information in the management discussion and analysis (MD&A) and specifying that the disclosures be written in "plain English," which generally means using the active rather than the passive voice and writing in straightforward prose. For example, instead of "It is expected that raw material prices will be under pressure," a plain English sentence would read "We expect that our raw material prices will increase."

The SEC's requirements—along with investors' desire for more analytical information—have caused CFOs to focus more on the clarity of their MD&A and other disclosures, including the description of the company's strategies and competitive positioning. It has also motivated accounting professionals to sharpen their writing skills.

Risk Factors

Consistent with their greater emphasis on enterprise risk management programs, CFOs are also focusing on the "risk factors" that are required in the 10-K. Companies generally are adding more discussion of risks, erring generally on the side of disclosing more, rather than fewer, risk factors.

This additional disclosure does not seem to faze investors, who recognize that companies are inevitably exposed to several risk areas; however, they appreciate reassurances that management and the board of directors are focused on the appropriate strategies for accepting or mitigating these risks.

Tax Disclosures

Taxes are another source of increased disclosure requirements. In particular, the adoption of Financial Accounting Standards Board Interpretation No. 48 (FIN 48) in 2006 and subsequent accounting changes have demonstrably increased the amount of information provided to investors, including a summary of the company's unrecognized tax benefits.

In the past, tax professionals generally argued against disclosing information because of the potential impact on future tax audits; they felt that the disclosures could provide a road map to the tax auditors, which would compromise their ability to negotiate a favorable settlement. However, their concerns have been overruled by FIN 48 and the other new requirements that have mandated more disclosure.

Given the greater transparency in their financial statements, CFOs must now be fully prepared to explain their company's tax status to investors. Furthermore, many audit committees are reviewing tax-related contingencies with more regularity and in greater detail than previously.

Fair Values

The accounting rules and financial reporting requirements clearly are trending toward more "fair value" disclosures—providing more information on the market values of assets and liabilities. Notable examples in recent years include fair value determinations related to investments, debt obligations, and pension funds. In addition, goodwill and intangibles are subject to market tests.

This movement toward fair value accounting is likely to persist, especially given the plan to converge GAAP with International Financial Reporting Standards (IFRS). As a result, financial reports are likely to become more volatile, which will create additional accounting and communication challenges for CFOs.

Given these trends, CFOs need to establish appropriate and consistent methodologies for performing these market valuations, in some cases supplementing their internal reviews with third-party validations.

Proxy Filings

Another trend worth noting is the increased disclosure in annual proxy statements concerning executive pay, including the compensation discussion and analysis (CD&A). As a result, CFOs have been assuming greater roles in the preparation of the annual proxy filings, especially the computation and presentation of the metrics used in executive compensation programs.

EXTERNAL AUDITORS

Given the stricter regulatory environment, obtaining timely completions of the external auditors' reviews can be a potential stumbling block in preparing SEC filings; indeed, it is not uncommon for the external auditors to request revisions to the financial statements in the time period between the company's earnings announcement and filing its 10-Q or 10-K with the SEC.

CFOs often lament that their external auditors can bring up new items at the last minute and that their engagement team must obtain input and approvals from their national office. Without question, the more demanding regulatory climate has caused greater oversight from the national offices, which can be frustrating for all concerned. As a result, there is more uncertainty concerning accounting judgments and more time is required to obtain them.

At the same time, the external auditors often cite the failure of their clients to get their work papers and draft materials to them on a timely basis. Indeed, the new regulations have caused many companies to be more circumspect in sharing early drafts with their auditors. The engagement team has a lot of hoops to get through each quarter and they often feel pressured from too little time to address potential accounting issues.

Suffice it to say that the overall process of preparing and approving the financial statements has become more difficult, requiring greater coordination between CFOs and their auditors' engagement partners. In response, CFOs should consider action steps to streamline the communications and avoid last minute surprises.

For example, the CFO can request that the external auditor provide a memorandum midway through each quarter to highlight potential issues in that quarter's financial statements. This memorandum can then serve as the agenda for a meeting with the CFO and corporate controller to discuss the issues and to determine what can be done to expedite their resolution—presumably well in advance of the filing deadline!

In general, CFOs should seek to forge a constructive and productive relationship with the lead partner on their account, identifying potential ways to streamline communications and expedite the work flow.

 AUDIT COMMITTEE

CFOs will also want to ensure that they keep the audit committee up to date on their financial reporting policies and potential accounting issues. By regularly reviewing their key accounting policies and procedures, they can reduce the risk that the committee will feel pressured to approve the filings without sufficient time to review the numbers and the accounting judgments that underpin them.

In particular, CFOs can partner with the chair of the audit committee to schedule agenda items that will educate the committee concerning the company's significant accounting policies. For example, they can schedule reviews of items such as:

- *Reserves*, including those pertaining to the tax provision, litigation exposures, and bad debts.
- *Intangibles*, including the balance sheet entries for goodwill, as well as the amortizing balances for intangibles such as customer relationships, technology systems, and internally developed software.
- *Revenue Recognition*, including bundled products and services and long-term contracts.
- *Fair Values*, including the methodologies and assumptions used to estimate the market values of assets and liabilities.

Furthermore, they should make the audit committee aware of their rationales for selecting specific accounting policies where different alternatives were evaluated. The external auditors are required to discuss these alternative accounting policies with the audit committee and it helps if the committee members have a prior understanding of the reasons behind the company's choice of its accounting methodologies.

 NOTE

1. "Interactive Data to Improve Financial Reporting" (January 30, 2009, Securities and Exchange Commission Release Nos. 33-9002; 34-59324; 39-2461; IC-28609; File No. S7-11-08), p. 8.

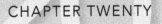

CHAPTER TWENTY

Communicating
Financial Results

OR ALMOST ALL PUBLIC COMPANIES, the announcement of their
quarterly and annual results is punctuated by a web-based conference
call that permits the management team to highlight the key items from
the financial statements, update investors concerning their accomplishments
and challenges, comment on their future plans and business outlook, and
entertain questions from analysts and investors.

Private companies likewise have developed routines for communicating
their results, but it is harder to generalize with respect to the specific steps that
are followed. Nonetheless, it is undoubtedly true that like their public company
counterparts, private company CFOs typically view the quarterly and annual
results as important junctures that require some effort to put the results in
context and to provide the color that helps investors to understand them as
clearly as possible.

EARNINGS CALL

In anticipation of announcing their results, CFOs will usually lead a process
that begins a few weeks earlier and culminates with the conference call and

follow-ups with analysts. The process generally follows a similar routine in most companies, although CFOs will adapt the routine for their particular facts and circumstances.

Identify Message Points

The process typically begins with the identification of the issues that will be on investor minds and the key points to address in communicating the financial results. Based on the forecasted results, CFOs will have a good idea of the way that the numbers are likely to finish and this allows them to get a leg up on the preparations.

Much like a politician preparing for a press conference, the financial and communication teams try to predetermine the key points to be emphasized each quarter. This includes focusing on the accomplishments during the quarter and the progress being made against the company's strategic objectives, as well as anticipating the issues and questions that will need to be addressed.

In particular, CFOs will try to identify any areas in the financial results that may come as a surprise to investors.

Prepare Draft Materials

The team will prepare a draft press release, which generally should follow a similar format from quarter to quarter, but should also include key message points, where appropriate. The press release forms the foundation for all of the company's communications, and thus it is helpful to get an early start on this document, even if there are holes to be filled in later.

Most companies use quotes from the CEO to communicate any information that involves subjective interpretations or expectations for the future. Otherwise, the press release should be based totally on objective facts.

Assign Potential Questions

Starting with the questions and answers from the previous quarter, CFOs will solicit potential questions that might arise during the earnings call and determine which of the questions from the prior quarter are no longer applicable. They will then assign the questions to various people throughout the company, asking them to update the previous answers and to prepare draft answers to the new questions that have been identified.

The practice of preparing draft answers in written form is a useful discipline—although the intent is not to read them. Instead, management uses the written answers as background for developing the extemporaneous responses that they will provide on the call. In some cases, however, the answers will be incorporated into the press release or prepared remarks, thus preempting likely questions.

Prepare Draft Scripts

The earnings call typically begins with prepared remarks in which the CEO provides general commentary about the quarter and the future outlook and the CFO provides a review of the financial statements. However, for some companies—especially very large companies with diversified businesses—the CFO will deliver most or all of the prepared remarks. In another variation, companies with chief operating officers will usually give them a prominent role in communicating the business results.

The prepared remarks will be transcribed verbatim by third-party services and made available to investors through the Internet. Thus, the scripts offer an invaluable opportunity for companies to highlight their key message points, provide context for their financial results, and identify the specific factors that affected the company's results during the quarter. It is also a chance to explain any technical accounting or one-time events that may not be easily discernible from the press release.

The scripts typically go through several drafts and are carefully reviewed by legal counsel and external auditors.

Review Draft Materials

The next step is to review the draft press release, the draft scripts, and the draft questions and answers. In addition to the CEO and CFO, the group that conducts this review typically includes members of the financial, communications, and legal teams, as well as representatives from the business units, often the business leaders. Their goal is to make sure that all of the facts are correct and that everyone is comfortable with the way that the quarter is described to investors.

In addition, the process of reviewing the draft materials invariably will reveal topics that need further elaboration and potential questions that should be added to the list. Furthermore, the group will consider any areas where the actual financial results are deviating from the forecast.

Finally, they will discuss the likely reactions from investors, comparing the company's results against investor expectations, and considering any earnings announcements that have been made to date by competitors.

Obtain Sign-Offs

The press release and scripts typically will be reviewed by various business unit and corporate staff leaders. In addition, the company will need to receive sign offs from the external auditors and the general counsel, who often will have the materials reviewed by an external lawyer who specializes in securities law.

The press release must also be formally approved by the audit committee of the board of directors. Because the audit committee includes people with financial expertise, they can serve as a sounding board, not only for the contents of the press release, but also concerning the proposed message points that will be delivered through the scripts and in the answers to likely questions. They can also suggest areas where the communications may need to be clarified or augmented.

Prepare Webcast Slides

A minority of companies prepare slides to accompany the webcast of their earnings call. The CFOs who take this approach generally argue that the visuals help them to communicate clearly with investors. However, many investors will be participating by phone and not over the web. Furthermore, using slides necessarily involves extra layers of review—especially by legal and compliance professionals—which may require that extra time be built into the timeline in preparing for the call.

If CFOs include slides, they should take steps to expedite their preparation. For example, the slides typically will follow a fairly standardized format, with relatively consistent information that is presented from quarter to quarter.

Rehearse the Call

The presenters should rehearse their prepared remarks, identifying any sentences or words that look good on paper, but which do not work as well when communicated orally. For example, the scripts normally should not use contractions and should avoid parenthetical phrases or complex sentence structures.

In addition, it is very helpful to review the draft answers to potential questions, with the goals of identifying who will answer each of the questions, converting the draft answers into extemporaneous responses, and maintaining the flexibility to adjust the answers to the various ways in which a question may be asked.

Contact People in Advance

In advance of the earnings call, CFOs typically will determine who should receive a "heads up" concerning the results.

Many companies provide an "embargoed" advance copy of the press release to selected news services—such as Bloomberg, Dow Jones, or Reuters—and offer to conduct a brief interview in advance of the call. Since the news services are working on tight deadlines, this gives them an opportunity to clarify any open questions and to obtain some commentary—usually from the CEO or CFO—to supplement the release. This is a fairly common practice and generally safe, although there have been rare occurrences where a draft release has been distributed prematurely, creating havoc for all involved.

Especially if the company's debt ratings are on the watch list for a potential downgrade or upgrade, or if the earnings announcement contains significant new information concerning the company's financial condition, CFOs will often provide an advance copy of the press release to the rating agencies and hold a brief call to answer their questions. This can avoid surprise reactions from them and helps to cultivate a constructive dialogue with the ratings team.

Other examples of people whom CFOs might want to contact in advance include financial advisors, regulators, major customers, or important suppliers. However, they should be careful to avoid any potential misuses of the insider information.

Conduct the Call

The conference calls typically last about an hour and are normally scheduled before the market opens in the morning or after the market closes in the afternoon. The participants are usually in "listen only" mode for the prepared remarks and then the lines are opened, enabling them to ask questions according to a queue that is managed by a moderator.

The questions are normally dominated by sell side equity analysts, although the company may get questions from major shareholders or debt holders, especially if the company has a transaction pending. Representatives of the media should not ask questions on the call and, if possible, they should be screened from entering the queue.

Companies often have additional management people in addition to the CEO, COO, and CFO—such as business unit heads and the general counsel—available to answer questions. This can help provide detailed responses, but requires more dexterity in orchestrating the call.

Employees can normally participate through the webcast. In addition, companies will often schedule a follow-up call with management, who can then cascade key message points to their organizations.

Follow-Ups

Subsequent to the call, the company's investor relations and financial people will usually make themselves available to the equity analysts to clarify the information and answers that were provided during the call—but they are careful not to provide any new information that could be deemed a violation of the Fair Disclosure regulation (which prohibits selective disclosure of material information). In most cases, the analysts will be updating their earnings models and confirming the points that they heard on the call.

The sell side analysts will typically issue a report to investors within 24 hours of the call. In addition to highlighting the information provided by the company, the analysts will summarize their impressions and note any updates to their earnings forecasts or target stock prices.

The call is recorded and posted as soon as practicable on the company's website, where it can be accessed by investors, employees, and other stakeholders.

NON-GAAP MEASURES

The Securities and Exchange Commission (SEC) has decreed that generally accepted accounting principles (GAAP) should be the primary methodology for communicating financial results—including in press releases and investor presentations. Nevertheless, many CFOs have advocated the use of non-GAAP measures as supplementary information, with reconciliations to their GAAP results.

They argue that non-GAAP measures provide useful information to investors, especially if these alternative metrics are in fact used by the company in managing its business and by analysts when comparing companies in their industry. The SEC has generally acquiesced to this practice—provided that GAAP information is presented and that any non-GAAP information is fully reconciled to the GAAP results.

Adjusted Earnings

A relatively common practice is to compute "adjusted" earnings that exclude certain expenses. For example, CFOs may choose to exclude restructuring expenses, legal settlements, and gains or losses on divestitures. Other examples of potentially excluded items are amortization expenses that arise from intangibles due to purchase accounting adjustments in acquisitions or non-cash write-offs of software due to obsolescence or a company's decision to consolidate on another technology platform. They may also exclude or provide breakdowns of the impacts due to fair value accounting, such as the changes to debt valuations pursuant to FAS 159.

Providing adjusted earnings seems to be fairly well accepted by the financial markets, with many analysts using them in their earnings per share forecasts. However, CFOs need to be careful not to overdo the exclusions, thereby losing credibility. For example, while excluding episodic restructurings can be justified, analysts will look more askance at serial restructurings, which can be construed as a recurring cost of doing business. They should also apply the adjustments consistently from one quarter to the next.

Industry Norms

The other common use of non-GAAP information is to provide measures that are typically used by analysts and investors in an industry. For example, CFOs of capital intensive businesses may present earnings before interest, taxes, depreciation, and amortization (EBITDA). As another example, frequent acquirers may emphasize earnings before interest, taxes, and amortization of acquisition-related intangibles (EBITA).

Although the financial markets generally appreciate this supplemental information, CFOs should be careful not to deviate too much from accepted norms. For example, Groupon's attempt to present a novel earnings measure in its original initial public offering (IPO) filing highlighted the risk of running afoul of accepted practices or SEC constraints. As a result, if CFOs are going to introduce a new non-GAAP measure, they will need to build in time for legal counsel to review the draft materials and to be cautious in defining measures that deviate too greatly from the conventional alternatives.

In addition, analysts and investors can be naturally skeptical if it appears that a CFO is manipulating a company's presentation materials so as to "spin" the financial results and future outlook. For this reason, CFOs should use non-GAAP measures sparingly and should emphasize consistency in their investor communications—resisting the temptation to "cherry pick" the metrics that make the company look good.

 ## EARNINGS GUIDANCE

Another key issue that CFOs of public companies must address is whether to provide guidance concerning their expectations for future earnings. Investors—and especially sell side analysts—often profess their preference for such earnings guidance. Furthermore, it is often argued that providing guidance can add shareholder value by the additional information that is communicated to investors.

However, a 2006 McKinsey study did not find this to be the case, reaching the following conclusion:

> Our analysis of the perceived benefits of issuing frequent earnings guidance found no evidence that it affects valuation multiples, improves shareholder returns, or reduces share price volatility.[1]

Given the countervailing views, there is no strong consensus among CFOs on whether to provide earnings guidance and, if so, what form it should take. And while there definitely has been a reduction in the number of companies providing guidance—especially in the wake of the 2008 financial crisis—CFOs continue to take varying approaches to their guidance practices.

The primary alternatives are to provide both quarterly and annual earnings guidance, to provide annual earnings guidance only, or to provide no earnings guidance at all.

Quarterly and Annual Guidance

The most expansive approach is to provide guidance for the upcoming quarter and the full year. This was the prevailing practice in the past, but it has become less common in today's market environment, especially given the volatility and uncertainties introduced by the financial crisis and economic recession.

The principal argument for this approach is that it helps to avoid volatile reactions in the stock price if earnings fail to meet analysts' expectations. By providing guidance, management can share its best thinking about the outlook and lessen the probability that the analysts will develop unrealistic expectations. It also makes it easier for CFOs to have conversations with analysts and investors about the company's outlook without violating the Fair Disclosure constraints.

However, providing this guidance can be problematic. First, management exposes itself to the risk of unintentionally misleading investors, especially if much of the revenue and net income drivers in any quarter are outside the company's control. In fact, providing guidance that turns out to be wrong can exacerbate rather than ameliorate the stock's reaction to disappointing results. It also can cause management—especially the CFO—to lose precious credibility with investors.

Second, if it becomes apparent that the company is likely either to exceed or to miss its guidance, the question arises as to whether the company should pre-announce its earnings (by issuing a press release during the quarter to update the market concerning its revised earnings expectations). In contrast, if it has not provided guidance, the company is under less legal and market pressure to make a special disclosure in advance of the earnings announcement.

Third, it can increase the company's vulnerability to shareholder lawsuits. With the benefit of hindsight, the likelihood of an earnings miss can appear to have been obvious and lawyers can often find public comments by management that can seem to be incriminating after the fact.

And fourth, investors may become skeptical if the company has a propensity to provide "lowball" estimates that it almost always exceeds. This in turn can produce *"whisper"* numbers in the market, making it confusing to discern whether the company has in fact met or exceeded the market's expectations.

Annual Guidance Only

Given the disadvantages with regularly providing guidance, some CFOs choose to take a middle ground: providing annual guidance only, typically estimating a range of expected results for revenue and earnings per share. This eliminates some of the company's exposure to quarter-to-quarter volatility in the results (e.g., if software sales are deferred into the next quarter) and generally reduces the company's vulnerability to unforeseen events.

CFOs who take this approach typically provide the annual guidance at the beginning of the fiscal year—when their budgets have been completed—and either reaffirm or update their range of expected outcomes at each earnings call. Therefore, as the year progresses, their guidance gradually becomes more precise, with fewer periods in which to make up shortfalls or to fall further behind. Furthermore, CFOs taking this approach often define their guidance to exclude certain items—focusing on "adjusted" rather than GAAP earnings—which reduces their vulnerability to wide swings in the estimates.

Providing annual guidance generally represents a compromise between the desire to guide investor expectations versus the risk that the guidance can be misleading over the short term. It is consistent with the goal of providing greater transparency to investors, but it still exposes the company to legal risks and potential loss of management credibility.

No Guidance at All

The final alternative is to provide no guidance whatsoever. This has been the growing trend, especially among companies in economically sensitive industries or whose mark-to-market accounting can significantly affect their results.

During the financial crisis, many companies suspended their guidance due to the extreme uncertainty in the economy and have not resumed the practice. Moreover, some analysts and investors who previously applauded the policy of providing quarterly guidance have become accustomed to a world without guidance and are less adamant in their belief that it is advantageous for investors.

Earnings Drivers

Whatever their policy with respect to providing formal earnings guidance, CFOs generally are providing more information concerning the variables that drive their results. By providing additional information about the company's earnings drivers, CFOs can assist analysts in deriving forecasts and can reinforce their reputation for transparency.

For example, CFOs can explain their company's exposure to foreign exchange or interest rates and quantify their sensitivity to hypothetical percentage movements. Likewise, they can provide more information concerning the exogenous and company-specific factors that drive revenue (such as sensitivity to pricing for products or services), their programs to lower the cost base (such as expected trend lines in major cost drivers), and the potential impact from material accounting assumptions (such as the pension fund discount rate or the depreciation schedules for major assets).

In taking this approach, CFOs should also use their earnings calls to update investors concerning any unusual factors that will be affecting the results in the upcoming quarter or year. For example, they may indicate an expected gain on an asset sale or highlight an exposure due to a legal settlement.

In addition, they can provide guidance concerning parts of the income statement that are especially unpredictable. For example, tax rates are notoriously volatile given the requirement to update the expected effective tax rate each quarter; for clarity, the CFO can inform investors on the call what the expected tax rate will be for the next quarter or the full year.

CFOs should be similarly transparent concerning the key performance metrics that will drive future revenue and earnings. For example, they can update investors concerning the number of customers, the company's headcount trends, or the anticipated spending on advertising. Investors will appreciate knowing the metrics that the CFO thinks are important, as well as the company's current performance against those metrics.

 NOTE

1. Hsieh, Peggy, Koller, Timothy, and Rajan, S.R., "The misguided practice of earnings guidance" (March 2006, *McKinsey Quarterly*, www.mckinsey quarterly.com), p. 1.

CHAPTER TWENTY-ONE

Implementing Sarbanes-Oxley

T HE SARBANES-OXLEY ACT (SOX) was enacted on July 30, 2002, in the wake of a raft of notorious corporate scandals—including Enron, Tyco, and WorldCom—as well as the dissolution of Arthur Andersen. The enactment of SOX has resulted in profound changes in the priorities for CFOs and their financial organizations, as well as the nature of their interactions with boards of directors—especially audit committees—and external auditors. It also has caused significant changes in the financial organization's procedures.

OVERVIEW OF PROVISIONS

The main provisions of SOX—which apply to public, but not private companies—include:

- **Accounting Oversight:** Establishes the Public Company Accounting Oversight Board, which provides independent oversight of public accounting firms.
- **Auditor Independence:** Sets forth standards for limiting conflicts of interest with external auditors.

- **Certifications:** Requires that a company's CEO and CFO certify the quarterly and annual financial statements.
- **Financial Reporting Controls:** Imposes new testing and reporting requirements concerning the adequacy of a company's financial controls.
- **Disclosures:** Stipulates increased disclosures such as off-balance-sheet transactions, material contracts, and insider transactions.
- **Analyst Conflicts:** Defines codes of conduct for securities analysts, including disclosures of conflicts of interest.
- **Whistleblower Communications and Protections:** Mandates whistleblower hot lines, establishes criminal penalties for interfering with investigations, and provides protections for whistleblowers.

In some companies, the development and implementation of these new requirements have been led by the internal audit staff, while in other companies the responses to SOX have been coordinated by a specific individual who has been assigned responsibility, usually reporting to the corporate controller. In still other cases—particularly within financial services or other regulated companies—the primary responsibility for implementing SOX has rested with the chief compliance officer.

Irrespective of the method of implementation, the compliance with the new requirements has been a major effort—resulting in altered behaviors and new ways of doing things—and a significant investment of resources. It has also changed the nature of the CFO's relationships with the external auditors and the audit committee, generally causing their interactions to be much more formal and arm's length.

Of all the changes wrought by SOX, the most impactful to CFOs have been the provisions related to auditor independence, financial statement certifications, and internal controls.

 ## AUDITOR INDEPENDENCE

Title II of SOX establishes requirements for auditor independence, including prohibitions on many types of consulting services for auditing clients, acceleration of the rotation of auditing partners on an account, procedures for approving a company's external auditing firm, and requirements for regular communications by the external auditors to the audit committee.

As a result of these new requirements, the external auditors generally have a more arm's-length relationship with the CFO, more direct interactions with the audit committee, and additional safeguards against any conflicts of interest. For example, external auditors can no longer provide internal audit outsourcing for their clients. However, they can perform certain audit-related activities, such as providing tax and acquisition services.

To comply with these restrictions, audit committees regularly review the activities performed by the external auditors and have established procedures to pre-approve any services to be performed by the external auditing firm. They have also instituted formal procedures for approving all fees paid to the external auditors.

In addition, they have established processes for approving the renewals of the auditor engagements each year, including due diligence reviews and investigations of any potential conflicts of interest. For the most part, CFOs have advocated continuity in their auditing firms, but they must consciously and deliberately renew their recommendation each year. However, while CFOs can offer their recommendation, under SOX the responsibility for the engagement and compensation of the external auditing firm explicitly rests with the audit committee.

At this stage of the SOX implementation, the audit committee's enforcement of auditor independence has become fairly routine; however, this topic typically requires some attention by the committee at nearly every meeting and the committee chair is often called on to approve actions between meetings.

In addition, the auditing firms have instituted formal procedures for communicating with their clients, ensuring that their written reports conform to the regulations or guidelines set forth by SOX, the Securities and Exchange Commission (SEC), and the PCAOB. They also provide mandated written communications to the audit committee on a regular basis.

Because of the sheer volume and the time-consuming nature of all the procedural requirements, audit committees are hard-pressed to focus sufficiently on the material issues related to a company's financial statements and its control environment. Therefore, in partnership with the audit committee chair, CFOs should help to ensure that the agendas do not become too bogged down in procedural details and should seek to facilitate rich discussions concerning the company's key accounting and control issues.

 ## CERTIFICATION OF FINANCIALS

Another major change in SOX was the requirement under Section 302 for the CEO and CFO to certify the quarterly and annual financial statements, stating that they are "responsible for establishing and maintaining financial controls" and "have designed such internal controls to ensure that material information relating to the company and its consolidated subsidiaries is made known to such officers."

In most public companies, it is virtually impossible for the CEO and CFO to comply with this requirement without relying heavily on other executives, as well as the officers and managers throughout the financial organization. Therefore, CFOs have instituted two procedures, in particular, to provide comfort to the certifiers of the company's financials.

First, they have established *disclosure committees*, consisting of representatives from all parts of the company who can discuss any items or events that potentially should be disclosed in the financial statements or otherwise. By routinely reviewing the potential disclosure requirements surrounding business, financial, or legal developments, these committees provide an early warning system concerning potential issues and ensure consistency in the criteria and processes for their review.

As a best practice, the disclosure committees operate independently from the CFO, providing an objective source of information and judgments. They are a valuable source of intelligence and positive contributors to enterprise risk management.

Second, they have established *internal representations* whereby the layers within the financial organization certify the financial information under their purview. Most companies now have procedures in place to obtain these cascading certifications in writing each quarter—usually through emails—thereby bringing to light any potential issues that could cause someone to hesitate, or even refuse, to certify the financial statements.

These formal requirements for each person to certify results give substantial comfort to CEOs and CFOs, who appreciate the affirmations that the financial information has been carefully reviewed at each stage of its preparation. This process also reinforces a culture of accountability, which is the bedrock of a robust control environment.

ASSESSMENT OF INTERNAL CONTROLS

Effective as of 2004, Section 404 of SOX established a requirement for management to provide an annual report to the SEC that assesses the "effectiveness of the internal control structure and procedures of the issuer for financial reporting." Without question, this has been the most burdensome of all the SOX provisions, requiring a major effort by CFOs to comply with its requirements.

It has resulted in material incremental costs for most companies and has caused significant alterations in routine processes, especially in the requirements for additional testing and documentation. To the critics, these requirements have been more form than substance and their benefits have been outweighed by the costs.

Nevertheless, it is indisputable that some good things have emanated from the Section 404 requirements. They have caused CFOs to focus on their key control processes—identifying cumbersome processes, faulty procedures, or inadequate technology. Moreover, they have motivated further automation in processes, substantially reducing the risk of errors.

While the initial assessments were a major distraction for the financial organization, it is irrefutable that they have led to improved processes, including greater documentation, which can facilitate outsourcing and other efficiency gains. Whether these benefits were worth their costs is another question, but at least it wasn't a total waste of time and resources.

Furthermore, the costs of compliance have declined over time. First, as companies have gained more experience in implementation, they have been able to reduce the number of control processes that are considered "key" and that require annual testing. Second, once the processes have been revamped, they generally require less remediation going forward. Third, when the PCAOB approved Auditing Standard No. 5, this allowed the external auditors to rely more on the companies' tests—reducing both the cost and the time commitment to achieve compliance.

Identification of Deficiencies

As part of the of the Section 404 requirements, the testing procedures have highlighted areas of weakness in a company's control environment. This in turn has helped CFOs to focus their management oversight in areas of higher concern and has led in many cases to targeted investments in technology tools that can enhance the accuracy and timeliness of their financial statement preparations.

The control issues are arrayed each year according to the following hierarchy of definitions that is set forth in Statement of Auditing Standards 115:

- **Control Deficiency:** A deficiency in internal control exists when the design or operation of a control does not allow management or employees, in the normal course of performing their assigned functions, to prevent, or detect and correct misstatements on a timely basis.

- **Significant Deficiency:** A significant deficiency is a deficiency, or a combination of deficiencies, in internal control that is less severe than a material weakness, yet important enough to merit attention by those charged with governance.
- **Material Weakness:** A material weakness is a deficiency, or combination of significant deficiencies, in internal control, such that there is a reasonable possibility that a material misstatement of the entity's financial statements will not be prevented, or detected and corrected on a timely basis.

Because material weaknesses must be disclosed in a company's external financial reporting, they are anathema to CFOs, who usually establish a stated goal of having none. Likewise, while significant deficiencies are not as serious a blemish as material weaknesses, the fact that they must be disclosed to the audit committee gives them undesired visibility. They also run the risk of turning into a material weakness.

Understandably, CFOs will seek to remedy a material weakness or significant deficiency as soon as possible, especially if it can be accomplished before the end of the current fiscal year. Until the remediation has been achieved and confirmed by the company's external auditors, it will be a continuous topic for discussion with the audit committee—which is not how CFOs like to spend their time with the committee.

Compared with most other financial functions, the tax area has been a relatively frequent source of significant deficiencies and material weaknesses in the SOX reporting. As a result, many CFOs have felt the need to escalate their focus on tax accounting—in some cases shifting the leadership from a tax planning specialist to someone with a background in financial reporting. They have also strengthened the ties between the tax and controllership functions.

Ongoing Assessments of Controls

At this stage of implementation, CFOs are generally reconciled to their ongoing commitment to comply with the Section 404 requirements; indeed, they may need to guard against complacency within the financial organization. They generally need to ensure that their processes continue to be brought up to date and that they are functioning consistently and accurately, as verified by the annual testing procedures.

Furthermore, CFOs should reinforce the advantages of robust processes throughout the financial organization, including the geographic locations and business activities that do not meet the thresholds to require verification through the Section 404 assessments. Greater automation, for example, is likely to be valuable wherever it's applied.

Application to Smaller Companies

After a series of postponements, the SEC has *permanently exempted* smaller companies (non-accelerated filers) from the Section 404 requirements. This makes sense because the fixed costs of compliance make it hard to justify the cost/benefit trade-offs for these smaller companies. Nevertheless, both smaller public companies and private companies, including nonprofits, can benefit from the disciplined approach to internal controls that is encouraged by the SOX legislation.

In particular, the CFOs of smaller companies can take to heart the best practices from the SOX procedures: namely, the greater focus on automation and the need to document methodologies and processes. Especially as the accounting standards become more focused on fair value determinations, it also makes sense for all CFOs to ensure that these judgments are applied consistently and appropriately.

CHAPTER TWENTY-TWO

Reinforcing
Compliance and Controls

CONSISTENT WITH THEIR ROLE IN RISK MANAGEMENT, CFOs are charged with the responsibility to encourage and perpetuate a focus on compliance and controls. This has always been a priority for CFOs, but undoubtedly this focus has become much more important since the adoption of Sarbanes-Oxley and the greater emphasis on enterprise risk management.

Boards of directors are acutely sensitive to regulatory trends in jurisdictions throughout the world and recognize that any lapses in compliance and controls can cause significant damage to a company's reputation and financial well-being.

U.S. companies are especially mindful of the "Federal Sentencing Guidelines" that apply to both public and private companies, including non-profits and specify that an organization shall:

1. Exercise due diligence to prevent and detect criminal conduct; and
2. Otherwise promote an organizational culture that encourages ethical conduct and a commitment to compliance with the law.[1]

CONTROL ENVIRONMENT

CFOs can play a major role in creating and reinforcing healthy control environments that meet the heightened expectations of today's regulatory climate. Along with the CEO and management team, they can influence the company's adherence to high standards by setting a positive "tone at the top," promulgating a "code of conduct," and establishing a "zero tolerance" attitude.

Tone at the Top

The CFO's role begins with setting a "tone at the top" where his or her resolute commitment to high ethical standards is unquestioned throughout the financial organization. Indeed, *integrity* is usually cited as an essential quality for the modern CFO.

CFOs will also enlist the support of their CEOs and business leaders to reinforce the tone at the top. An annual email from the CEO can be a powerful reminder, raising compliance and good business practices to a top-of-mind priority.

They should also include control-related topics as part of the standard agenda for business reviews. For example, reviewing a status report on outstanding audit issues is an excellent vehicle for highlighting the importance of controls, which otherwise might be perceived as a mundane issue. They also can highlight potential regulatory developments in their strategic and risk management reviews.

Code of Conduct

A "code of conduct" can be another valuable tool for inculcating the right culture throughout the company. With dispersed locations and several business lines, companies often view their code of conduct as a way to reinforce a "one-company" attitude—where everyone applies high standards and exhibits mutual trust—among colleagues, customers, business partners, and communities. It complements the company's "values statement" by extolling the principles that should guide behavior.

As a best practice, companies are converting their codes of conduct from the traditional legalese into common sense *plain talk* that is easily understood. They are also promoting their codes of conduct through several means, including posting them on the web, sending out targeted emails, providing a hard copy version to every employee, translating them into several languages, and creating a video. Furthermore, they are sponsoring training programs and requiring annual online certifications that employees have agreed to abide by the code.

Zero Tolerance

Given their mandate to reinforce a culture of compliance and controls, CFOs typically seek to instill a zero tolerance attitude toward any ethical lapses and to establish processes for achieving compliance with applicable legal requirements throughout the world. Similar to the *"broken window"* theory of police work, CFOs usually encourage a focus on even minor violations of a company's code of conduct, thereby reinforcing a culture of adherence to good business practices. Just as a focus on broken windows can improve the crime environment, so can attention to small matters enhance the control environment.

For example, travel and entertainment (T&E) policies can be a good vehicle for instituting a zero tolerance attitude. Although they generally are minor infractions, T&E issues can represent a large percentage of audit findings and can be an indicator of potentially serious issues such as fraud or a possible violation of anti-corruption laws. Therefore, CFOs can get good visibility by setting a goal to reduce their frequency.

In addition, many CFOs have realized benefits from the implementation of an Internet-based T&E system; it can facilitate procurement savings, in addition to fostering a strong control environment. In some cases, CFOs have further reinforced the need for compliance by outsourcing reviews of T&E submissions to a low-cost site like India—thus reinforcing their focus on small as well as large infractions.

AUDITOR AND BOARD SUPPORT

In fulfilling their compliance and control objectives, CFOs should work in tandem with legal and compliance professionals throughout the company. In addition, they should leverage the support of internal auditors, external auditors, and the board of directors—especially the audit committee—in monitoring potential issues and ensuring that compliance and controls remain front-and-center priorities.

Internal Auditors

Internal auditors can play a vital role in achieving the CFO's compliance and control objectives. Like the cavalry in nineteenth-century warfare, the internal auditors can serve as the company's eyes and ears in detecting potential issues throughout the world. Furthermore, their comprehensive audit findings can identify conditions that may violate a company's policies or otherwise pose risks to the company's reputation.

Internal auditors can also bring specialized expertise to the assessment of risk. For example, they have been emphasizing skills in information technology and fraud detection. Also, by tapping into outsourcing services, they can bring in specialized talent to complement their internal skill sets.

Finally, by keeping good records concerning their audit findings across business units and geographic locations, the internal auditors can identify pockets for improvement that deserve special focus by the CFO and the audit committee. For example, they may perceive patterns—such as information technology issues—that are growing in importance; the internal auditors can recommend actions to address the issues before they migrate to other areas of the company, often suggesting best practices that have been applied elsewhere.

External Auditors

External auditors are another valuable source of input. They can highlight potential issues, bringing to bear their experience with other companies in similar situations. For this reason, audit committees especially value their chance to have candid discussions with the external auditors in executive sessions, often learning of potential issues that could fester if not properly addressed.

The external auditors can also inform the CFO of situations where the financial staff is being stretched or where their skill sets may not be equal to the tasks to be performed. Their candid, off-the-record feedback can be a godsend to CFOs, who may be oblivious to the strained conditions in the field.

Finally, the external auditors can play an instrumental role in developing internal audit's annual plan, helping to identify the areas that deserve particular attention. Because the audit staff is stretched in most companies, prioritization is crucial in dedicating the right resources to the right places. Given their broad-based experience, the external auditors can be a font of helpful input to the allocation of limited resources.

Board of Directors

The board of directors can be an effective ally for CFOs in establishing the desired culture. Through their interactions with the business leaders and through the prioritization of their agendas for audit and risk committees, the board members can elevate the importance of compliance and control issues within the company's overall hierarchy of priorities. For example, by regularly receiving summaries of all significant audit findings, they can signal their expectation that the issues will be addressed promptly and fully. The board can also request in-depth reviews of ethical or regulatory issues—especially if they involve violations of law—and determine if any changes should be made in the company's procedures, policies, or personnel.

The audit committee, in particular, can be an indispensable source of support. For example, by regularly including compliance as a topic in their agendas, audit committees can highlight the company's commitment to high standards and exemplary conduct. Like a Congressional hearing, an audit committee review of a topic sends a signal that this should be an important priority for business and financial leaders; furthermore, the preparation for this review can be a healthy exercise for the people involved.

In addition, if the CFO regularly provides updates to the audit committee, these reports can serve as a mechanism for ensuring appropriate follow-up on control issues. For example, by providing a scorecard showing open audit issues, the CFO is conveying a tacit reminder that these issues need to be addressed in a timely manner.

If the board has compliance or risk committees, they likewise can be excellent forums for accentuating the CFO's compliance and control priorities.

Board members are also increasingly interfacing directly with governmental agencies. This is especially true with respect to financial services companies, but it's likely to become a growing trend in most other industries as well. As a result, CFOs and management teams should make sure to keep the board fully informed concerning any regulatory developments or emerging issues.

FOREIGN CORRUPT PRACTICES ACT

In cultivating their control environment, CFOs should pay special attention to compliance with the Foreign Corrupt Practices Act of 1977 (FCPA), which imposes strict anti-bribery standards with respect to the international activities of all U.S. companies—both private and public—as well as non-U.S. companies that file reports with the Securities and Exchange Commission.

FCPA can present challenges as companies expand into countries that have differing norms concerning the way that business is conducted. In response, companies must ensure that their desire to adapt to local customs does not cross the line of violating this U.S law. The fines and penalties can be steep and the cumulative impact on a company's reputation can be severe. Consequently, the standard of compliance should be *"non-negotiable"*—absolute conformity with the law.

CFOs should familiarize themselves with the application of FCPA to various situations that can arise. For example, representatives of state-owned enterprises are treated as government officials under the law. They also should ensure that effective controls are in place in the hiring of third parties, including adequate due diligence and well-defined limits of authority.

In addition to focusing on potential FCPA issues, CFOs should be cognizant of the rules emanating from non-U.S. regulators. For example, the U.K. Bribery Act criminalizes commercial bribery as well as bribery of foreign government officials. Indeed, CFOs are likely to be increasingly challenged to stay abreast of new regulations and guidelines that are promulgated by jurisdictions throughout the world.

COSO Report on Corporate Fraud

In 2010, the Committee of Sponsoring Organizations (COSO) of the Treadway Commission's report on corporate fraud concluded that financial fraud continues to be a significant issue. Based on 350 alleged accounting fraud cases investigated by the SEC during 1999–2007, the report included the following conclusions:[a]

- "Financial fraud affects companies of all sizes, with the median company having assets and revenues just under $100 million."

- "The median fraud was $12.1 million. More than 30 of the fraud cases each involved misstatements/misappropriations of $500 million or more."

- "The SEC named the CEO and/or CFO for involvement in 89 percent of the fraud cases. Within two years of the completion of the SEC investigation, about 20 percent of CEOs/CFOs had been indicted. Over 60 percent of those indicted were convicted."

- "Revenue frauds accounted for over 60 percent of the cases."

- "Many of the commonly observed board of director and audit committee characteristics such as size, meeting frequency, composition, and experience, do not differ meaningfully between fraud and no-fraud companies. Recent corporate governance regulatory efforts appear to have reduced variation in observable board-related governance characteristics."

- "Twenty-six percent of the firms engaged in fraud changed auditors during the period examined compared to a 12 percent rate for no-fraud firms."

> ■ "Initial news in the press of an alleged fraud resulted in an average 16.7 percent abnormal stock price decline for the fraud company in the two days surrounding the announcement."
> ■ "News of an SEC or Department of Justice investigation resulted in an average 7.3 percent abnormal stock price decline."
> ■ "Companies engaged in fraud often experienced bankruptcy, delisting from a stock exchange, or material asset sales at rates much higher than those experienced by no-fraud firms."
>
> [a]"Financial fraud at U.S. public companies often results in bankruptcy or failure, with significant immediate losses for shareholders and penalties for executives" (May 20, 2010, COSO News Release, www.coso.org).

 FRAUD PREVENTION

CFOs are well aware of the truism that despite their best efforts to instill a culture of compliance—and notwithstanding the good intentions of Sarbanes-Oxley and other procedures—fraud will continue to be a risk to the organization. Therefore, they need to be ever-vigilant in detecting and eliminating fraudulent activities that may arise.

Given the prevalence and consequences of financial fraud, internal audit teams have been enhancing their expertise in fraud detection and CFOs, as well as audit committees, have been escalating their focus on fraud prevention. This includes support for whistleblower procedures within the company and sponsoring additional training in *forensic accounting* and other fraud detection skills. Unfortunately, fraud is likely to be a continuing, if not growing, issue for most companies, requiring continuous attention.

In addition, the continued presence of financial fraud provides further evidence that companies need to ensure that their management practices and compensation programs do not provide undue incentives to attain financial targets. Moreover, it highlights the singular importance of hiring finance professionals who are paragons of probity.

 WHISTLEBLOWERS

The implementation of the new Dodd-Frank Act rules undoubtedly will have profound effects on financial services companies, compelling them to comply with various restrictions concerning the amount of capital required and the types of business transactions that can be conducted. And the "say on pay" provisions clearly will be significantly influencing the way that public companies manage their compensation programs.

However, the provision in Dodd-Frank that is likely to have the most far-reaching impact is the "whistleblower" provision that became effective in August 2011. This provision provides that mandatory awards of 10 to 30 percent of the amount recovered will be paid to a whistleblower who voluntarily provides "original information" from "independent knowledge" of a violation that is successfully enforced by either the SEC or the Commodity Futures Trading Commission (CFTC) for a penalty of at least $1 million. The whistleblower does not need to be an employee of the company involved.

The implementation of this provision is a source of consternation within many companies—due to the financial incentives to bring up an issue and the ability of whistleblowers to bypass the company's internal processes. The fear is that these awards may encourage more issues to be raised in an independent process—which may in fact weaken, rather than strengthen, the procedural safeguards that are currently applied within companies. Furthermore, they may cause issues to be disclosed prematurely, before the relevant facts and circumstances have been ascertained.

In response, companies are taking steps to emphasize their existing internal processes. They are strengthening their tone at the top, encouraging an open atmosphere for raising issues, and emphasizing a clear anti-retaliation policy. They also are re-examining all of their internal investigation processes and ensuring that they provide a viable alternative so that whistleblowers will not feel the necessity to proceed directly to the SEC or CFTC with their concerns.

COST OF COMPLIANCE

Given the explosion of new regulations in the past decade, the cost of compliance has definitely increased for the vast majority of companies—with no end in sight to the additional burdens that legislators and regulators will be imposing in the future. However, few companies today can quantify their total costs of compliance, much less compare their costs from year to year. This undoubtedly will change as CFOs focus more on this cost category going forward.

The costs of compliance include expenses related to prevention and detection, as well as those related to remediation of issues. CFOs should scrutinize the mix of spending, remaining mindful of the proverbial adage that an up-front investment in prevention is much more cost-effective than spending to cure a problem.

CFOs should determine whether they can reduce their company's expenditures through streamlining processes, eliminating redundancies, implementing staffing strategies, or realizing other efficiencies. Because the costs of compliance tend not to produce any incremental revenue, any savings that can be engineered likely will flow directly to the bottom line.

 NOTE

1. Section 8B2.1 of the U.S. Sentencing Guidelines Manual: "Effective Compliance and Ethics Program."

PART SEVEN

VII

Leadership

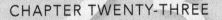

CHAPTER TWENTY-THREE

Achieving Finance Transformation

VERY FEW FINANCIAL ORGANIZATIONS have remained static during the past decade. Given the mounting financial and regulatory pressures, CFOs have responded with a series of initiatives to streamline their communications, standardize their processes, and enhance their analytical capabilities.

Frequently, CFOs refer to their organizational aspirations as achieving *"finance transformation,"* a term that can have a generalized meaning, but typically and more specifically is associated with:

- Revising the organizational structure
- Implementing technology systems
- Reengineering financial processes
- Outsourcing financial functions
- Emphasizing analysis versus data

 ## ORGANIZATIONAL STRUCTURE

The CFO's first objective in finance transformation typically is to revise the reporting relationships, creating more centralization and specialization among the financial functions. These changes can occur quickly—especially in response to severe cost pressures or control issues—but more likely will be implemented gradually, with incremental revisions over several years.

Traditional Structure

In most large companies, the financial organizations traditionally have been organized according to business units. In this traditional structure, each business unit has a financial leader—typically with the title of division chief financial officer or division controller—who in turn has people reporting to him or her who are responsible for the various financial functions.

For companies with international operations, the reporting structure usually has reflected a geographical focus as well, with a country serving either as the dominant organizational unit or as a secondary form of organization in a matrix arrangement with the lines of business.

This traditional structure has the advantages of simplicity and consistency, with a series of decentralized financial organizations that are linked through a hierarchical chain of command. It also fosters close working relationships between the finance professionals and the business units.

However, as companies have expanded their operations—moving into new business lines and expanding their global footprints—this decentralized form of organization has proven to be too costly. It is often associated with inflation of job titles, lack of specialization, and redundancies among activities and locations. Moreover, while a decentralized structure can help the finance professionals stay connected with the business, it can also result in sub-optimal controls and a loss of objectivity in financial reporting and analysis ("going native").

Alternative Structure

In response to the dual demands for stronger controls and lower costs, financial organizations generally have been evolving toward more centralization of activities and stronger reporting relationships. This trend toward greater centralization in the financial organization—both regionally and globally—first appeared for truly specialized functions (such as treasury and tax) and then became commonplace for operational activities (such as accounts payable, accounts receivable, and procurement), which were often organized as shared services.

In recent years, this evolution toward more centralization and greater specialization has spread to the controllership functions—including an explicit separation of accounting and financial reporting from financial planning and analysis (FP&A).

Modern Organizational Structure

The modern organizational structure emphasizes more centralization and specialization in the reporting relationships than in the traditional structure. For example, the financial organization might be organized as shown in Figure A.

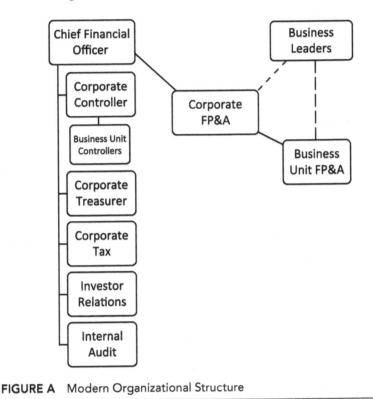

FIGURE A Modern Organizational Structure

In this alternative form of organization, the business unit controllers report directly to the corporate controller on a straight-line basis. However, they may continue to have a dotted line reporting relationship to their business unit— either a line of business or a country—and they may continue to be located physically in the field.

In addition, the controllers often continue to be responsible for operational activities such as payables and receivables, although increasingly companies are housing these operational functions in a shared services organization, which may also include other functions such as procurement and facilities administration. These operational activities are normally clustered in centralized or regional locations.

The FP&A activities—which consist primarily of budgeting, forecasting, performance measuring, and business analysis—are separated from the controllership functions under a head of FP&A, who normally reports directly to the CFO. Alternatively, the FP&A people will continue to report to the business units, with dotted line reporting to the financial organization.

Among the CFOs who have implemented this alternative structure, there is not a strong consensus concerning the reporting relationships for their FP&A functions. Some CFOs advocate straight-line reporting throughout the financial organization, perhaps with dotted lines to the business units. Others prefer to maintain a predominantly business unit focus, usually with dotted line reporting to the financial organization. And still others conclude that a dual reporting structure is best, with shared responsibility between the business units and the financial organization, including shared responsibility for performance reviews and compensation decisions.

Irrespective of the formal reporting arrangements, CFOs invariably will argue that they should have a strong say concerning the compensation decisions and career paths for the FP&A professionals and that the FP&A functions should maintain linkages with the rest of the financial organization.

Benefits of Reorganization

As CFOs have gained experience with these alternative organizational structures, they have realized significant benefits, including:

- **Lower Costs:** The alternative structures are inherently a more efficient form of organization for most companies, requiring fewer and often less expensive people. They can lead to fewer layers of management and more efficient flows of information.
- **Enhanced Controls:** A centralized controller organization facilitates the reengineering of accounting processes and fosters greater objectivity and consistency in accounting judgments. For this reason, audit committees typically prefer controllership functions that feature straight line reporting relationships to the CFO.
- **Differentiated Skills:** The revised organizational structure recognizes that the requisite skill sets for a controller position will vary from the skill

sets for FP&A and other financial positions. This can enhance the recruiting of highly qualified people to fill specific openings.

- **Analytical Capabilities:** The division of responsibilities makes it more likely that finance professionals can focus on analysis and value-added activities. The FP&A skill sets typically are enhanced through the greater focus on business analysis.

- **More Standardization:** The centralized structure facilitates the adoption of consistent accounting procedures (such as the chart of accounts) and standardized performance measurements (such as the business unit financial reports and metrics). This promotes efficiencies and timely information flows.

- **New Technologies:** A global financial organization also makes it easier to implement new technology systems. More top-down direction and tighter reporting relationships can overcome some of the active or passive resistance that otherwise might frustrate major changes to existing processes.

The bottom line is that the reorganization of reporting relationships can be a significant step forward for the financial organization. The benefits are tangible and well worth the effort.

Obstacles to Reorganization

Given the potential benefits from a revised structure and the success that companies have achieved to date, why do all CFOs not adopt a centralized form of organization? The answer is that they usually need to overcome some obstacles, such as:

- **Inertia:** Reorganizations are disruptive, and there never seems to be a good time to implement the changes, especially in light of competing priorities. CFOs need to drive the process and to take some risk.

- **Business Unit Resistance:** Many business leaders prefer to control all of their staff functions, including financial reporting. They may resist changes that will give them less autonomy over their financial statements and their people. This is especially true for their FP&A professionals, who often serve as their trusted lieutenants in running the business.

- **Division Controller Resistance:** Division controllers often like to manage all of the financial functions for their business unit and do not want to choose between accounting and analysis, preferring to do both. Also, they may have concerns about their status (including their title), their level of compensation, and their future career path.

- **Insufficient Size:** Smaller companies or business units may not be able to realize the benefits from greater specialization. It may be more cost effective for finance professionals to perform multiple responsibilities.
- **Technology Limitations:** The ability to implement the changes may be impeded by limitations in the company's technology infrastructure. Consequently, the reorganization often must be accompanied by investments in new technology systems and tools.
- **Career Development:** The greater degree of specialization can make it harder to groom well-rounded financial leaders. The CFO's talent development programs need to explicitly address this challenge, employing development tools to broaden the skill sets of finance professionals.

The bottom line is that it is not easy to implement the organizational changes. CFOs need to communicate the benefits and solicit support for the transformation. They also need to proceed with deliberate speed, building on interim successes and quickly resolving issues that undoubtedly will surface along the way.

 ## TECHNOLOGY SYSTEMS

A common lament among CFOs is that it is hard to get data in the form that they need it and that the financial organization is inordinately focused on producing data rather than providing business analysis. Finance transformation responds to this issue by upgrading and standardizing information technology systems.

The good news is that technology providers have been developing sophisticated products to improve the efficiency and effectiveness of financial information systems. But the bad news is that implementing these technologies can be difficult.

Therefore, CFOs should follow some best practices that increase their odds of success in finance transformation. In particular, they should communicate a business plan and focus on project management.

Business Plan

CFOs should communicate a clear *road map* for the scope of the project—including the time frame for its implementation and the benefits to be achieved—and set forth a realistic assessment of the financial and human resource commitments that will be required. This will help get buy-ins from the CEO and business leaders, who can be indispensable allies in getting things done.

In addition, they should set forth the goals for their financial information systems—articulating the end state that will define success. These *system requirements* typically include:

- A consistent chart of accounts.
- A single general ledger system.
- A comprehensive data warehouse.
- Software for extracting and manipulating the data.
- Automated electronic transfers of data and information.
- Tools to facilitate consolidations of financial statements.

Finally, CFOs should estimate the annualized *cost savings* to be realized from the project. Much of the benefits of the transformation will be qualitative, but the technology investments also should produce some quantifiable savings, usually in the form of greater productivity and lower headcount. These savings can help sustain support for the project in the face of the challenges that inevitably will arise during implementation.

Project Management

CFOs can also enhance the odds of success by focusing on proven project management strategies. These best practices include the following seven rules:

Rule 1: Establish manageable goals. Do not try to do everything at once, particularly if it expands the number of people who need to be coordinated. For example, CFOs may choose to implement one business division or one technology improvement at a time and to establish interim milestones.

Rule 2: Fix the underlying problems. CFOs should not expect the technologies to fix underlying issues in their financial processes. Instead, the best practice is to fix the problems first (such as establishing common definitions for the chart of accounts) before implementing a new technology system.

Rule 3: Provide top-down leadership. While consensus-building is normally a laudable goal, this kind of project needs firm direction to succeed, including the support of the business unit leaders who will benefit from the greater analytical capabilities that are made possible. It is absolutely critical for the CFO to provide strong top-down leadership.

Rule 4: Standardize; don't customize. Instead of trying to replicate existing reports, the best practice is to settle on some standardized approaches that are used throughout the organization. Insisting on standardization is much more cost effective and can dramatically reduce the potential complications in implementation.

Rule 5: Make someone accountable. Ideally, the project leader should know the financial organization, be adept with technology, and possess superb project management skills. It is important to appoint the best person available and to make it clear that he or she is in charge of the project—with the CFO's unequivocal support!

Rule 6: Hire a consultant. It helps to have people involved who have been through this process before. And consultants' specialized know-how and technology expertise can be invaluable to project management. However, while the consultants can play a vital role, it is not their project: The accountability still lies with the CFO and the project manager.

Rule 7: Celebrate and reward success. New and evolving technologies inevitably will be fundamental to maintaining a first-class financial system into the future. Therefore, CFOs should cultivate, recognize, and reward those people who demonstrate the ability to execute technology projects in a timely and effective manner; it's likely to be a valuable skill set that is coveted by financial organizations for the foreseeable future.

Reinventing the CFO

In his 2006 book *Reinventing the CFO: How Financial Managers Can Transform Their Roles and Add Greater Value* (Harvard Business Press, 2006), Jeremy Hope suggests ways to "liberate both finance and business managers from huge amounts of detail and the proliferation of complex systems that increase their workload and deny them time for reflection and analysis."

Hope puts forth the following vision:

- Reduce targets, measures, and controls.
- Improve business analysis skills.
- Enable local managers to respond to events.
- Eliminate costs that add no value.
- Measure to learn and improve.
- Manage risk by raising competencies.

PROCESS REENGINEERING

A persistent theme is that CFOs are challenged to reduce the costs of their financial organizations, while at the same time continuing to maintain a high level of professionalism and service to their stakeholders. And to a very great extent, they have been succeeding: It is estimated that the financial headcounts have come down about 30 percent in the past decade.

These cost reductions have not been easy, resulting in large part from the concerted efforts by CFOs to introduce more specialization, eliminate redundant activities, and achieve greater economies of scale.

Without question, cost pressures will continue to be a fact of life for CFOs. As with most corporate functions, financial organizations will be expected to deliver continuous improvements and productivity gains. Moreover, because of their leadership role in managing the company's cost structure, CFOs will be expected to exemplify a cost consciousness that can be emulated throughout the company.

Therefore, like it or not, the CFO's playbook must include a relentless and never-ending focus on the reengineering of financial processes.

Set Aggressive Targets

Although various benchmarking studies can provide some comparative data, it is hard to get true apples-to-apples comparisons for the overall costs of the financial functions. Companies can vary a great deal in their business mix, their geographical locations, and the functions that are included in the finance organization. For example, corporate development may be included in some organizations, but not in others. Furthermore, the treatment of payments to service providers—such as audit or banking fees—may not be consistently included or excluded by the companies in the survey.

In addition, the benchmarking may not reflect differences in the quality of service provided by the financial organization. For example, a greater focus on business analysis can result in higher costs, but also increased profitability.

Therefore, while general benchmarking studies can broadly indicate an average level of spending—the general rule is that finance should be around 1 to 2 percent of revenue—it cannot provide a specific road map for managing the cost structure. A more fruitful approach is to look at benchmarking for specific financial functions—such as transaction processing or treasury functions—for similar companies in similar industries, but even here the information is likely to be directional and not dispositive.

An alternative approach is to set aggressive targets against the company's baseline budget for the finance organization. The goal should be to achieve continuous savings, but to set the bar high enough so that it cannot be achieved without some radical improvements.

If the CFO can get the finance organization's buy-in for ambitious objectives, then the financial leaders can focus intently on the action steps that are required, and worry less about the potential implications for their current status or career prospects. This approach has worked well in many financial organizations and is likely to be the best alternative for CFOs to pursue.

Introduce More Specialization

The trend toward more centralized reporting relationships undoubtedly has helped financial organizations to achieve more specialization, which in turn has enhanced their level of expertise and knowhow. The need for increased specialization has been magnified by the seemingly endless proliferation and growing complexity of governmental regulations and financial reporting requirements; specialization has enabled CFOs to fulfill these added compliance responsibilities in a capable and efficient manner.

As an acknowledged best practice, companies are centralizing both financial and operational activities within geographic regions or even at a single worldwide location. For example, a company might centralize all of its account reconciliations in one location, which can facilitate smooth communications and timely adjustments. Of course, specialization can deliver further savings if the activities are concentrated in a lower cost location.

Finally, establishing centers of excellence also benefits a company's controls (e.g., by avoiding potential issues related to separation of duties in small operations). Moreover, the greater reliance on specialized expertise enhances the likelihood that a company will keep up-to-date concerning new regulatory requirements and will stay current with best practices in processes, methodologies, and technologies.

Eliminate Redundant Activities

Establishing regional or centralized locations can also produce significant efficiencies through the elimination of redundant activities. The potential savings can be especially pronounced in the case of repetitive operations such as accounts payable, accounts receivable, and the administration of compensation and benefits plans. Although the relocation of functions can be disruptive—

especially if much of the accumulated knowhow has not been documented—the potential benefits are usually well worth the hassles.

In addition to the direct cost savings from the reduction of headcount, CFOs have often been able to achieve dramatic improvements from the adoption of best practices among the units that have been combined. Bringing the functions together makes it much more likely that these best practices will be embraced, especially if the operations are starting with a clean slate.

Furthermore, documenting the procedures and practices can be a useful exercise in itself, helping to identify steps that can be eliminated and highlighting instances where employees are achieving results through heroic, but ultimately, inefficient "workarounds"—such as the use of offline spread sheets. Eliminating these workarounds will greatly enhance the integrity of the processes and pave the way for further automation and streamlining.

Achieve Economies of Scale

The combination of activities in a centralized location can produce further benefits through greater economies of scale. For example, a consolidation of activities can lower the costs for facilities, technology tools, and administrative support. In addition, the larger scale can facilitate the assignment of activities to full-time specialists, who can work more efficiently than the part-time efforts of the people who were doing the activities previously.

Even greater savings are usually possible if the financial operations are included within a broader shared services organization, especially if they are combined with other company-wide activities such as information technology, facilities management, and procurement. By elevating the status of shared services, companies can attract managers who have an aptitude for driving operational efficiencies and create a separate career track for people who have specific skills in shared services. Probably the biggest disadvantage with co-locating the shared service functions is the greater risk of a disruption due to a natural event (such as an earthquake or hurricane) or a labor issue (such as a slowdown or strike). Therefore, CFOs should consider the risk of potential business disruptions in deciding where to locate the shared services and ensure that they have back-up plans to mitigate the risks.

OUTSOURCING ADVANTAGES

The use of outsourcing arrangements is another growing trend among modern finance organizations, although not without some controversy and risks.

In many ways it is a natural outgrowth from finance transformation, as CFOs seek more specialization, centralization, and economies of scale throughout their financial organizations.

Traditionally, CFOs have outsourced functions such as payroll, tax filings, internal audit, and collections. The unmistakable trend is now for CFOs to consider a much broader array of potential outsourcing arrangements, including core accounting and financial reporting activities and operational functions such as accounts receivable and accounts payable.

Lower Costs

The cost advantages to be derived from outsourcing are well-documented at this stage. The arrangements usually reduce a company's all-in expense due primarily to lower labor costs, greater economies of scale, and perhaps a lower capital commitment.

In addition, CFOs can achieve cost advantages from the service provider's greater level of expertise. In effect, the outsourcer can leverage the knowhow gained from its work with other companies and pass on some of the learning curve benefits from its accumulated experience.

Enhanced Quality

Outsourcing can also result in improved quality, usually arising from the superior qualifications and training of the people involved. For example, an outsourcing firm in India can attract a well-educated and highly motivated work force. Furthermore, the outsourcing companies emphasize continuous learning in their specialized areas of expertise.

CFOs can reinforce the focus on quality by establishing performance metrics that are defined precisely, documented thoroughly, and monitored regularly. When CFOs experience quality issues in outsourcing, it is usually due to improperly designed metrics or with a lack of clarity in the tasks to be performed. Therefore, CFOs who include outsourcing in their playbook should ensure that much careful thought goes into the "*statement of work*" that governs the outsourcing relationship.

Improved Controls

For similar reasons, many CFOs also consider outsourcing to be a source of improved controls. A decision to outsource does not relieve a company from its responsibilities to maintain an effective control environment for the functions that are transferred. However, CFOs can take comfort from the outsourcing company's expertise, the quality of its people, the extensive documentation in its statement of work, and its intense focus on consistently delivering the performance metrics.

Furthermore, each year the outsourcing company will provide a report pursuant to Statement on Auditing Standards No. 70 that confirms the effectiveness of its controls.

Greater Flexibility

The transfer of work to a location in a different time zone can be advantageous if it facilitates continuous processing—often allowing a transfer of data back-and-forth between two or more distant locations. Combined with the efficiencies of broadband communications, the difference in time zones can reduce cycle times and allow more flexibility in meeting deadlines.

Moreover, an outsourcing arrangement can also provide more flexibility in preparing for disaster recovery or other disruptions to the company's work flow—providing alternative locations where work can be accomplished. This is particularly true where the outsourcing company maintains back-up sites that can service several of its clients.

 OUTSOURCING IMPLEMENTATION

Much of a CFO's success in outsourcing relates to the manner of its implementation. It is not without risk, and therefore CFOs should carefully review the best way to accomplish their outsourcing objectives. In particular, they should fix their problems first, take a gradual approach, review the tradeoffs in using an offshore provider, consider the potential ramifications to various stakeholders, and continue to evolve their outsourcing strategies.

Fixing Problems

Probably the most common mistake in outsourcing is to transfer the operations before the problems are fixed—expecting the outsourcing provider to rectify the issues. Instead, the best practice is to identify the problems and then not to transfer the functions until the problems have been fixed or there is a well-defined road map for addressing them.

CFOs should view an outsourcing decision as a golden opportunity to review all of the processes and to determine what steps need to be improved and what steps can be eliminated. If CFOs need help in making these assessments, they can bring in people with specialized expertise, who typically are different people than the people who are adept in managing outsourced operations.

In addition, many CFOs have learned—often the hard way—that they should not transfer the operations until they have fully documented all of the processes and have determined the performance metrics by which the operations will be managed. Otherwise, the statement of work will be unduly vague, which can lead to miscommunications and flawed execution.

The outsourcing arrangements simply will not work properly unless the expectations are *reasonable* and *certain.*

Gradual Approach

CFOs are also well-advised to move gradually toward the outsourcing of their financial functions. Usually, it is best to gain experience with outsourcing routine functions such as payroll and accounts payable, and then proceeding into more sophisticated functions such as accounting and financial reporting.

Managing an outsourcing relationship requires different skills than managing operations directly. In particular, it takes a different style of communication, usually requiring more precision in the instructions and more clarity in the objectives that are sought. Therefore, before entrusting more extensive or higher value activities to the outsourcing provider, CFOs should ensure that their organizations have had sufficient experience in managing through performance metrics pursuant to a statement of work.

Furthermore, because the outsourcing contracts typically extend over several years, a gradual approach allows the CFO to test the relationship before expanding the company's financial commitment. It is relatively easy to add new services to an existing relationship, while it is usually very difficult to unwind a relationship after the activities have been transferred.

Consequently, CFOs should generally err on the side of caution, including an incremental approach to an expanded relationship.

Offshore Alternatives

Many CFOs have had a positive experience in contracting with outsourcers who conduct their activities offshore. Such offshoring typically results in even greater cost savings than a domestic alternative due to cheaper labor and superior quality due to more specialized expertise. Also, they can offer economies of scale by co-locating several clients in the same vicinity.

However, the vendor may be challenged to sustain these advantages as its labor markets become more competitive and its employee turnover escalates. For example, labor costs and turnover have been rising in Bangalore, India, where a number of outsourcing companies are located.

As a general rule, CFOs are likely to have greater success in outsourcing if they are an important client of the vendor. If the vendor is allocating its best people, CFOs will want to be on its list of priority clients.

Furthermore, communications can be a barrier. This certainly can apply to oral communications where language skills may be an issue. However, it can also be an issue in written instructions, which need to be extremely precise to avoid the risk of miscommunications. This is why the vendor normally will house a number of people at the client's place of business—who serve as intermediaries in communications with their colleagues at the offshore location.

Finally, it should be noted that it can be difficult for CFOs to manage activities that are being conducted in a distant, remote location, especially if travel arrangements are limited. This can make it hard to maintain a hands-on understanding of potential problems that may be percolating. Also, travel can represent a significant cost of outsourcing, both the out-of-pocket transportation expense and the opportunity costs of management's time.

Stakeholder Relations

CFOs should be sensitive to the potential impact of outsourcing on the company's relations with its stakeholders, including governments, communities, customers, and employees. This is especially true when the activities are being transferred to an offshore location.

Given high levels of unemployment, communities and customers may react negatively to an offshoring decision, perhaps damaging the company's image and its reputation for corporate responsibility. And depending upon its business and customer mix, the public's reaction can have a discernible impact on the company's revenue and business results, especially if it markets its products or services to governments and their agencies.

In addition, the decision to outsource—either a domestic or an offshore alternative—can have a negative impact on employee morale, causing the people not directly affected to feel less secure about their own status. Therefore, it is very important for CFOs to be extremely transparent with employees, letting them know as soon as an outsourcing decision is made and providing candid descriptions of the future plans to the extent that they are known. They should not be learning of decisions through the grapevine.

Employees can handle the truth; it is uncertainty that they find most vexing. They will appreciate being kept informed and being treated with trust and respect.

Evolving Strategies

Without question, CFOs will continue to pursue outsourcing as a fundamental way of doing business in an increasingly global environment. The question usually is not whether to outsource, but how much and with whom? However, given the potential issues involved—especially in a decision to use an offshore provider—it is also likely that most CFOs will be gradually evolving their outsourcing strategies over time.

Furthermore, the pros and cons of outsourcing are likely to be continuously in flux. Because the technology, labor, and political environments remain very fluid across the globe, a strategy that makes sense today may not make sense tomorrow.

For example, the locations for outsourcing may need to shift with the changing labor markets; today's low-cost location may be uncompetitive tomorrow—making it desirable to engage in a continuous migration to the next frontier of service providers. And a change in tax rules could make a difference in a comparison between locations.

The bottom line is that CFOs need to emphasize continuous improvements in their outsourced functions and to remain flexibly adaptive to changes in the environment.

ANALYSIS VERSUS DATA

Given the escalating demands for financial organizations to produce frequent and detailed financial reports, there is a natural tendency for finance professionals to become overly preoccupied with process and to focus on data rather than analysis. This is particularly true if, like most companies, their methods of generating data are cumbersome and time-consuming. The financial organization can become numb due to the constant need to produce data on a tight time schedule and too accepting of their limitations in providing financial analysis.

A focus on data rather than analysis was confirmed by an APQC study that found that 47 percent of financial analysts' time was spent on collecting and validating data; 30 percent on administering the process; and only 23 percent on providing value-adding analysis. Certainly, this is not the ideal allocation of time and CFOs are constantly seeking ways to tilt the balance toward value-adding activities.

Finance transformation can be a partial antidote to this dilemma, with its changes—reorganization of reporting relationships, investments in technology, and reengineering of processes—all intended to free up resources for higher value activities. However, the solution also lies with finance professionals who possess superb analytical skills and a passion for solving business problems.

In leading their financial organizations, CFOs should continuously reinforce the message that budgets, forecasts, and reports are simply tools in managing a company's performance and not ends in themselves. Their mandate is to facilitate timely and effective responses to business issues that are identified through a systematic and thoughtful communication of pertinent financial information.

They should also focus resources on higher value tasks, and accelerate the evolution toward finance professionals who are business partners. They should:

- Eliminate reports and processes that are no longer necessary or that have lower value compared with business analysis.
- Emphasize analytical and communication skills in staffing the financial organization, seeking people who can produce impactful analyses.
- Align objectives and rewards among finance professionals to reflect impact rather than process.

This requires a financial organization that is more adaptive and more focused. In other words, less is more.

CHAPTER TWENTY-FOUR

Developing Financial Talent

C FOS UNIVERSALLY BELIEVE THAT developing financial talent is one of their highest priorities and confirm that they are spending more time than ever in hiring, retaining, and training the finance professionals in their organizations. However, it is a priority that can be especially challenging in the current environment

First, the focus on reducing headcount has led to financial organizations that are more risk averse to transfer people to unfamiliar areas or to expand their responsibilities too quickly. It is simply less risky to keep good people safely ensconced in their comfort zones.

Second, the greater specialization that comes with finance transformation can make it harder to develop well-rounded finance professionals. Unless proactive steps are initiated, high-potential people may spend the preponderance of their careers in a particular functional track, such as controllership, financial planning and analysis (FP&A), audit, or treasury functions.

Third, there are fewer entry-level positions due to the automation of routine activities; the greater use of outsourcing; and the heightened emphasis on analytical skills, which usually require a higher threshold of prior business experience.

Fourth, given the competitive marketplace for talent among a mobile work force, finance professionals may be reluctant to accept a lateral transfer to a new area, preferring to accept an offer from another company in their current area of expertise—usually involving an increase in responsibility, a loftier title, and additional pay.

In the face of these challenges, CFOs are devoting more of their personal time to recruiting and developing their people. In particular, they are playing a highly visible role in implementing talent development programs throughout their financial organizations and encouraging their managers to take risks for the benefit of the organization's future talent needs.

This effort can produce an exceptionally high return on investment and can be one of the most personally fulfilling aspects of the CFO's job.

 ## RECRUITMENT STRATEGIES

Without exception, CFOs will proclaim the importance of having quality people in their financial organization, and they unanimously will agree that hiring highly skilled talent is a *sine qua non* for executing their playbook. Unless they can recruit people who have the requisite skill set—including the potential for continuous learning and advancement—no amount of development effort is likely to succeed.

Nevertheless, while there may be universal agreement concerning the "ends" of a recruiting program, there are considerable differences in viewpoints concerning the "means." To a very large extent, these differences in approach will reflect differences in philosophies, traditions, and cultures, as well as the CFO's specific priorities and needs at the time.

Entry Level or Lateral Hires

In virtually all cases, a company's financial organization will comprise a mix of people who were hired for an entry-level job versus those that joined after prior experience elsewhere. However, companies can differ markedly in the extent to which they emphasize either approach.

The advantage of entry-level hires is that these home-grown professionals can become steeped in the company's business and culture. Moreover, they can gain valuable insights and perspectives from starting at a relatively low-level position within the financial organization—enabling them to be more effective and empathetic leaders later in their career.

The advantage of lateral hires is that they can bring useful experience to the job, especially if they have gained technical skills and broad-based business exposure in their prior positions. For example, companies have had success in hiring accounting, FP&A, and internal audit people from the major accounting firms, which deservedly are well renowned for their training programs. As another example, companies can staff their treasury and corporate development groups with well-qualified lateral hires from investment and commercial banks or consulting firms.

Of course, many of the laterals are hired from other financial organizations, which is a practice that coincides with the growing proclivity for young professionals to make frequent job changes. CFOs should incorporate this infusion of talent into their career development programs, making sure that they have robust on-boarding procedures and ways of fully integrating the newcomers into their organization.

In addition, they will want to ensure that these lateral hires do not become range bound in their technical specialties for too long and that they are provided opportunities to play broader and higher-level leadership roles.

Hiring of MBAs

Although few companies require an MBA for advancement to a leadership role in their financial organizations, some CFOs actively recruit MBAs directly from business schools—as a way to strengthen their financial talent base and to import analytical and strategic skills.

The advantage of this hiring strategy is that the people have a proven track record from their prior business experience, and they likely will have benefited from the education and broadening provided by the business schools. It is also a particularly good way to recruit non-U.S. talent who can help to define and execute a company's global strategies.

However, while hiring MBAs undoubtedly can increase the pool of high-potential people in the financial organization, it can also create some management challenges.

First, their higher salaries can cause budget issues for the department that is hiring them; this can be overcome by a subsidy from the CFO, but at the risk of fairness issues if two people in the financial organization are receiving different pay for performing the same or a similar job.

Second, to recruit MBAs, companies often need to offer a distinctive early career track—such as a rotational program during the first few years—which can create conflicts with the non-MBA professionals, who may resent the unequal treatment.

Third, they may have unrealistic expectations concerning their upward trajectory, with them often expecting to run a business at a relatively early stage in their career. If these expectations are unmet, they may become disgruntled and leave the company.

This is definitely an area where a company's prior experience and culture can make a big difference. If a company has a track record of success in hiring MBAs, then the CFO is likely to enjoy success going forward. However, if a company has not recruited MBAs in the past, then there may be some growing pains if the CFO's plans are too ambitious; in this case, the CFO may want to take a more gradual and cautious approach, perhaps focusing initially on lateral hires of MBAs from banks or consulting firms.

Evaluations of Candidates

Companies can use a variety of methods for identifying potential hires, ranging from postings on job sites and social media networks, to referrals from existing employees, to active on-campus recruiting programs at targeted schools, to engaging professional recruiting firms using either a dedicated or a contingency arrangement.

By employing these various methods of recruiting, companies generally can obtain a good pool of candidates who meet the job requirements—at least as indicated by their resumes. The harder task is to determine whether the individual is a good fit with the company and whether he or she is likely to thrive in the environment over the long term (or at least for the next two to five years).

Traditionally, companies have used serial interviews to evaluate candidates—focused primarily on the person's background, prior experience, and technical skills. This has usually worked well, but given the stakes of making a bad hire, some CFOs are now incorporating other techniques for assessing prospective employees.

For example, they may ask the candidate to meet with a panel of interviewers for an in-depth discussion, thus creating constructive dynamics from having several perspectives represented in the questions asked of the candidate. Each member of the panel benefits from the answers elicited by the other panel members.

As other examples, CFOs may request writing samples from the candidates or may ask them to discuss a business case provided to them in advance. And, of course, there is the stress interview that focuses on an intellectually challenging question.

Whatever the method used, it definitely makes sense to learn more about the candidate than can be gleaned from the resume, with the overarching goal of determining not only whether the person can do the job, but whether he or she will be happy doing it. References can help in some instances, but their candor is often constrained by legal considerations or their desire to be helpful to the candidate's prospects.

The bottom line is that CFOs should seek to learn as much as possible, not only about the candidate's education and prior experience, but also about his or her motivations and definitions of success. Furthermore, it is important to evaluate the person's potential to progress beyond the current job—to broader and higher responsibilities within the financial organization—rather than focusing too much on the current position being filled.

Emphasis on Soft Skills

Another question is how much emphasis should be placed on evaluating the candidate's technical skills and relevant prior experience versus the "soft skills" that may not have much direct relevance for the current role, but that could be crucial for the individual's long-term advancement.

What are these soft skills? While opinions can differ, one CFO has provided an especially cogent description of the attributes that he seeks in recruits—what he calls the four "Is." In reverse order of importance, they include: *intellectual skills, intensity, interpersonal skills, and integrity.*[1]

CFOs increasingly are emphasizing these soft skills, recognizing that when a new hire does not work out, it is usually not due to technical shortcomings, but more likely is due to intrinsic characteristics that make the individual a poor match for the organization. In addition, they are evaluating personal qualities—such as integrity—that are absolutely essential, irrespective of the position being filled.

Expatriates versus Locals

In staffing their overseas operations, CFOs need to address their preference for relocating expatriates versus hiring local recruits. To a large degree, this preference may depend on the stage of development in their international operations and the availability of local talent who can satisfy the technical requirements.

As a general trend, CFOs are relying less on expatriates and recruiting more local talent, especially as their operations become more global and less home-country centric. However, most CFOs of U.S. companies still strongly prefer, or may even require, that finance professionals speak English.

When local talent is hired, it is usually desirable—if financially feasible—that they spend some time at the corporate or regional headquarters early in their tenure. This orientation—which can be accomplished either through a formal training program or through a special visit—can make a real difference in their ability to work effectively with the rest of the financial organization.

 ## DEVELOPMENT OBJECTIVES

Assuming that CFOs have identified and hired well-qualified finance professionals, their next challenge is to develop this talent to its full potential.

CFOs often develop checklists of the basic skills that their finance professionals should seek to master and identify the personal qualities that they want their people to exemplify—often relating these qualities to the brand attributes that they are seeking to instill throughout the financial organization. However, these checklists can be daunting—indicating a large number of skills and attributes that are deemed to be desirable—and may be misleading concerning the way that talent is actually evaluated for financial leadership positions.

Therefore, it can be helpful to emphasize the overarching objectives of the development program: expertise, experience, and leadership skills. All three are essential for advancement within the financial organization or in a broader management role.

Expertise

The first objective is for finance professionals to demonstrate a high level of competence within their area of expertise. In most cases, this requires a minimum time commitment—probably two to four years—for finance professionals to master their current job duties and to add distinctive value. They should spend enough time in the position to achieve a high-quality work product and to achieve a superior level of performance, as evidenced by their annual performance appraisal.

If a finance professional moves too quickly from job to job, he or she may not have the chance to master a set of skills and can become known as a "jack of all trades," which generally has a pejorative connotation within the financial organization. Instead, it is incumbent on finance professionals to exhibit a commitment to their functional area. This includes focusing on technical skills and staying current on best practices.

However, it is also important that they not become pigeonholed—too strongly identified with a particular area of expertise and not considered as a candidate for a different or broader role. Thus, finance professionals need to strike the right balance between demonstrating superior skills in their current area, while remaining open to new challenges outside their comfort zone.

Experience

The second objective is for finance professionals to broaden their experience base through a series of positions and, if possible, a variety of situations. For example, it is generally desirable for finance professionals to balance a headquarters position with a position in the field or to take a position within another functional area in the financial organization.

For example, a high-potential individual may go from an accounting role at headquarters to a similar role in a business unit location or else may take a job in another area such as treasury or investor relations. Of course, this objective can be constrained by circumstances that limit the person's ability to relocate. However, CFOs are often able to devise creative solutions to accommodate an individual's specific requirements.

Given the increasing globalization of markets and supply chains, CFOs often want their finance professionals to gain experience outside their home country. Becoming exposed to international operations can help the individual gain a fuller appreciation for the company's scope of operations and a greater sensitivity with respect to the challenges of operating in locations with varying cultures and business practices.

In addition, CFOs often emphasize the value to be gained through experience in business operations, typically through an FP&A or a shared service position. This can prepare people for future roles within a business unit—perhaps in a general management role—as well as enhance their effectiveness within the financial organization. In fact, many companies consider business unit experience to be a prerequisite for the CFO position.

Internal audit is generally considered a good vehicle for gaining exposure to business operations, especially in the case of audits that involve extended visits to a field location. Many companies have introduced programs whereby their finance people can participate in audits on a rotating basis, thereby giving them exposure to business operations without having to make an extended time commitment to an internal audit position. These are very worthwhile programs, and a particularly good experience for the people involved.

Finally, finance professionals should seek to learn more about the company's business and financial strategies. In particular, they should familiarize themselves with the capital allocation and funding policies, the shareholder return objectives, and the enterprise risks, as well as the way that the company's strategies are communicated to investors.

Understanding the broader business and financial strategies will help finance professionals to perform their current jobs and will provide evidence that they have the ambition and capabilities to assume greater responsibilities.

Leadership

The third and most important objective is for finance professionals to develop their leadership skills. Most of these skills can be considered "soft" and thus can be more difficult to measure objectively in a formal development plan. Nevertheless, they probably represent the attributes that are most crucial in determining an individual's long-term career trajectory.

What are these leadership skills? Certainly, they include *communications*: the ability to write succinctly, yet comprehensively, to make compelling presentations, to take complex topics and reduce them to their essence, to speak confidently and persuasively to both large and small groups, and to listen carefully. Ironically, in a world that is increasingly moving toward shorthand communications such as tweets and text messaging, the focus on traditional communication skills is more important than ever, and they offer one of the ways that young finance professionals can stand out among their peers.

The required leadership skills also include the ability to *organize and motivate* groups, often where there are unclear reporting relationships and ambiguous scopes of responsibility. For this reason, CFOs often assign high-potential people to special task forces and project teams where they can gain experience in working within an unstructured environment. Most finance professionals are very good at working within well-defined parameters; however, to excel at higher levels within the financial organization, they will need to be equally comfortable with ambiguity—working with a clean sheet of paper on an unstructured task that has a "to be determined" definition of success.

In addition, they should have *management capabilities* as well as leadership skills, not just with respect to their direct reports, but more important, with people outside their span of control—often outside the finance organization. The most successful managers pay attention to the details, but don't get bogged down. They know how to set realistic objectives, when to follow up, and when to intervene with a mid-course correction.

They also know how to *manage upward*, recognizing that managing their boss is vital to their success and having a sixth sense as to when and how to bring problems to his or her attention. Moreover, they cultivate realistic expectations concerning the results to be achieved within a given time frame.

Finally, leadership skills include the ability to transcend narrow, technical skills and to make meaningful contributions with respect to broader responsibilities, including the formulation and execution of value-enhancing *business and financial strategies*. Given the greater emphasis on partnering with the CEO and business leaders in delivering shareholder value, finance professionals will be expected to become more strategic in their thoughts and actions.

Continuous Learning

In addition to a tripartite focus on expertise, experience, and leadership, CFOs should also emphasize the importance of continuous learning. This includes maintaining an intellectual curiosity about new developments, especially in a person's area of expertise, and being openly receptive to new ways of doing things.

Continuous learning should also include business and financial history. Knowing the historical context—of economic cycles, market bubbles, ponzi schemes, accounting frauds, business booms and busts, inflation and interest rates, depressions and recessions, mergers and acquisitions, financial theories, and so forth—can provide invaluable perspectives for assessing current developments and making considered judgments.

In other words, the old adage that "there is nothing new under the sun" applies to finance as well as to the rest of life. And knowing the historical track record can help financial leaders to respond effectively to the challenges of the present.

From CPA to CFO

In a 2009 article in the *Journal of Accountancy*,[a] Matthew G. Lamoreaux listed the five prerequisites for CPAs seeking the top job in finance. As paraphrased, these five skills include:

Skill 1: *Strategist*. Look at the organization holistically.

Skill 2: *Translator*. Communicate information and strategies.

Skill 3: *Leader*. Motivate people in the organization.

Skill 4: *Technical Generalist*. Gain experience in several jobs.

Skill 5: *Facilitator*. Help groups to realize their objectives.

[a]Lamoreaux, Matthew G., "CFO 101: Five Prerequisites: Veteran CFOs give advice to CPAs seeking the top job in finance" (September 2009, *Journal of Accountancy*).

DEVELOPMENT TOOLS

CFOs can use a variety of tools to advance their development programs, often in concert with human resource programs that are used throughout the company. However, even if participating in a company-wide program, CFOs should adapt the program to the particular needs of their financial organization and take a direct personal interest in its implementation.

CFOs typically use a blend of proven strategies and best practices in their talent development programs, ranging from formal processes—such as development plans, talent assessments, and succession planning—to mentoring, recognition programs, and informal communications.

Development Plans

Development plans are essential to the CFO's playbook and should be required for everyone in the financial organization.

At least annually, all finance professionals should specify their development objectives and then discuss them with their managers. These plans can include technical skills to obtain, courses to take, or areas of self-improvement to emphasize. They should reinforce a commitment to continuous learning and foster greater self-awareness.

They can also facilitate a productive dialogue between managers and their team members, providing a vehicle for an ongoing dialogue about each employee's career aspirations and development needs. This can make a difference in retaining high-potential people, who generally seek the individual attention that these plans can deliver.

Although many companies use computerized templates for preparing the plans, they are just as effective—if not more so—if summarized in a single page of bullet points. If they are too elaborate or too bureaucratic, they can lose some of their impact—which should be squarely focused on the individual's needs and not on the form to be completed.

It is a best practice to separate the discussion of the development plans from the individual's annual performance reviews. Although the two discussions are obviously related, they should serve different purposes and should not be combined.

Talent Assessments

CFOs often administer a program for assessing their talent each year—typically reviewing each of the finance professionals at a specified level and above (e.g., managers and above). Usually, these assessments use a three-by-three or two-by-two grid to measure professionals along two dimensions: (1) their performance in their current job and (2) their potential for higher levels within the organization.

This bifurcation helps reinforce the distinction between the skills needed to perform today's job versus the skills needed for tomorrow's job, and highlights the difference between a performance review and a development plan. A sample format is shown in Figure 24.1.

The talent reviews are then shared among the senior management team to raise awareness of the talent base throughout the finance organization—including the identification of high potential individuals—and to ensure that there is a consensus concerning the evaluations. The group will also identify areas where developmental actions should be considered for individuals, including potential movements to another position that will broaden their experience.

CFOs have differing views as to whether they should share the results of the talent assessments with the people being evaluated. On the one hand, it is good feedback for the people, who can benefit from learning the objective assessments, especially the appraisals of their long-term potential. It can help

GROWTH POTENTIAL

Low	Medium	High	
7 Pro in Position	8 High Potential	9 High Potential Future Leader	High
4 Solid Performer	5 Hold for Development	6 High Potential	Medium
1 Watch List	2 Watch List	3 Unusual Case	Low
			PERFORMANCE

FIGURE 24.1   Talent Reviews

manage their expectations and perhaps indicate development actions that would be especially desirable.

On the other hand, communicating the specific evaluations can imply more precision than is warranted and may be discouraging to an individual, especially in the early stages of his or her career. The danger is that the assessment can be self-fulfilling and perhaps can prematurely curtail a person's upward potential.

In either event, it is important that the "process" for assessing talent be transparent, which should give everyone comfort that the financial leaders are focused on facilitating their career aspirations and meeting their long-term development needs. Furthermore, describing the process can reassure people that the financial organization is a meritocracy based on performance and skills—and not overly influenced by cronyism or personal exposure to the decision makers—which can be particularly important as financial organizations become more diverse.

Succession Plans

For each position at a specified level and above (e.g., the director level and above) CFOs often will sponsor an annual exercise whereby candidates are identified who could fill each of the key financial leadership positions—either immediately, within the intermediate term (say, one to three years), or within a longer period (say, three to five years).

These succession plans are then reviewed by the senior management team to confirm that the candidates make sense, to discuss any development steps that would help an individual to succeed in the position, to identify gaps where there are not sufficient candidates for a position, to encourage candidacies from other functional areas, and to assess the financial organization's progress toward its diversity objectives.

360 Reviews

Either routinely or occasionally, CFOs may institute "360 reviews" that look at a professional from several vantage points: managers, peers, subordinates, and either internal or external customers. These reviews are usually conducted anonymously, then the results are shared confidentially with the individual.

The 360 reviews can enhance self-awareness, helping individuals to understand third-party perceptions of their strengths and weaknesses. They typically are accompanied by a candid self-appraisal, sometimes with the help of a coach who works with the person to develop a game plan for the future.

However, it is important that the CFO encourages a positive attitude toward these assessments, avoiding any defensiveness or consternation that an individual may feel about this relatively intimate mechanism for providing feedback.

Mentors and Coaches

High-potential employees are often assigned a mentor (typically a more senior member of the financial management team) who meets regularly and confidentially to discuss the individual's career aspirations and to offer career advice and encouragement. These mentors are usually supplementary to an individual's informal mentoring relationships throughout the finance organization; they help to ensure that everyone has someone who is looking out for them and provide a framework for discussing career alternatives.

Some CFOs will go further by hiring a "coach"—usually a trained professional with experience in career counseling—who will work with an individual to construct a personalized development plan. However, if CFOs take this approach, they should clearly communicate that having a coach does not indicate a problem, but rather is a sign that the person is considered to have the potential to play a larger leadership role within the financial organization.

Recognition and Rewards

Given the flattening of most organizations—and the concomitant reduction in opportunities for promotions—CFOs are sponsoring more awards that recognize exceptional efforts and superior performance. This is especially important to the newer generations of young professionals, who generally have more desire to receive frequent positive feedback than did the preceding generations.

Whether participating in company-wide programs or sponsoring specific finance programs, CFOs are enthusiastically embracing these opportunities to recognize the contributions of their people. The programs are particularly powerful in celebrating an achievement that has added shareholder value—such as a cost reduction idea—or in recognizing the contributions of team members who have worked well together.

Although these programs often come with a financial award—typically cash, a gift certificate, or restricted stock—most employees respond more positively to the recognition itself than to the size of the monetary award, especially if the CFO communicates the award winners throughout the financial organization. The CFO should communicate not only the names of the winners, but also describe the reasons for their recognition.

External Courses

Companies may choose to send their high-potential people to external seminars or business school management programs where they can interact with professionals from other companies and enhance their technical or leadership capabilities. This type of recognition provides tangible evidence to the individuals selected—as well as to the rest of the financial organization—that they are well-regarded by the CFO and the other financial leaders.

Furthermore, although an MBA or other advanced degree is certainly not a prerequisite for advancement in most finance organizations, CFOs may want to encourage and support their people who choose to pursue these educational opportunities—usually during nights and weekends—and recognize their initiative toward self-improvement.

However, CFOs should be cautious in directly sponsoring an executive MBA, as the explicit or implicit quid pro quo for this financial support can be quite tricky. For example, it can foment jealousies and fairness issues unless the criteria for this special treatment are well-understood and well-accepted by the organization. In addition, it can be very awkward if the individual accepts another position shortly after completing the MBA.

Informal Dialogues

Most CFOs spend a considerable amount of their time in informal interactions with their financial organizations—ranging from brown bag lunches, to town hall meetings, to one-on-one discussions. For example, a CFO may schedule monthly breakfasts or lunches, with invitations going to all of the members of the finance staff who have birthdays that month.

These types of informal settings provide opportunities for the CFO, as well as other financial leaders, to discuss their philosophies concerning career development, and to offer encouragement and advice to finance professionals in varying stages of their careers. It is also a great way to learn what is on their minds, perhaps surfacing morale or organizational issues that otherwise could go undetected.

Handwritten Notes

With the revolution in communication technologies, it is easier than ever for CFOs to use electronic tools to communicate broadly throughout the finance organization and to bypass traditional chains of command. For example, CFOs often send emails to announce organizational changes or to recognize individuals who have received awards or otherwise have achieved a noteworthy success.

However, given how ubiquitous and facile these electronic communications have become, CFOs have surmised that handwritten notes can actually be more powerful than ever. Sending handwritten thank you or congratulatory notes can go a long way toward making their people feel special and appreciated.

 ## DIVERSITY

A theme that permeates the development programs in most financial organizations is a focus on diversity—of gender, race, religion, ethnicity, sexual orientation, disabilities, geographies, backgrounds, and ideas. CFOs have embraced the notion that diversity is crucial to their company's business objectives and to the vitality of their financial organization.

In most companies, CFOs are sponsoring actions to reinforce their commitment to diversity and to retain and develop the individuals who can help achieve and sustain a diverse culture. They also are visibly reaching out to support the trailblazers who are leading these efforts and serving as role models for others in the organization.

The overriding point is that achieving their diversity objectives will not come naturally to most financial organizations; CFOs usually will need to establish goals and hold managers accountable for achieving them. It's the right thing to do, and it's certainly the best way for CFOs to ensure that they have access to the full array of talent.

 ## FUTURE REQUIREMENTS

In developing financial talent, CFOs should be focused not only on their current organizational needs, but more important, on their requirements for the future. Of course, no one knows with certainty how the financial organizations will evolve, but it is a good bet that certain trends will continue, including:

- **Analytical:** Finance professionals will focus less on preparing information and more on adding value through their analysis and insights.
- **Externally Focused:** Finance professionals will be more focused on competitors, investors, customers, vendors, regulators, and governments.

- **Global:** Finance professionals will demonstrate global perspectives—as markets, products, supply chains, labor pools, and ideas integrate seamlessly across geographical borders.
- **Technologies:** Finance professionals will embrace rapidly changing technologies to stay cost competitive and to achieve continuous improvements in their capabilities.
- **Communications:** Finance professionals will emphasize effective communications—to ensure organizational alignment, to facilitate timely decision making, and to cut through the clutter of competing messages.
- **Unstructured:** Finance professionals will be comfortable with a less structured organization—with less emphasis on chains of command and organizational boundaries.
- **Leadership:** Finance professionals will lead through persuasion and not by command and control—as they drive performance and change.
- **Integrity:** For the finance professionals of tomorrow as well as today, integrity will continue to be the number one prerequisite for success.

In short, the corporate finance playbook will continue to broaden, will grow increasingly complex, and will escalate in its criticality. But the essential CFO will remain the same.

 NOTE

1. Lange, Cliff, CFO of Boston Mutual Life Insurance, at an Argyle Executive Forum, as reported by David McCann in "The Four 'I's of Talent Management," CFO.com (April 26, 2011, CFO Publishing LLC).

About the Author

B RUCE NOLOP RETIRED in 2011 after a 35-year career as an investment banker and corporate executive, including more than a decade as chief financial officer of Pitney Bowes and E*Trade Financial.

He has been a board member of Marsh & McLennan since January 2008 and currently serves on the audit, compliance and risk, finance, and corporate responsibility committees.

His education includes a B.A. in political science from the University of South Dakota, a J.D. from Stanford Law School, and an M.B.A. from the Stanford Graduate School of Business.

He lives in New York City with his wife, Susan, and has two sons, age 22 and 21.

Acknowledgments

URING MY CAREER AS AN investment banker and corporate executive, I was privileged to know many outstanding chief financial officers. It is their collected wisdom that is reflected in this book.

In particular, I want to call out the members of the CFO Roundtable—a group sponsored by the Center for Corporate Innovation—who shared their insights and best practices during our rich discussions of corporate finance topics.

I also have been fortunate to have had many outstanding mentors and bosses. While the list of my benefactors is long, I especially want to acknowledge Darwin Smith and Don Hibbert of Kimberly-Clark, Mike Critelli of Pitney Bowes, Don Layton of E*Trade Financial, and Steve Hardis of Marsh & McLennan.

For helping with this book, I must start with a thank you to my sons, Michael and Nathan, who assisted their technologically challenged father in navigating Word and PowerPoint and gathered financial statistics from Bloomberg, where Nathan was a summer intern.

In addition, I want to thank Yuk Ping Ng, Alan Bieler, and Scott Gilbert for reviewing certain chapters.

Finally, I want to acknowledge Sheck Cho of John Wiley & Sons, who took a chance on a neophyte author and provided steady guidance.

Index